L.A.
IS THE
CAPITAL OF
KANSAS

STEPHEN — YOU ARE
A HECK OF A SWELL
GUY (TRUE).

Richard B. Walter 89

L.A.

IS THE
CAPITAL OF

KANSAS

Painful Lessons in
Post-New York Living

R I C H A R D
M E L T Z E R

HARMONY BOOKS

NEW YORK

Enormous THANKS to James Vowell for encouraging me to write much of this stuff; to Bill Reed for forcing me to stack it all together; and to Bud Holiday and Michael Pietsch for making the ultimate fact of the thing as a book more than remotely feasible.

Pieces in this book were previously published, in somewhat different form, in *The L.A. Reader, L.A. Weekly, Coast, Boulevards, Stuff, San Diego Reader, The Village Voice, Chic, Playgirl, Forced Exposure* and the book *17 Insects Can Die in Your Heart.*

Published by Harmony Books, a division of Crown Publishers, Inc., 225 Park Avenue South, New York, New York 10003, and represented in Canada by the Canadian MANDA Group.

HARMONY and colophon are trademarks of Crown Publishers, Inc.

Manufactured in the United States of America

Library of Congress Cataloging-in-Publication Data

Meltzer, R. (Richard)
    L.A. is the capital of Kansas.

    1. Los Angeles (Calif.)—Social life and customs—
Anecdotes, facetiae, satire, etc. I. Title. II. Title:
LA is the capital of Kansas.
F869.L85M45   1988   979.4'94053   87-30820

ISBN 0-517-56867-5

10 9 8 7 6 5 4 3 2 1

First Edition

To my sister

CONTENTS

Well, it's not the capital of *Norway*, is it?
                    —Dirk Dracout, *The Book of Spoons*

INTRODUCTION

In the spring of '75 I turned 30. As ages were going for me it was really just another number, though a better one, whatever that means, than anything from 26 to 29. For a four-year stretch I'd been bearing the burden of paired numerals that *meant nothing* to me, 'cept maybe as football scores (three touchdowns, a field goal and a safety; four touchdowns with a missed extra point) or so-and-so's jersey i.d. with the New England Whalers, but literally nothing—whatsofuckingever—re any *living me* I could bring myself to consider. Owing to a feeling in my cliché gut that I'd been making no progress in the business of this here life, they stood instead, when they stood at all, as numeric adjuncts to the ostensible *dying* me. And while their sequence as dealt never seemed particularly additive—I felt no *older* at 29 than at 28 or 27, nor closer to actual graves of the heart, mind, etcetera—the cumulative oompah of such unfriendly arithmetic was enough to superannuate my metaphoric ass. At cutting-edge 30— how do you 'splain it?—age-coded matters felt instantly friendlier. But, what the hey, not for long.

'Cause the moment 30 years of a life not yet really lived got to feeling *less* devastating than 26 through 29 of same, a calendar crisis

I'd so far avoided zoomed in to replace the old one in spades. THREE DECADES IN A SINGLE TOWN—and what a town: New York—were suddenly, drastically the issue, and by early summer their psychic weight approached that of a geologic epoch, a Pleistocene—or something—of the regionally delimited soul. Geotemporal poetry's a pisser, and we're talking *severe* geotemporal poetry, which by August I was tumbling to, verse, line and sinker: *Out!*—I think you know this one—*Get the hell* out *while you can!!*

Other factors, equally compelling, a tad more concrete (and far less hokey), certainly contributed to the scenario: the inevitable, perhaps even imminent, breakup of a multi-year live-in relationship, coupled with the grim longshot of ever finding a suitable *local* replacement apartment; a growing disaffection for Manhattan sleaze, the final gimcrack in the city's cultural arsenal with any claim to my interest or passion, personal or writerly; an escalating bitterness over my editors at the *Village Voice* having branded me an "anti-intellectual," a heretic and apostate who in saner times would by now have been tarred, feathered, run out of town on a rail. A trio of hot ones f'r sure, motivation no doubt for *some* kind of move (a change of hobbies?), but without the three-decade horseshit to paint my options not only urgent but grandiose, to prod the submacho chump in me into making *his* dumb move, I might never have reached Jersey City. "Hey chickenshit"—an interior harangue, circa September— "you are one worthless toad unless you extricate yourself *utterly* from all vestiges, semblances and simulations of [shall we say] mommy." Which sounds kind of like far, *far* away. So sure, fine, that's settled. But where, for inst, might that be?

Okay. In my five-plus years as a rockwriter of note, even if the note was frequently an asterisk of renegade repute (reviewing albums by their cover rather than "content"; leaping in a fountain at a Rolling Stones press party; splashing wine on a de Kooning at a Country Joe reception at the Museum of Modern Art—little things I fancied I *must* do lest the ever-dwindling rock-roll "flame" flutter out), I'd fortuitously managed, along with most of my rockwrite cohorts, to get flown places, many places, umpteen times over. The record biz was feeling fat in those days, and it was not unusual for even second-string reviewers to average eight-ten trips a year in the name of company-artist relations. Ultimate record sales be damned: if in the course of a long and boring tour a wide-eyed upstart band got interviewed by (or merely intoxicated with) an inkstained lout from *Creem* or *Changes* flown in at company expense, said band would at least in theory buy the notion that the company *cared*. (Narrow-eyed non-upstarts alike were ofttimes deemed susceptible to the ruse.)

As bearer of such ersatz attention I got shipped to Dallas for Three Dog Night, to Aspen for the Nitty Gritty Dirt Band, to San Francisco for RCA/Grunt patsies Jack Bonus and Black Kangaroo, to Boston for something called Gross National Product (or possibly Productions) on Metromedia (now defunct) Records & Tapes. For a dizzying run, the spit holding the whole setup together flowed incredibly freely, and I *saw places*, Jack, sampled the wares of cities and townships—Tampa, Buffalo, Wilkes-Barre, Minneapolis—I might otherwise, through all possible lifetimes, have passed on completely. In the process I developed a taste for return visits (at my own expense) to outposts where I'd formed acquaintances with homebred rockscribblers and/or rockscribble groupies (yes, there *were* such beings), thus granting New York an adventitious *usefulness*—as a viable "base of operations"—which, prior to my 30th, could easily have been the catalyst nipping all thoughts of leaving at the gitgo.

Anyway, after five solid years of this nonsense, with a remarkable acceptance ratio as visiting gadabout-unleashed, I'd been to Los Angeles and, of all places, Montreal more times than anywhere else—seven, maybe eight visits each. Since I felt I could count on more "lasting friendships" in these two towns than the rest of the continent combined, and since I wasn't about to take on a *new* continent without a rock-junket freebie to pave the way, an unlikely prospect in view of my plummeting ratio vis-à-vis the *biz*, by autumn's first whatsis my range of choices seemed limited, clearly, to one of the two (gadabouts love security).

Montreal, but an hour from LaGuardia or JFK in case I got homesick, boasted at the time an offbeat, essentially French-flavored rockscene only I, among U.S. anglophones, had chosen so far to chronicle, thus appealing to the elito-archaeologist in me. In addition they had this real *wowser* of a sportscene, deep both in content (major-league hockey and baseball; CFL football; TV access to the usual American crap) and consciousness (hipper fans than I'd seen for *anything* anywhere else; sportswriters, some of whom I'd had drinks and laughs with, who seemed to know their ass from Uranus), which appealed-ain't-the-*word* to my latent sportswrite pretensions. Hey, here was my chance to finally kiss this teenage rock-roll bluh bluh *goodbye*, to at least *begin* to finesse a transition, and what better timing than the Montreal Olympics, on tap for the following summer? And that summer, that year: '76. Did I *really* want to endure the BICENTENNIAL in America? I did not. (Points for Montreal.)

But, much as I'd always liked snow, even slush, Montreal winters were Something Else; muffle up, I'd been told, or *lose your earlobes*. And I'd have to learn French, really learn it, not just rehash a couple-three verb drills from high school, or run the risk (come the Great Quebec Heave-Ho) of being one lonely *chien anglais*, my bilingual French pals no longer willing to English me (and my Anglo chums long gone to Toronto). Plus I'd probably have trouble with work papers, customs charges on my possessions and shit—so scratch Canada.

Leaving me—was it really ever a contest?—with L.A., and on 10/15/75 I took the big flight west and south. As a sign of how hopeful and foolish my Decision had made me, I'd chosen that date to give me time to get invited to some *great* Halloween parties. (In, y'know, Hollywood.) En route I sipped white wine, though I usually preferred red, musing on the twin New York themes of L.A. as Tinsel-Turd Central and San Francisco, an option I'd never for a moment entertained, as acceptable True California, and chuckled. But flying with chuckles is one thing; landing's another. No sooner had I deplaned, 98% of my worldly goods in a Bekins truck somewhere in (perhaps) Ohio, than I began to *notice things*, dire and highly unpleasant things, things which had somehow escaped my eye when I was just a rockin'/rollin' out-of-towner with a beer in each hand and a penis for brains . . .

SKIMMING
THE
SURFACE

For starters, there were airheads like I could not believe. I'm not talking laid back, slow on the draw—I'm talking bubbleskulls, insensates. Any gathering of five-six people would invariably include at least one raging dodo cum oaf, either (I at first assumed) because Angelenos were flexible, "tolerant," less rule-governed in respect to wiggy abstractions like human thought, or (a better working premise, one I tried hard to repress) because sun-and-fun might ultimately cook *anyone*'s brain until full-service mentation became a tricky and functionally meaningless calisthenic, one less vital (on a regular basis) than signaling a lane change. On my second day as a resident a new acquaintance labeled me, semi-derisively, an "intellectual," as if the breed were as rare, freakish—and locally unwelcome—as an anti in New York. I had split the Seriousness Capital of the World, it was quickly becoming evident, for the Dummdumm Capital of Same.

The ramification of this which I could easily have taken most personally—the fact that here I was, a goddam writer in a town where nobody *reads*—actually bothered me less than spillovers to local culture and epistemology. To service all the dummdumms, willful or otherwise, you had trendy mindstuff *galore*—as product, pastime, veil of enlightenment, from Nichiren Shoshu to past-life therapy to Born-Again Christian lunacy—to professionally tackle their need for A-implies-B. On my first visit to an L.A. dentist, I caught the tail end of a hot one between receptionist and hygienist: "I just can't *wait* to be enlightened"; "Be patient—sometimes it takes a few weeks"; "Weeks?!"—gosh, I hoped she could make it. After a couple months of this, I half-expected to see a neon (or billboard) for "Mindology—it's a science."

Which is maybe cute 'n' charming in a 90-minute film about Mars or the 1960s, but not when you're living it, not when it's foreground, background or at least frame most parts of most days. (Two of my so-called friends had succumbed to est; my first regular sex partner was an ex-Hare Krishna.) Nor was it much fun to see, or to have to constantly deal with, most folks' *disinclination* to distinguish illusion from reality, surface from substance, or a wretched hand-as-dealt from a viable one. With these distinctions ultimately mattering so little, and with surface (as such) so unrecognized, overesteemed or misjudged, it was hardly unusual to see the superficial jump a track and *run deep*, to hear "Have a nice day" four-five times an hour, to receive autopilot smiles (from waitresses, bank clerks, etc.) that wouldn't've fooled a retard back in New York. There was this news piece, "Happiness Quotient Soaring," wherein it was claimed that 89% of Southern Cal adults boasted of being "pretty happy" or "very happy" with their hand: what a bunch of simps, feebs, Republicans, robots and *children*.

'Cause the hand, hey, well let's look at the hand (as I saw it):

The Sun. *Fuck* the Sun. Even though I'd once lived in (Rock, Rock) Rockaway Beach, I had never gotten a tan, nor did I want one, now or ever. Early November, even mid-November, still felt like what *I* considered summer. My least favorite season. Would it ever be winter? (Did fall exist?) Had I only been here previously in cold spells (and/or air-conditioned limos)? Would it ever *rain*?

The antisepticness of it all. No litter anywhere; people threw even gum wrappers in the trash. Everybody took showers all the time (in any event, more than twice a week). No women had armpit hair; males with exposed face *shaved every day*. Lawns were like putting greens; no weeds the eye could see. A house with one cockroach was considered infested. Unwashed cars—any age—were assumed to have been abandoned.

No bars. Even a clean and stupid place should have 'em, but there were none. Least not of the friendly, functional "neighborhood" sort I'd come to regard as my trans-urban birthright. Just glitzy *cocktail lounges*, with a sprinkling of Skid Row scuzz; nothing in the middle far as I could tell. Except for bottles right in hand, I'd probably only gotten drunk in rock clubs during shows, and 2 A.M. closing time—'s 4:00 in New York—took me by surprise and struck me as *absurd*, as did the zeal which generally accompanied its enforcement. But as denials of pleasure go, that was minor compared to the *10* o'clock closing time—on Fridays! Saturdays!—of most *restaurants* I had any fondness for. This was Babylon?? (How had it ever got the name?)

Womanlove: ha. [See: "Gonads and Chablis."]

Money. As culture. As opposed to what it can "buy." Maybe in '88 it's all anybody in America cares about, but in '75 it was more on a topical back burner. In L.A., though, it was already front and center. At the only Halloween bash I managed to get invited to, the first stranger I met asked me, "How do people like you survive?" (I had holes in my jeans.) The first woman I spoke to asked if I was a doctor. When I told her no she promptly left the room.

Jogging. Sailing. Racquetball. Golf. None of which I'd come here to "do."

So what *had* I come for? Beats me. What I *did*, though, was grumble, groan, eschew the same shit I'd already kissed off in New York—museums, galleries, concerts, plays—and basically continue, on alien soil, a New Yorkish lowlife creep. I crawled, crept, found my little oases of not-much, usually on the mainstream's under-underbelly, presuming that to be where the "substance" was. On mainstream turf, whenever feasible, I kept an eye out for the benignly, the *superficially* superficial. (I had, after all, reviewed LPs by their sleeves.)

But in many ways I wasn't really looking. The years, a few of 'em, crept by. By which time I still didn't especially "like" living in L.A., though I wasn't about to pack up, pack in and "return east." (I'd been too deprogramed from crowds, noise, etc. to even consider it.) But for all the local input my N.Y. eyes, and N.Y. blinders, were as yet letting in—neutrally, nakedly, without N.Y. "judgment"—it mattered little that I'd ever moved west of Staten Island. (If the tarrers, the featherers, could see me now!)

Then: the dawn. The day, with ur-crucial assist from L.A., something *national* happened to send my N'Yorkocentricness down the drain; to force me to behold, once and for all, neither askance nor askew, the Not New York; to convince me that, except possibly emeritus, New York wasn't the anything capital of *dick*. Actually it was more like a week. The week (remember?) when Carter chose to reinvent the Cold War, which would soon be handed to a pus-headed former Angeleno named Reagan, and during which I realized I was living in the heart, belly, anus of a Beast. A beast rarely noticed— uppercase or lower—on the sidewalks of New York, where rats-in-a-cage commonality makes one far more aware of the Cage. A beast called America.

Off the coast of which New York is but an *island*.

But *of* which, meantime, L.A. is capital in let me count the ways.

BARBER
SHOP
ZEN

Patricia Fripp, 35-year-old sibling of Brit guitarist Robert Fripp, has been barbering for a living since one week shy of her 15th birthday. Among her early clients were Hayley Mills and Princess Ann of Denmark (whoever *she* is), but since '66 when she went to work for eventual Manson snuffout Jay Sebring she's been a men's clipper and nothing but ("Hair is the frame of the male face, women can *cheat* with rouge and things"). Just two of her satisfied sitters-still since then: U.S. Senator (and rightwing semantics prick) S. I. Hayakawa and Jack Rosenberg a/k/a Werner Erhardt, founder of the self-indulgence training scam *est*.

"I knew Werner about 1970 when he used to come to Sebring's shop. One day he was late for whoever was doing his hair at the time, so I did his hair. There was always a certain *presence* about Werner that made you realize he was a little different from the average bloke, you could really tell that he was not, quote-unquote, *normal*. And one day I said to him, 'What's new, groovy and exciting in your life?' and he told me, 'I've just taken this course called Mind Dynamics and it's so fabulous I'm learning how to teach it.'

L.A. Is the Capital of Kansas

"It sounded interesting so I went and did it and it really was a powerful and interesting experience for me. Then 18 months later, after he left Mind Dynamics and went on his own, I took a review in the est training, and they wouldn't let me go to the bathroom and stuff like this that I didn't *totally* enjoy or appreciate or see the necessity of. Then I did it again in '75 and the only reason I didn't leave was because I was goin' out with a guy that was on his staff who was givin' me hell because I wanted to leave, I guess he didn't think it was *okay* for his girlfriend to leave and all this stuff. Let's just say I *support* est but I don't shake a tambourine."

Not for est perhaps but she sure does shake it, shakes it for this big mouthful called Dale Carnegie's Adventures in Achievement, which alone shoulda been enough to give me second thoughts about letting this stranger come in my house and give me a freebie—for "review purposes"—worth $17.50 plus tip. Shoulda been, but there was more. Like she tells me her sign ("Aries women are independent and ambitious and flirtatious and energetic") tho I won't tell her mine (wouldn't for even *two* haircuts). Then she says, "What fascinates me now about hair is the marketing aspect of it, how to sell the fact that *your* haircut is better than somebody else's, and the motivational aspect of how you can show barbers and hairdressers that they can improve the quality of their lives by doing a better job and *thus* serving the public better." Goodies like that plus the fact that she's got one the stoooopidest hairdos on earth* (more irrationally short and misshapen than Pet Clark or Joey Heatherton or Angela Lansbury) shoulda made me hesitate, but there's something about her chairside manner that seduced me (nobody takes courses for nothin') so I let her punctuate the rap with some ongoing scissor & snip.

"See, I believe in *miracles*, the miracles that we have performed every day. Like a while back a guy called Gary Barionelli came into my shop. He was a computer programer for Levi-Strauss making about $18,000 a year. He was a little overweight, plainly dressed, kinda greased-down hair. I did his hair, it looked fabulous. He looked

---

*This was pre-punk '76.

good, not only did I think he looked good, his wife thought he looked good and all the women in the office thought he looked good and he felt GOOD!

"He lost weight, got some trendy clothes, became more outgoing and his bosses saw the *change* in him and offered him a job as a salesman even though he had no prior sales experience. Now the way it works with sales is you can't make any more than your sales manager and at Levi-Strauss that's $55,000 a year. So every time he'd get up to making $50,000 in sales they'd split the territory. Gary Barionelli has had his territory split *four times*. And I'm not saying it *is* because of my haircut *but* giving him the haircut made him feel differently about *himself.*"

Turns out tho that she's down on "superstar haircutters" like Sassoon whose main concern is "image" (as opposed to "hair for hair sake") so I ask what she thinks of all these gallant small-time ethnic locals carrying on the neighborhood cheap-cut tradition: *nothing* as there's not one *artist* among them. Ask her about baldies: "I personally *excel* with men with receding hairlines. You don't have to have hair to come into my shop, you just have to have the price of admission. Just because you don't have a lot of hair doesn't mean you can't have the wonderful *experience* of being in my shop and experiencing the service that we give."

Ask her next what she likes in the way of rock-roll thatchery (brothers excepted) and she don't actually care for *any* of it: most notable male SHOWBIZ hair she ever actually "dug" was PAUL NEWMAN'S after Sebring got done with him. Hmm.

Gradually I'm losing confidence in the sculpture being performed on my very own head, losin' it by the minute, especially after she claims she's taken my "casual lifestyle" into account so it won't make my forehead sweat even if I don't choose to comb it.

Finally the moment-o-truth as I survey the results in the mirror, tho first I have to wait for her to piss (turns the faucet up *full* as she does). Finally: *youch.* There's this pompadour-looking thing on top and nothing in back and all kindsa shit hangin' over my ears like a country-western dipshit. And since she's already packed and finished all I can ask or beseech is *whuddo I do with the goddam thing, huh?*

13

L.A. Is the Capital of Kansas

Great answer (dig *this*): "Oh, just brush it back." Haw haw and I'm stuck with the worst butcher job my locks've got since "Uncle" Jerry, Camp Cayuga '58—get *outa* here, lemme try 'n' salvage this disaster . . . where's my scis?

NO WAYLON,
NO WILLIE,
NO GOAT

"We're *loaded* with perverts tonight," announces pot-bellied, be-sweatered Harry Newman of KLAC, the spotlight accenting mole-like nose growths like you sometimes see in paintings of obscure Italian nobles by long-dead, too-honest bozos with a brush. Another weekly talent showcase at North Hollywood's Palomino Club is about to unwind: all the pathos and bathos that Thursdays up Lankershim way have been entailing for the past 17 years; beehives and bandanas from Simi to San Dimas pouring their hearts and lungs out for the $100.00 grand prize.

Some slight interference tonight: simultaneous doings (and undo-ings) across town at the Academy of Country Music Awards fan-dango will be vying for relevance with the contestants' valiant, mournful look-at-me. No big deal when Harry reveals that (1) he's failed to win deejay of the year honors "for the seventh year in a row" and (2) Billy (not *the*) Graham, fiddler tonight in the makeshift band required to back up all the wide-eyed amateurs, has copped *bassplayer* of the annum kudos, but the proclamation that "Waylon Jennings will be here after the awards with his lovely wife Willie Nelson" *just might be construed* as willfully detracting from the urgency and poignancy of high-school opener Laurie Canterman's brace-faced rendition of the Linda Ronstadt version of the Everly Brothers' "When Will I Be Loved?"

Yes, Linda's gotta be the number one source this evening, with Karen Blair in her white-flowered Mama Cass sarong contributing "Love Has No Pride" and Jody Chelik in red and black (a Stendhal fan?) getting her 2¢ in with "You're No Good." But Ray Price is also drawn from (earringed Gino Vanelli lookalike Jamie Wayne with "Crazy Arms"), as are Jeannie Sealy (Joanne Alexander, her features as psychically maimed as one ever gets to see on a *nightclub stage*, eyebrows narrow, lips too cold to kiss ice cream, lending a dash of hard meaning to "Don't Touch Me"), Kris Kristofferson (balding, work-garbed Chuck Schaefer stalling through the final chorus of "Help Me Make It Through the Night" until Harry orders his hippie butt off stage but *pronto*: "maximum of four minutes per act"), "Teenager in Love" (sloppy/slobby David Caleb, T-shirt sticking out from under his bland beige "business" shirt) and even "Abraham, Martin and John" (former winner Scott "T," Troy Donahue-like in the white three-piece leisure suit chances are he squandered his previous winnings on at C & R Clothiers, struggling to find his groove *a cappella*) . . .

Then of course there are those who'd rather *write their own* (just as crucial as *rolling* your own): Michael E. Strain (dull-sheened western shirt with an "I've had my troubles" tune the band can't follow nohow), Chuck Curtis from San Juan Capistrano (immaculate work duds; reverent lyric about Hawaii), Connie Birdwell (long skirt, flirty, eyes way too big for her face; a "town we were born in" item that falls on dead, deaf ears), Steve Shannon ("no stranger to the Palomino," your perennial loser, "Some Man Will Never Know," a title and everything: stoic with a soft center of stale, mushy cornflakes), etc., etc.—*many* etceteras.

And lest we forget our fine not-yet-employed country *comics*: Tiny Brooks ("three hundred pounds of rompin'-stompin' love"—more like three-fifty—her jokes what you might call, um, *racy*), Lee

Coleman (black, "I'm a nigger impressionist," a George Wallace routine drawing hoots of "Three cheers for George!") and the "aptly named" L.A. Knockers (five "country sluts" in dancehall scanties, "I screwed more cowboys than I can count," Harry Newman becomes *unglued*) . . . yawn.

Talent, talent *galore* you'd have to admit. But nothing to *compare* with the awesome artistry of this gent Harry welcomes right after he's called attention to a post-awards Mel Tillis and Tom T. Hall entering the men's john together: cat name of *Goat*. Goat! Wild! Shades of Peter Wolf! The blues! In black! Scruffy beard! Boots to his knees! Grungy! Scuzzy! Out on the dance floor! "Gun at my side" inane lyrics! Crawls on the floorboards! Clucks like a chicken! Insults the band! Shoves his mike in audience mouths: "Testify!" Go go Goat!

Looks like a man a hundred bucks richer *for sure* but before the results are tabulated there's time for Messrs. Hall and Tillis to strut forth their *professional* variety of eternal country verity but funny 'cause Tom—seriousness ringing his cowlike phiz—*ain't really no better* than a good two-thirds of the amateurs (true). Steve Shannon for random instance could easily have outdone Thomas's unstirring, lacklustre "Clayton Delaney" with rolled up napkins up his snoot (I wouldn't lie to ya, Steve, keep up the blah blah etc.). Melvin though, his famed stutters and stammers working overtime, is simply *ace*: "I didn't expect to get up and sing—this is my *night out*. I've had too much to drink, I'm like Don Ameche." Spotting the bulbous Tiny Brooks down front: "I *like* you, who are you?" Tiny: "Moby Dick." Mel, quick with a *good'un*: "You're the only g-girl I know where I could run through two inches of hair and two inches of fat and run out of d-dick . . . is it okay to say 'dick'? There goes my image, baby!" Don't worry Mel, your image is safe with us patrons of the "Pal"!

Okay, down to six finalists and Goat is among them, lookin' good. Shouts of "Goat! Goat!"—lookin' better. Runner-up ($50) is named: David Gross (ponytail and straw hat, sang "I Can't Stop Loving You"), at least they're not denying Goat his full hunnert smackers. FIRST PRIZE: John (whuh?) Anderson (huh?), yoyo who did

L.A. Is the Capital of Kansas

Waylon and Willie's "Good Hearted Woman" and reminded this word jockey *strongly* of the guy who used to sing for NRBQ (i.e., a goddam *pro*!). We wanna recount! At least an applause meter!

And—hey!—where're Waylon and Willie for cryin' out loud?!

Sheee . . . (gal's room has a Li'l Legs pantyhose dispenser though).

WONDERFUL
NOSE

I'm at Trader Vic's in Beverly Hills. Don't ask me why. No, that's okay, go ahead, ask me.

I'm at Trader Vic's because a crony *dragged me to Trader Vic's*. One of us is enjoying the hors d'oeuvres. Not far from our table stands a pyramid.

A chintzy wooden pyramid. Actually just the frame of one— unpainted. With a wine rack underneath or you might call it inside only it's too wide open. Real, real hokey but this is hokesville. Kind of "goes" with the South Seas decor, one more bold allusion to foreign exotica. I then spot a fine brochure which tells me otherwise.

"Trader Vic's Pyramid Wine" reads the legend. 'S right there next to the wine list. "This may sound silly," it begins, "but I've done it and it works. No doubt you've heard about Pyramid Power, so I'll just give you a few of my thoughts on the subject based on my own experience." This is the Trader himself talkin', god's gift to the Polynesian sparerib industry, and he goes on to yodel about Cheops and how this advanced civ from Atlantis, see, built it or possibly the aliens. He advises a good stiff read of *The Art of Terra Cotta Pottery in*

L.A. Is the Capital of Kansas

Pre-Columbian Central and South America by Alexander von Somesuch as it will explain (and then some) where the Central Ams in fact got their pots from: excellent reading. He then whips out his slide rule and figgers dimensions should you need a pyramid of your own six feet tall (base, 9.4248 feet; sides, 8.9674)—thanks, that's helpful.

Gettin' further down to biz he has, he sez, put milk in his own personal 'mid and it's turned to yogurt, fruit and it's turned to... didn't turn, stayed fresh. Most hifalutin So. Cal. use is you take a bottle of local [shitty] wine and lay it in a pyramid facing north. Cork end north? Victor doesn't say. "I did the same thing with Almaden Pinot Noir and inside a week I had a Pinot Noir that was nice and soft and it had a wonderful nose." No nose like a wonderful nose!

"Each of our restaurants," he concludes, "will have various wines from under the pyramid for you to try. We hope you have as much enjoyment as we have." Okay, T.V., you're on! Garçon, pinot noir s'il vous plait! Whatever in heck it is (red?) this boy will have some maintenant!

Have it and it is red but nice & soft? 'Tis. Wonderful nose? Possibly. Sip it, drink, finish it, nice, soft, very quite possibly wonderful. FUCK, NO, I *HATE* WINE, GIMME A MARGARITA!

YOU DON'T HAVE TO GO TO LONG BEACH TO GET TATTOOED

No because there's some my-t fine colorful hole drilling for your arm or chest or back or calf or buttocks available in L.A. proper. Four neat-isn't-the-word emporiums in Tinseltown dedicated to permanent painted designs that you'll wake up one morning and hate for the rest of your life and on any grand tour downtown's got to be the very first stop: West Coast Tattoo Studio, 507 S. Main. "Oldest & Biggest Tattoo Studio in Calif" sez the peeling sign and elder it sure do be (respect your elders they always say). "WE BUY OLD COINS" and if they've got the first coin they ever earned it must be from the far side of WWI unless eyes are capable of lying through their teeth 'cause most of the graphics seem to date from that famous major skirmish.

Even the WWII and Korean Konflict drawings on the wall have that real swell "prehistoric" look like they're based on ancient prototypes that no tattooist in his conventional right mind would beg to differ with. Bulldog face with the inscription MY OLD SARGE. Worn out dog/soldier carrying a USMC duffel bag: NEVER AGAIN. Human-faced soldierboy with a big bad bullet through his noggin and a cross upon his deader-than-dogdoo shoulder: MY LIFE FOR GOD & COUNTRY. Sieg-heiling goosestepper with ACHTUNG instead of a head.

As I'm mulling the art the establishment's two artistes're engaged in animated tat-parlor dialogue, the fat bald tattooed-to-the-gills one in blue banlon asking the greased-blond tattooed-to-the-diz beatnik one, "Is this your pen, if it is I'll pay you for it." One of those 19¢ cheapos but Maynard G. Krebs isn't taking credit for ownership that is not his: "No it's not, you can have it." "You sure it's okay?" "Yeah it's not mine." "Absolutely sure?" "Keep it." An arthritic seahag staggers in to join the fray, tattered wool hat over her ears, ski jacket over plaid lumberjack shirt (springtime and it really ain't cold), her tongue protruding at some new experimental angle. She wants to know if so-and-so's been in lately, the boys tell her the party is in F-L-A but surely a postcard will be forthcoming. "Ha," she laughs, "he doesn't even have my address." "Well he could just mail it to Shirley, Broadway, Downtown L.A., ha ha ha." "Ha ha ha ha ha." (Tattoo hideaways are *great* places to hang out now that barber shoppes have gone the way of the hoss & buggy.)

In eventually walks a disgruntled recent customer not totally satisfied with his purchase. Guy has almost no hair and what he's got was cut with a pocketknife (or butter knife), age about 19 or 20 very hard years old. Lots of scabby red patches which he insists weren't *finished* when he was in for his original sitting. They squeeze his arm, look: "Okay, let it heal first, then come back." His wounds have not yet healed.

Back on the walls the action is fast and it's furious. Harley-Davidson logo with a skull and "3-D" swastika. Different skull with rabbit ears smoking reefer. Yet another inside a cocktail glass, signifying juice will kill you if ya don't watch out. A pair of skunks: DRUNK AGAIN (animals do not fear cirrhosis). Nude honey stabbing the shark she's riding like a bronc, blood *gushing* from the poor doomed fishy. *Lotsa* Jesus stuff (ornate!). An El Grecoesque ghoul with a shovel at the local cemetery. IN MEMORY OF MOTHER (angel type broad with a crucifix). Che. Y'know Guevara. Fist with POWER on the cuff (cuff?). CROSSED EQUA-

TOR (ship), to commemorate crossing it either after or before shipping out but before would be *cheating* and tattoos're matters of honour Mr. Sailorboy, don't you forget it!

Men responsible for the various & sundry scribbles d'arte that our two boss aces of their profession (Baldy & Beaty) are fully capable of inscribing on your living breathing flesh so you never need fear getting stuck in the same Judaic burial plot as mom & pappy are in some instances listed beneath their efforts. Ernie Sutton 53. Sutton & Lewis 56. Capt. Jim 69. Spanning lotsa years and speaking of years IF NOT 18 SCRAM reads another calligraphic masterwork above the doorway to a backroom containing ???? UNDER SUPERVISION OF DR. J.D. NELSON M.D. so you know the filth of the place is healthy and no grisly horrible hepatitis will invade your bloodstream from electric needles scraping your skin like a sharpened ballpoint dragging across with muscle behind it causing blood to seep in small to moderate eruption which they then wipe off with a kleenex so as not to interfere with their unobstructed view of the remainder of the work which lies ahead, no debilitating hep to keep you from hitting the bottle for upwards of six lousy horrible drinkless months in bed or walking around turning yellow.

Speaking of which, the yellows on *many* an illustration at the upstairs tat dive at 6758 Hollywood Blvd. are washed out like they've been fading in the sun streaming in from the great big window overlooking John's Pipe Shop, Star-Lite Pants and the Hollywood Wax Museum across the street. Sun could be the culprit but careful inspection reveals photocopying's to blame. Copied from (sure looks *familiar*) the downtown branch (seen it *all* before) of (somewhere just *hours* ago) West Coast (I *remember* that name) Tattoo Studio as this is just the Hollywood offshoot so why bother redoing everything with ink & quill? No reason so same stuff—copied. Tattooist's of an unsame ilk though (dress shirt, simple gold earring) and the clientele's your standard Hollywdblvd. jive-joe deadbeat flotsam 'stead of scab-arms and drooling slatterns.

Some newies on the wall though like that famous Li'l Red Devil or whatever his name is riding a bike with a big 13 (signed Dave Hollywood 75). And Goofy with SEA DOG in script beneath his famous mug. And MAN'S RUIN, a stockinged gam straddling a skull with dice, cards and a fifth of something off to the side. And TOKYO JOE, a slant-eyed skull with one of them *Chinese* braids on top. And rabbits "doin' it."

Hygiene's as conspicuously good as let's say Johnny's Steak House in the gen'ral vicinity so no "under supervision of" sign is necessary to ease the mind of hypochondriacs paying a visit with needles in possible mind. Signs are for readers anyway and tattoo premises, gen'rally speaking, are not. They are for three types of people: 1. tattooists; 2. tattooees; 3. people having looksees at the tats, the tooists and the tooees, in other words MUSEUM GOERS either conscious or in spite of 'emselves which is another something these swell dens of culture are *good for*, especially considering the outrageous $1.50 or whatever ungodly price to ogle worthless Commie oils from Moscow, USSR, at the crowded and germ-ridden (earl painters are known for their rots) L.A. County Museum of Crap.

The Hollywood Tattoo Studio at 6317 Hollywood Blvd. is not only better-ain't-the-word than said canvas graveyard but 's admission free to boot. Real neat framed oldish B&W snaps like from an overpriced antique shoppe of oldtimey seafarers of the bounding main with their bodies tattooed to a fairtheewell adorn the window beside a vintage "Ladies Tattooed in Private" sign so you know before entering this place is as contempo as tomorrow. The gentlemen of this jukejoint (BOB-PHIL-TODD-LARRY & BOBBY 76) have done something none of their competitors have thought to do: "update" the graphics. So you get the same awesome themes done with a post-1945 hand if not downright mid-'70s 'cause that's how new the artwork "looks."

F'rinstance: nipples on the nudies resemble succulent red-tinted low-watt bulbs like y'might find in an "underground" comic. Ditto on the dog soldiers: comix doggies like a San Friscan might choose to draw without a shotgun even pointed at his head (freedom of expression = solid guarantee of permanent needlework to your person persisting in the "now" department for at least fifteen months). Homo sap warriors in like manner have that Nam look or even Rhodesian mercenary. So you can join the marines in *style* for a change.

Even the *total* originals are literally busting a gut with originality. Mahatma Gandhi (himself) smoking a waterpipe with you-know-what in the barrel. Skull with a syringe poking its eye socket containing a wide range of possible you-knows: smack, speed, coke, STP for inst. Al "Scarface" Capone poised as big as life above the silhouette of a submachinegun. A buxom redhead of the feminine persuasion with a green skull on her lap and her pudenda exposed as rosy red as a Valentine's Day heart.

Another plus for this top-drawer tatjoint is prices are listed on each whatsit so you know without asking how much of a hole it's gonna make in your pocket to beautify your boring bod till death do you part. Prices on the above: $31.50, $24.50, $32.00, I forgot to write the last one down. Superman insignia: a mere $26.00.

Meet Mr. Needle-Man: young, personable, no earrings or pierced nostrils, reeking of concerned hipster and counterculture orientations, used to work for Spider Webb in Mount Vernon, N.Y., where I once got charged $35.00 plus tax for something that here might only set me back a half to a third as much, it's too bad you can't trade them in!

Speaking of which, tattoos are of course indelible and unremovable unless you want some doc to scrape it off with a grindstone. In which case you've got yourself a nasty horrible *scar* where once multicolored loveliness flourished so you've gotta be a fool to have it removed. Point is you've only got one body to mutilate and one lifetime to mutilate it in so why not use the lifetime while it's still around to mutilate that one body in a manner of your choosing before the worms're digesting your entrails and tonsils and the sinews around your hubcap, make that kneecap. I mean once you're dead you're *no longer alive* and think of all the personal bod art you'll have missed out on. But. But it's hard to stop at *just one* once you've broken in that virginal epidermis with tat ink which sometimes makes the area swell up real bad when you're showering (solution: fewer showers) so you really must decide in advance how you're going to allocate the available parts of your surface anatomy. Like once you've got DEATH BEFORE DISHONOR on your left forearm that's it for that sacred spot, no replacing it with ANCHORAGE 2012 and an anchor superimposed on a map of Alaska.

Not that you can't have Cliff Raven of Sunset Tattoo Studios, 8418 Sunset Blvd., work his magic 'round and about what you're already stuck with and in so doing create an overall *composition* of flowing majesty that'll take him maybe three or four weeks worth of tedious painful sitting time on your tail to complete. Bigstuff such as whole arms and backs and torsos and abdomens and even the male meat are his oeuvre and prices even for butterflies the size of a shamrock *begin at fifty bucks* so figure it from there if you want both thighs psychedelicized by a goddam authentic skilled tradesman. Cliff is now in the process of obliterating the memory of Bay Area superspud Lyle Tuttle whose employees used to haunt this address. They took their wallstuff with them so if you want the museum treatment you'll just have to settle for this turquoise-earringed weasel flipping plastic-covered photos of what Cliff's done with the body parts of satisfied clients (if you're fond of artwork on the male unit he's got some *doozies* to show ya). Tigers and dragons and snakes and eagles and drapery and clouds and foliage and Cliff does it all *free hand.* So you don't get all that messy *graphite* like they usually use with stencils on your gorgeous groovy hide.

But as mentioned it'll run you a pret-ty penny so take the advice of my good buddy Doug Zoot of San Quentin and *do it yourself*: "Take the staples out of a magazine. Straighten them and sharpen the ends on the cement around the bottom of the toilet in your cell. If you haven't got cement many times the steel of the flat cross-rails or the bottom or corners of your steel bunk can also put a fine point. Then take some threads from your towel and wrap the newly made needle to a matchstick, using enough thread to hold ink. Make the needle no longer than necessary so you can stash it in a light fixture or behind the sink or any other tight place so it won't be found in a shakedown. Take some paper (newsprint is best), burn it and crush the ashes to dust, add water and you've got an outasight ink. Shredded pencil lead is highly toxic and makes a lousy tattoo. If you get chained out to the joint you can usually get sewing needles from the laundry. Heat a toothbrush, insert needles and wrap with thread to make a more permanent needle but I recommend the other kind as it is easier to hide and there are usually stiff penalties for getting caught with this equipment. Also you can make lots of commissary and have all the dope you want if you can tattoo good. Anyway if you ever get in a bind it is better than playing cards and you'll have everything you need available at your particular jail." Thanx Doug, sounds good to me!

Coast mag's own Marsha Boone however would have none of this homemade hokum, choosing instead to visit a skilled professional to have her big toe tatted (a tat-toe) with three colors across it like a rainbow but as fate would have it our valiant storefront pros were unwilling to perform the service on account of hands and feet're illegal in this here state (too close to the bone). One gent however was willing to do the pedal digit for an extra remuneration far in excess of its worth (asked for 25 clams) plus the promise of total anonymity. A promise is a promise: his name was "Marv," age 26, place of origin Wyoming, nationality Greek-American. That's all you'll get from me—I'll go to the *gallows* to protect this tatman's identity so lawmen lay off 'cause my lips're sealed . . .

As Ms. Boone describes the experience (guy wouldn't perform with witnesses, told me to "stay here" while he took her off by her lonesome to *another room* from which sounds of drilling for female hemoglobin issued forth): "He started drawing rings on my toe with a Bic pen. Then he went through this crisis, should he or shouldn't he, he's afraid he'll lose his job. Then I persuade him, I say please, please, I *licked my lips* and things, moved my body in *certain ways*. From that point on there was lust involved in his manner, which I could put up with because I've had to put up with it in acquiring other things, ha. A *man* would've had to offer him a lot more money because he was obviously heterosexual.

"So finally he started doing it, he takes this needle out, *ooh*. He put black ink in it and started doing these lines on my toes. The needle didn't scare me when I saw it at first, it was only when he turned it on and it started making that noise, it felt and sounded like a lawnmower, I felt like my toe was being mowed, it felt like he was drilling down to the bone. There was this one part he got to towards the outside of the toe that actually was sort of excruciating—so I bit my knee so I wouldn't yell. I asked him if people ever got up in the middle of it 'cause they couldn't take it, he said yes, sometimes they even pass out.

"Then he hadda do the colors [red, green, yellow], he already had the lines on. The color didn't hurt as bad but my toe was beginning to feel like hamburger. It all took twenty-five minutes. When he was done he put this ointment on and told me to go buy a bandage 'cause he didn't have one that small and he didn't want me showing anybody out front where the tattoo was by means of a too-big bandage.

"I'm glad I didn't get a tattoo that I'd have to sit on—'cause it *hurts*. I'm contemplating whether to go buy a pair of appropriately stylish shoes that don't put pressure on my toe because I have a busy social schedule this week and don't wish to wear a tennis shoe with a toe hole cut out. Limping around is no fun."

Asked about future permanent defacements, Ms. Boone replied: "Absolutely, just not for a while." And what she thinks of people who're scared to get 'em: "They're candy-asses. What's a little *pain*?" Bravo Marsha, you've got yourself a good'un!

L.A. IS THE CAPITAL OF KANSAS

> ..."society"
> which is just a name
> for that great Milwaukee
> the entertainment business dreams up
> and calls America
> —Tom Clark, "To Lenny Bruce"

The news is out and the news is: (hick).

You sit for five minutes, at most ten, in the Farmer's Market off Fairfax, all these tourist-priced postcard and jade ashtray shops, you're reading the paper, sippin' your tourist-priced carrot-coconut juice and without fail (it matters not what day, season or week) a full-fledged YOKEL from Des Moines, Sioux City or Dubuque (for inst) will exclaim to a fellow hick he or she has met on the Gray Line bus: "Lookit what *I* got, Irma—a Bo Derek poster!!!" As if they don't got 'em back in Walnut Falls and maybe they don't; I've never asked. Three years ago it was blowups of Farrah, the Fonz, now Bo, and they go home smiling that appleknocker SMILE (you've seen it in films), blowup in hand and tales on their lips of an unforgettable visit to the land of Dreams: a scumbag town that it beats me how anyone but a walking metaphor from Des Moines or Walnut Falls could actually be dreamin' about. REAL-LIFE HICKS AS META-PHORS INCARNATE (AS REAL-LIFE HICKS-AND-A-HALF). Or something like that.

But outside hicks, hick tourists, ain't even *needed*. Tourist stores need 'em, sure, but hardly the town. 'Cause the town would be hick on its own without any assistance: the biggest HICK TOWN (per se) in all the hick land. Biggest in area, population, but a "city" . . . "big town" . . . "major venue"? Surely you're kidding. Name me another major (I'll settle for Europe, even Australasia) that needs brass-rimmed stone STARS to certify, to its *own inhabitants*, the achievements of its local achievers. (I mean outside of kindergarten.) Hicks, both real and imagined, regardless of whatever else they are or aren't, are *easy marks*. L.A., not only bigger but easier, goes small-town hick one better: gawking touristhood redirected unto ITSELF. ("Yes, Seymour, a sidewalk memorial to one of our *greats* . . . Ozzie Nelson.")

For bulk SQ—susceptibility quotient—L.A. scores high. It buys its own shit. By it I mean principally its "citizens," its resident *lower-stratum* hicks. (Tho uppers have been known to buy as well.) In any event, like most anyhickwhere else, homebred lowers tend to *love* their uppers—"authority"—and what does L.A.'s homehick Author-ity love? It loves, currently, to shoot Kneegrows, altho they did shoot a nude whiteperson recently—claimed he'd struck a martial-arts POSE! Martial LAW meantime is *extremely popular*, so when I see L.A. *under* martial law (as if it's ever not!) in the fifties film *Them* I realize someone around here once had a keen sense of irony. Few today mind a shakedown for I.D. en route HOME from their car parked down the street ('s for yer own safety, dig?), fewer still mind LAPD 'copters waking 'em, shining brightlights in their window at 4 a.m.—and by don't mind I mean don't MIND. Incredibly few actually do. (Hick as a one-town Old West Preservation Society, with townspeople deputized to Eat Shit on selected dotted lines.)

You could fool ALL of L.A.'s underhicks ALL of the time, to

L.A. Is the Capital of Kansas

paraphrase one of history's more persuasive bumpkins. But you hardly need "persuasive powers" to sway *this* electorate; you needn't be an Honest Abe (nor an Andy Hardy's dad) (nor a Sgt. York's preacher). All you need is ruthlessness and money. Local lobbyist/ politicos *know* they're dealing with hicks (with *morons* too but at bottom just basically hicks), pulling numbers these days that make the Proposition 13* campaign look like the Lincoln-Douglas Debates. There's this Prop. 10 thing up for approval in the next election that's naught but a landlord con to finesse Angelenos into jettisoning the rent control they've miraculously lucked into and (once they buy the hype—which they will) will most likely never see again. Lying ads 'round the goddam CLOCK tell you Yes means "fair rents" when in fact it means an end to rent control once and for all—'ll shift control to the "community level" where the property-is-theft boys can tread merciless greed-water endlessly. And since richfolks KNOW BEST: no opposition!—would be tantamount to "treason." (Hick as, let's see, *Mr. Smith Goes to Washington* w/out Jimmy Stewart *daring* to impute scumbait venality to Claude Rains—and w/out Claude expressing an *ounce* of heartwarming Prot.-Ethic Guilt. I.e.: hicktown prospect-zero with no hick knight-in-shining to even redeem the STORY.)

Speaking of manipulation in the 20th century, there's *lotsa* places in the world that're *Alphaville*, lotta current dates that're really code for *1984*, but how many outposts of the soul can boast being real-life analogues to *THX-1138*? On any given night you watch Cal Worthington's used internal-combustion commercials or the mealtime/latetime local news and a non-myopic outsider would *swear* you were tuning your knob to the non-hologram version of those government-supplied "get off" stations in Lucas's first H-wood biggie. TV everywhere is like that more or less but here it's more or

---

*Approved by 67% of L.A. County voters in the state election of June 6, 1978, Prop. 13 awarded homeowners a sharp reduction in property tax in exchange for drastic cutbacks in such traditional public services as garbage pickup, aid to dependent children, and state-funded mental care. (See " . . . and Crazy for Loving You" for a ground-level blink at one aspect of its damnable wake.)

31

more: rubes tumbling f'r electrons like they were BORN YESTER-
DAY. Like it was 1947 and they were ogling tee!vees! in department
store WINDOWS. And why d'you think so many businesses in the
San Fernando Valley, the hickiest suburbia in the annals thereof
(anti-busing capital of the WORLD by the way), close at FIVE-
THIRTY? So their employers, employees, everybody can get home
in time to enjoy the blissful bliss 'n' agony of nuclear-family
mealhood and catch the evening's SHOWS with a fully digested
meatloaf already in their large intestine. The family that rooms
together consumes together? (Hick as nuke famine NOW MORE
THAN EVER.)

And praying/staying—that's hickstuff, right? Strictly from
Dogpatch. Well, a good 30-40-50% of L.A. TV fare (VHF and
UHF combined; either syndicated or local) is religious DOG*SHIT*.
In addition to the usual sick array of christmongery leisure-suited All
Smiles talkshow replacement-host types, that original Smiler the
goddam Maharishi has just landed on channel 18. His own show.
Bored-again Barry ("Eve of Destruction") McGuire has a show on
ch. 40, as does the *real* Jim Jones, Dr. Gene Scott. Over in Malibu,
Bob Dylan HIMSELF used to think he *was* God (now he's got
someone else—the Roadie in the Sky—doin' the dirtywork) but his
TV price is prob'ly too high but that's cool 'cause f'r godsakes the
true religion of this town, this frigging country, is godless CAPI-
TALISM (now you're talking). Or maybe—talking just the town—
it's the SUN. Sun: long before topical skin cancer, the first official
One God of that first official monotheist, Ikhnaton. Ray Manzarek,
late of the Doors, swears by him. Hicks for Ikh! (And who're bigger
hiiiiiicks than suntanned SURFERS?) If they ever go to solar power
L.A. & Ikh, hand in hand, will Show The Way—but he ain't got a
show yet so fug him. (Hick as oldtime/newtime not-insincere-ish
awe-grope in neurotic search of an Occasion and a Packager—you
can *never* trust yer own context.)

Hick? Hic! I've had a few. (Dwinks.) I am not debating-team
sharp. All you'd hafta do is yell "ONE-HORSE UNIVERSE" and I
would'not know what to say. One-horse universe! One-hor—! OK,
okay, I'll respond to that. 'S certainly a one-horse *nation*, no problem

there, 's even quite likely a one-horse "Big U"—not much of a thing called LIFE now, is it! (The Hick Upstairs—speaking of gods, speaking of One-Gods!—seems pretty much a one-size-fits-all down-on-the-farm'er.) So fine, oke, that much is settled: one-horse Neptune, one-horse Madagascar, one-horse Chicago. But what of *this* one-horser—does the hoss have herpes? are its withers arthritic? is there anything special (or strange) about its "corral"? In short, what's there to debunk about this jerkwater burg among many?—a very good question. Pour me another and I'll drink, er, think about it. Meanwhile, a quote:

> "Look at the Americans. They have invented some quality called un-Americanism just as though Americanism were a concept of an individual instead of a government's concept. There are strong resemblances between Americanism, Communism and Aryanism: all are government ideas and therefore will naturally describe characteristics of the easily governed."
>
> —Len Deighton, *Funeral in Berlin*

All of which starts HERE. Or finishes here. Certainly most of it. Maybe the "govt.," y'know D.C., *occasionally* supplies the frame, the theme, then L.A. comes in to paint the pitcher, flesh it out—when it oughta be *flushed* out. I'm speaking of its FILM biz of course (not its thriving huarache industry!) and I'm not just speakin' "for personal use"—I'm speaking *export*. (New York in comparison—these days—paints & exports equivalent *nothing*.) What it exports, with malice afore, is Standard Obsolescent American Hogwash writ LARGE: th' American so-called "Dream"; the whole wretched never-say-die American "Myth." That the dregs of this myth are churned up and packaged mostly by cynical, non-believing NON-hicks makes no diff, nor does it especially matter that the "real hicks" of our fabulous HEARTLANDS where even Kerouac had trouble getting laid must've stopped churning such hoss-shit on *their* own 'fore the advent of the hula hoop: they're gonna get it and like it and (according to *Variety*) they do. The balance of trade: they send us fresh and nutritionally bankrupt CORN FLAKES; we send 'em stale and mega-lethal LIES ABOUT THEMSELVES. All of which kinda takes on a certain, uh, *national significance* now, what with Prez Carter trying his ding dong darndest to give the U.S. *back* to the hicks (I mean *right?*)—thus making L.A. not only the CULTURAL CAPITAL of this outhouse of a republic but, for most or many intents and purps, the political cap as well.

Levels of the lie: sometimes it starts with the *title*. What, for inst, does anyone break away *from* in that latest helping of heartland hoke, *Breaking Away?* The main jerk doesn't even Leave Home!—sticks around w/ his maw, paw, bike helmet and terminal case of Indiana INERTIA. (Does Indiana exist? Sure, it's that *inertial place* yonder.) The message (to "Indiana," to the "rest of us"): inertia is cool; a mere quirky thought, a healthy "moment of doubt," is sufficient; why insult maw, paw and the neato/swello Order o' Things by forcing events to the point of, y'know, *realization?* Good boys don't do that, not good Indianamerican boys, so tell me, was it my imagination or were those *bad* boys, those mean-ass foreign-tongued cyclists who kayoed not only our goodboy's bike but his good ol' all-American *friendship* vectors, were they updated stand-ins (perhaps?!) for COMMIES? Or: Indiana lives down HAVING SPAWNED JAMES DEAN. . . and regresses to Andy Hardy. Fellow-traveling CRITICS meantime swear it's about "transcendence" or some such cornpone of *their* own reckoning (the *guise* of U.S. Freedom, of "options," is apparently still quite nec. to maintain); in any event, less one-dimensional than, ha, *Smokey and the Bandit* or *Gator*—contempo yokel "genre" films of a presumably, uh, frothier sort. (Or am *I* completely missing the point—tho I wasn't drunk when I *saw* it!—and it's really, oh, a heartland-based remake of *The Gradu- ate*????)

Anyway, okay, what does L.A. qua Hollywood GET for such falsification? (Other, that is, than money?) It gets to control a lotta shit. It gets, first of all, to shuffle itself in as PART of this country by exercising its option to *define it*. Huge chunks of it. It gets to *designate* America. And then *confirm it*. Deny it? Well, a Designated America qua *marketplace* underpins things (but propagates far more than profit). Succeed or fail, a film's destiny is so tied up in Lowest Common Denominator designated bullshit that hicks—designated or real (and what's lower than d. hicks, designated kids?)—are damned if they is, damned if they ain't: designated SCAPEGOATS for Hollywd.'s "miscalculations." Great moments in no-win, when a pic's a hit they're goat-goats: designated hicks will SWALLOW ANYTHING. Anything you feed 'em, leading to the question: if they'll swallow anything, if profit can (in principle) be made by *selling* them anything, why is the anything they're generally *asked* to swallow SO SHITTY? Only possible ans.: because Hwd. loves to see 'em smile their designated SHIT-SWALLOWING GRINS. (Keep those e-litist "hick jokes" a-coming!!)

Worst of all tho is their peddling of all this current godshit, fueling the sparks of the latest & sickest Judaeo-Christian Blight Upon Our Land. Or maybe not fueling, just *fanning*, running hand in *glove* with the fucker, giving "larger than life" designated flavor and SHAPE to it. Just when it was finally looking safe to be an AMERICAN ATHEIST, they dump these goddam *I Found Noah's Ark* docu-fabrications (proof! God drowned Man!) in our lap, not to mention all these horror pics in the wake of *The Exorcist* which insidiously shill for *exclusive* God/Devil causality—whatever happened to "monsters from the Id" and good, wholesome laboratory slime? (Horror pics should know better!) And these "one week only" UFO docu-whatsems, you think they're not being packaged almost as TRAIN-ING FILMS in redirected godhead orientation? (Dare I mention *Close,* ugh, *Encounters?*)

None of which would really add up to much more'n a major PAIN IN THE ASS—a pain, a *major* pain, an *incredible* major pain but no more—if it weren't for the fact that these scumbags have the gall to designate *bad guys* of the God World as well. To wit: Jim Jones, the *real* Jim Jones, the REAL real Jim Jones is, don't laugh, JIMMY CARTER. Like here's this guy who actually SUDDENLY one day decides to reinstitute the frigging threat of WORLD WAR, the wind hits him in a funny way and he thinks Afghan/Iran, yeah, that'll do it, or possibly oil for the executive coffee machines of America, he

35

figures okay, let's get tough, boycott the commie Olympics, let's all fucking DIE (if need be), what's the big deal, worst that can happen is we go to HEAVEN. I mean geez, just when it seemed like presidents weren't gonna *pull* such shit anymore, like it was strictly a thing of some godawful sick American PAST, and meantime 200,000,000+ (among how many billion worldian) American lives hang in the approximate BALANCE, maybe this sick fucking (suddenly macho) hick will PULL THE PLUG. And you don't think he's the REAL JIM JONES? Well neither do the movies. Their Jim Jones, if you can believe it, is *named* Jim Jones (and played by Stuart Whitman).

No, wait, I just realized, lemme look it up—he's *not* named Jones in the movie. A normal mistake after 2, 3, 4 . . . a few beers (maybe I should take a nap). Close enough tho: Jim Johnson. In *Guyana—Cult of the Damned*, a RED HERRING if ever there was one. I mean when in the last, oh, ten years have we been on the brink of such irrational internat'l catastrophe as right now with this Carter up-the-ante biz? And what INSTEAD gets focused on, designated, some jerk from LAST YEAR'S NEWS responsible for what, a mere 900-some-odd deaths? Seems like an obvious diversionary tactic, the release of the pic right now when Carter could USE some diversion, which is not even to *suggest* intent on any party's part, it's just too grimly *uncanny* the way this shit gets timed, like some cybernetic oversoul of god-bless-american-war-machine *thoughtfulness* pressed the precisely correct button at *precisely* the moment the program called for it. (We just call it Holly!wood!—to the rescue!—remember *Patton* and Nixon's Cambodia?)

Anyway, the two Joneses, er, Jims—Carter and Jones/"Johnson." You'd have to look far, you'd have to look wide for a more uniquely matched pair of *not* atypical Christian-American daddy figures hellbent on Death, yet not ONE reviewer in the thousand, ten thousand or however many we've *got* to keep us consumer-hip has managed to latch onto the super-obvious correlation 'tween 'em— looks like I'm first (shake my hand). But it doesn't end there, the comparison continues: it take *two* ends to play this, the Jim end and the mutton-to-slaughter end, the hick/rube/hayseed/yokel end (which is where, I believe, we CAME IN); in the case of the Jim who ain't dead yet: *our* end. Yep, it looks like we're potentially ALL HICKS for some deadlier aspects of plot, if not this week then some time SOON, unless (of course) Hollyshit SHUTS THE WHOLE SICK PROGRAM *OFF* ALREADY... and don't forget the former actual "ACTOR" gearing up (come November) to grab Carter's deathball and smash it in our hick-silly FACE... shuts it before we're boxed in a corner thinkin' the only good hick is a dead hick and that hick (forever) is US. 'S called "death wish," they made a film called that once, don't remember if it was one word or two...

The end of the world begins here? (Wake me when the "fun" starts.)

LI'L GLOBAL VILLAGE
IN THE SUN

Somewhere in the early eighties I tried to talk one of my old *Voice* editors into letting me do an L.A. column, or a West Coast column or whatever, on the premise that my take on the place would be different from that of your average expatriate writer schmo. "I'm the only writer I know," I explained, "who came here *not* to write screenplays." His response: "Yeah, sure, tell me another one." Well, heck, it was—and is—the only one I have to tell.

And people are sick of me for it, even with variations. "Words I've sweated over mean too much t' me to let some jerks *butcher 'em*" is one way I tell it; "Me—collaborate with the Death Culture? Never!" is another. Mr. Integrity-Till-You-Puke, that's me (and won't I please shut up?). 'Cause, yeah, most people I know *work* for the motherfucker, or would if they could: the *heart* of the heart of the beast. The film biz.

Which is maybe not *the* principal industry—auto repair? condo construction? gardening?—but certainly *a* major wellspring of local commerce 'n' revenue. If you live in Logan, West Virginia, you're bound to know miners and such; likewise, in Los Angeles, 'tain't really odd to have made the acquaintance of camerafolk, film editors, actpersons, film processors, grips, gaffers, studio lawyers and/or the occasional director. (Employed or un.) Some of whom sometimes make *me* sick.

I know people, for inst, who in various capacities, though not themselves buckets of scum, worked on *Rambo*, *Red Dawn* and *Top Gun*. People who, of course, "didn't have to" (they could, instead, indeed, have gone on welfare, collected unemployment, or made french fries at McDonald's). People whom, for what it's worth, I in fact care for, otherwise trust and would never call assholes. But when you find out they've done it, when *I* find out, it's like learning in New York that your friends are really slumlords—or cops. Shit, I've even decried complicity in such "well-intentioned" see-Spot-runners as *Silkwood*, *Under Fire* or anything about Cambodia. I can, I'm told, be a real ballbuster of an "idealist."

And prob'ly I am. So much so that as much as it bums me to view the effects of manipulative film fare *after* the fact, to see the devastation wreaked by its systematic falsification, distortion or "oversimplification" of reality, to sit and watch a world qua audience yanked, by the numbers, by a ring through its collective nose—as much as all that burns my *ass*, it bums me even more to cop eyefuls of filmish life-dance and throb *before* the fact, with no cameras rolling, with no such scams on the line. I'm referring, of course, to The Act. The sickish whatsit of all these actpeople always being "on," always "playing to the room," always behaving like line-trained automatons or, lacking scripting, like windup improv-ists on speed. Always? Let's say 80-85% of the time, of the times *I've* been in rooms with 'em. A roomful of act/ors and act/resses is about as dense with hardcore sincerity as a roomful of, I dunno, bankers? golfers? RV salesmen?

But, hey, let's be "fair"—they've gotta do it somewhere, perform their y'know, their *art*, something the biz wants from 'em the way it wants AIDS. An unpaid "role" at a party (or the post office) may thus be more "satisfying" than anything offered for bucks. (Man does not Act for bread alone.) And as self-dehumanization goes, professional act-humans aren't the only duds in town a-doin' it: playing roles, delivering lines, working overtime at "looking the part" (grooming! grooming! GROOMED!!), being "motivated" by considerations of GLAMOR in abeyance of all LIFE, etc., etc. 106% of the town's warm bodies have often, in this regard, Acted.

Nor are they, the pros, the only ones in pictures: I myself was in three. Or maybe four. Mea culpa, mea culpa—B-pics, Z-pics, low-budget, no-budget *bad* pics (the only good kind!)—as a walk-on—so *shoot me*.

I also worked for—no, it was against—the *aorta* of the heart of the heart of the beast: television. For three years, at a weekly throwaway sheet, I *reviewed TV*.

TV: a deathpump whose time has come. Back in the fifties, early sixties, you'd go to a movie, some little theater, and out in the lobby there'd be these petitions, something to do with the "threat" of TV. To the movies. The movies, or at least their handmaidens the neighborhood theaters, were scared that on Tuesday nights, Wednesdays, even Fridays and Saturdays, you would rather be home, saving money, watching some shit on TV. In time, the reasoning went, the profit base would dwindle, disappear, and wonderful, wonderful movies—boo hoo hoo—would no longer *be*. Movies, dig it, versus TV. Today, no more versus—movies *are* TV. One industry, one mega-mega-profit, one (for all practical purposes) vision. But no more little theaters, natch, and with TV in *irreversible* control of the pump.

In terms of numbers, and in terms of L.A., the vast majority of scripted-acted-directed-photographed productions are generated by and for TV. Maybe most films aren't yet the literal made-for-TV article, but more and more they (theatrical releases) are *looking* it. TV makes the *fact* of a film official, and the ultimate *destiny* of a film is to be seen, via VCR, on TV.

Anyway, TV *as* TV. Except, perhaps, for locally originated minor dogshit viewed by approximately no one, everything on TV equals everything else on TV—and everything on TV is a meticulously digitalized *major* lobotomy. The functional difference between David Letterman and Pat Robertson—or PBS and ABC—is hardly worth addressing. On a basic mind-control level, sitcoms and soaps are but the "entertainment" equivalent of the news. And likewise for the *bounty* of TV. JFK and Muhammad Ali are not likelier *outcomes* of TV than Reagan and Vegas. Sometimes you luck out—if you believe, that is, in luck.

Which, or some of which, maybe sounds like a bleak paraphrase of that dipshit McLuhan—who actually swore the Future would be benign. McLuhan: who might've been talking about a TV in *some* possible world—but not about *this* TV in this one. This TV: which has bashed us and trashed us and terminally sapped our will to resist; which (speaking of "futures"!) has returned us, not that most of us have noticed, to a non-ironic prospect-zero pre-rock fifties of the heart, mind, body, *soul*. (What's next—the pre-drug sixties???) Anyone vile enough to work for THIS TV should be nailed to a wall and eaten by rats.

And the Work and the Program start here. In this teevee town. It doesn't even have to be a "master" program, nor is a "conspiracy" required to explain the whole wretched thing. The conspiracy is more of people who Watch than of those who Broadcast, anyway. Big Bro hardly needs to spend your tax dollar watching *all* of you when all of YOU are already watching HIM.

Well, fuggit, for three years I watched—series, talk shows, specials, the whole pail o' poison—and wrote. I'd of course watched before, since age three or four (and in New York had in fact *hated* bohos who spoke disparagingly of "the tube"), but never with such direct knowledge of, or queasy proximity to, the Source Of Poison. So even at the height of the gig I could never force myself to watch more than 40-45 minutes, total, a week. Thirty seconds to a minute of any given show was usually enough to generate a paragraph. I'd mock shows, wheel out the humor, try 'n' keep 'em laughing at the medium's "expense." [A typical column: "*The Armenian Show* (Not to be Missed)."] After three years I found even these minimal doses too severe—and unplugged my neurons f'r the rest of their life. Okay, sure, I do still catch maybe 10-11 minutes some weeks—a minute of a tennis match, 19 seconds of a Korean who-knows-what ad on UHF—but in terms of the big stuff: none. I haven't watched the news since '83, or a trendy new series since '82. I have *never seen*— only heard about—*Lifestyles of the Rich and Famous*. (I must be a saint.)

MUTANT
LIKE ME

Through unfairly smallish holes in the yellowed ping-pong hemispheres that have been affixed to my eyes, I can just about make out the rest of Ms. Whatsthename's handiwork in the smudgy mirror before me. Whatever her name—Maggie? Molly?—she's already plastered my face with eight fake moles and half a dozen fake open sores in varying degrees of festerhood. Good grisly shit, and what the hell, *all* mutants have them—or at least are bound to by the year 3000, the time frame for New World Pictures' *Death Sport* (formerly *Death Sport 3000*), the long-awaited sequel to the highly not-bad *Death Race 2000*. It's a good bet there'll be mutants galore by then—and how valid could a sequel be if *it* didn't take advantage of all the r-a-d-i-a-t-i-o-n our gene pool might be privy to in the 1000 years that will have elapsed in the interim?

It's not at all certain, however, that mutants of the third (fourth?) millennium will be wearing prisoners' uniforms left over from *Papillon*, which is what we're draped in for the profit and glory of New World Pics. But—heck—aren't mixed metaphors the *greatest*? Especially on a budget of $600,000, of which non-mutant leadingman David Carradine is reportedly pocketing half. At least

45

they're not *lepers' shrouds* from *Papillon*, you know? In any event, the outfit is beginning to itch, and the oozing fake wound on my left palm is feeling strangely *authentic* or something. For added discomfort, the ping-pong eyeballs have not been properly aligned—I can see no better than one peeper at a time—and the points of contact threaten to force my contact lenses into real-life vitreous humor. Beside me, a fellow mutant (and aspiring Method Actor) named George mutters in his own makeup misery, "I don't believe Brando and De Niro had to start like *this.*"

I ain't really an actor myself, Method or otherwise, though I do resemble Robert De Niro—female bank tellers have told me so. My only actual connection with the making of things celluloid is my friendship with director Allan Arkush, whose previous credit, *Grand Theft Auto*, for which he second-unit directed, was also my own (and only). I had a bit part, for 15 bucks a day, as driver for a hit man, and walked away from it minus the ability to any longer watch a film in terms of *continuity*, minus any desire to actually "act." Though I'd sooner be a serious plumber than a serious actor, in all likelihood I'll be coaxed into another 2 or 3 such walk-ons before I'm done. But even if it's 4 or 5, or 9 or 10, I can't see *ever* having a more significant role handed me than the one I'm glued into now, a role I could not refuse . . .

Among my favorite movies (ages 0–15) were *Attack of the Crab Monsters*, *The Wasp Woman*, *Not of This Earth* and *It Conquered the World*. Monsters and such were—and still are—the coolest, the greatest. They're the only big-screen dramatis personae who/what/which, *regardless of the stiffs playing, staging, scripting them*, are consistently worth their weight in urine, film in/film out. As with dirty wrestling, I ate that stuff up. But, not being a *film buff*, a reader of credits, or any of that sophisticated *adult* crap at the time, I had no way of knowing that one man was responsible for all four pics, not to mention the gore-and-mayhem masterworks *Little Shop of Horrors* and *A Bucket of Blood*—quite a track record, don't you think?

The one man, of course, is Corman. Roger. Still with us, far from dead, no longer making the great, unadulterated junk with his own hands perhaps, but still auteuring a-plenty as chief bigwig atop the

New World scaffold. His personal coffers more on the line than when he actually directed, he inserts his restless snoot in every company project—master of quality shit-control you might say. Slated to follow *Death Sport* are *Girls' Gym* and *Piranha*: the flow of fine trash goes on. *Grand Theft Auto* was New World's as well, but even though it could taxonomically pass as Exploitation fodder, it was neither monsters nor gore, and I certainly couldn't use it to tell my grandchildren I WAS A MUTANT FOR ROGER CORMAN.

So okay, the finishing touches are at last applied to my pustule-laden face—Roger, through Arkush, has requested that we all appear "a little greener." It's taken a good three hours to do all the mutants, and lunchtime rears its head before we've managed a single scene. Bikers (death *sport* turns out to be off-track bikery), royal guardsmen, royal rulers (grand emperor has the red-hot moniker Armando Zirpola—shades of *Beach Party*'s Eric Von Zipper) and courtly courtesans (straight out of anything that ever starred Steve Reeves) are already lined up for a fab feed of gristly roast beef and store-bought potato salad as we, the punks of the monster world, take our place—at the back. Even at the ass-end of the line we're forced to endure mock-abuse—"Do we have to eat with, ugh, mutants?"— our filmic geekhood replicating itself on an off-screen cast-and-crew level. Plus, it ain't easy poking your plastic fork at slop you can hardly see, and *forget about* trying to chew without disturbing the latex slime on your cheeks, lips, chin.

Après le déjeuner they stick us inside the opening of this ridiculous wood thing painted grey to suggest a cave—the so-called Mutant Cavern. We're each given a hunk of rotten, smelly uncooked meat— a mutant's security blanket?—and the assignment to stagger into light expressing (a) "first breath of freedom" and (b) "total disorientation." Mostly, we just flail arms, rotate heads and stumble into each other. To distinguish us from the Keystone Kops, foamy mutant drool is simulated with Alka-Seltzer, full tab in mouth (no water), a system we find difficult mastering without swallowing outright or puffing our cheeks like Dizzy Gillespie (who's gonna *see* this shit, anyway?). Between takes, fake blood is applied by the quart to exposed actor skin and greying meat.

L.A. Is the Capital of Kansas

"What's my motivation?" asks Method George, half joking, half not.

"Motivation?" responds Arkush in stunned disbelief. "You're a lousy mutant!"

After several takes of us tangling with a handful of guardsmen, the last necessitated by the discovery of an enormous piece of off-color *tape* on the side of the cave, my lenses have become resting place for at least half a cup of off-track dust and grit, and there's no way to shed the ping-pong covers (and still remain a mutant). Ophthalmological distress: more *specific* a motivation than I bargained for.

And fuggit, a scene, a *big* scene: separate mutants. Time has come for each of us, one at a time, to run headlong into a *force field*. And since palms are part of what one tends to *press* against such an unseen obstacle, the festering rubbery mess on mine will be captured for all 35mm eternity. So I let those tears flow, tears plus dust filling my eyes now with *mud* . . . and I cope with it.

Next (ain't I tough?), we statically pose in designated spots to be "atomized."

Then we strut our stuff beneath Emperor Armando's private death sport booth and show him what we think, insofar as we *can* think, of his future-flavored tyranny, affecting mutants and non-mutants alike. "Make believe it's LBJ and you're a Berkeley peace-creep with the gift of a lifetime dumped in your lap—you're one-on-one with The Enemy!" But he hardly needs to direct me. I'm more than up for it: I get to go *home* when the scene is done. Even mutants deserve no worse than 9-to-5, and I've been on location since 7:00 in the miserable morn.

By now my meat (liver? tongue? whale pancreas?) is covered with flies, and I heave it straight at the overhead camera with my right hand while grasping my crotch with my left. I snarl and drool and scowl and heave and retrieve again and again, but Arkush still wants more. Nothing left but to take a Big Bite of dead mammal, so I *do it*, spitting the tender, disgusting morsel up at Armando. Cheers, cheers, a job well done and time for a beer—we each get *one*—which can't quite remove the sinews from between my teeth. Day's earnings come to the same $15 as last time (for eleven or twelve times the work), it takes a good half-hour to remove all the makeup and shit, and my meat-soaked, fake-blood-soaked garments are dumped on a pile for unlaundered repeat tomorrow a.m.

Day-the-second has us out at the Vasquez Rocks, where many a Western has seen the light of film. Naturally we're slated for some horseplay. We're to overtake a pony carrying a Shirley Temple-type brat and drag both off to a swell mutant feast. So what if the scene's scripted for *after* our atomization? Mutants, like German shepherds or collies, are largely interchangeable; we're simply playing *other mutants*. While our makeup is applied, we notice female lead Claudia Jennings, *Playboy*'s Miss November of 1969 and yet another entry in the Method sweepstakes, prepping herself chemically for her own arduous chores to come. This graduate of the Hefner School of Dramatic Arts ("Don't interfere with your *natural* dumbness; give *skin* lots of room to *state its case*") has an entire Winnebago to herself, while we, scum of the future earth, have been herded in a single RV like so many rabid sheep. Slightly before noon, she mounts her steed for the day, only to sufficiently complain about her saddle that lunch intervenes before she's had a chance to perform an actorly function, Method or otherwise.

The day's other fine actress, the brat we're supposed to snatch off the horsie, has been so cranky everybody's gotta humor her before she blows her cool and brings down child-labor wrath (she's only five) on crew and company. Nobody can stomach her, and we mutants are more concerned about hurting the cute little gluepot she's riding than about causing *her* any inadvertent bodily harm. Before we get at either of them, though, we've gotta set the scene by posing high atop a Vasquez Rock with bones in hand (no meat today) as if scouting prey. Arkush spits out a reference to a similar setup in John Ford's *Stagecoach*, so it's injuns we're emulating this time, prompting George to remark, "Mutants are the *real* Native Americans."

Arkush, whom I first met on a Hell's Angels boatride up the Hudson River, got his start in this biz by studying film at NYU under Martin Scorsese, a former Corman protégé who would ultimately deliver both Allan and Jonathan Kaplan (later to direct *Night Call Nurses* and *White Line Fever*) to Papa Rog' for armed combat in the Explo Brigade. By now Allan's developed a fair set of basic combat muscles, and he boasts of having at least begun to internalize Roger's message to young directors: "Anybody who can operate a lathe can direct a film."

Finally we're lathed and planted behind trees and brush, each with a definite task re rider and horse. George and I have scored dobbin, and on first take we discover even equines take objection to encroaching mutants. The fucker bolts upon catching sight and/or scent of us, carrying one screaming bimbo off into the desert— *whoops*. Fortunately for Roger, she doesn't fall or anything—he'd have got his merry ass sued by whoever *owns* her—and upon retrieval Allan tells her, "That was only *play* danger, it didn't *really* happen"— hardy har. On the reshoot, the snatch itself is accomplished without too much trouble, but horse minus girlie drags us much farther up the hill than we expected, and it takes us like five-ten minutes to lead the stupid nag back down (the things non-union actors must do). Anyway, I've managed to rub plenty of good fake blood all over the hoss's white butt, real neat improv so they better not cut me—I'm *good*.

Hey, we're *done*. All that's left is a little side entertainment involving Ms. Jennings. She's got this line—"This is what I think of your *death* sport" is how Arkush reads it—followed by clicking her ray gun at whomever.

First take: "This is what *I* think of *your* death sport." Try again. "This is what I *think* of your. . ." *No*, Claudia, it's . . . Okay: "*This* is what I think . . ." Not quite. Finally, on the seventh take, she *gets* it, only she forgets to pull the trigger, and the whole cycle of trial and error moves back to square one.

No, I haven't seen David Carradine, not even once. He hasn't had to interact with mutants (maybe it's in his contract), all his scripted concern with liberation evidently not extending to those with ping-pong eyes. But who, having *been* a mutant, a *proud* mutant, needs to eyeball a normal frigging *star*? Not I. (If you guys cut me, I'll never work for New World again.)

THE AUTHOR'S FAVORITE ACTRESS

Actingwise. Irene Forrest can *act*. Her way out of wet paper bags, locked safes, etc. Her most recent actpart, that of Wendy Cassidy— too bad you missed it—on the "Parent Week" episode of *Fame*, was, in the author's humble opinion, both existentially "pure" and existentially "correct." You can ask no more from an actperson.

But it hasn't been easy—the road—the dues—"getting there." No, she wasn't in *that* one (unavailable due to *Sitting Ducks*, her v. outstanding Hollywd. "vehicle," being shot at the time down in F-L-A), but CHECK these credits—Irene has starred in some HOT ONES: *THX–1138*, George Lucas's first (& finest) feature . . . the original *Night Stalker*, finest & greatest of all "TV movies" . . . the critically acclaimed *Heart Beeps* . . . *Intimate Strangers*, formerly *Battered Wives* . . . *The Boston Strangler* (co-starring Tony Curtis) . . . *National Lampoon Goes to the Movies* . . . the AFI version of Sartre's *No Exit* . . . *Curse of the Black Widow* (as "whore" to Sid Caesar's "pimp") . . . selected episodes of *Faith for Today* . . . you name it, she's been in it . . . a lineup of "hits" as long as your arm.

L.A. Is the Capital of Kansas

But it hasn't been easy—"Sisyphean" commitments rarely are—and thus it was quite a coup to coax this *actress's actress* away from her demanding schedule just long enough, over cocktails at the Chateau Chez Frou-Frou in Encino, to share—and bare—her innermost acting thoughts.

Q: First things first. How do you spell your last name?

A: F-double . . . no. F-O-double-R-E-S-T.

Q: Has it been spelled wrong?

A: With one R. It was spelled wrong on a credit once, for *Curse of the Black Widow.*

Q: Did you appreciate that?

A: No, I was upset. But I took it very maturely.

Q: Okay, Irene, what's the capital of Delaware?

A: Oh, Richard! I don't know *geography.*

Q: It's Dover.

A: Dover?

Q: Dover, Delaware. You didn't know that?

A: No.

Q: Okay, what's the square root of eight?

A: Well I know the square root of four. Two.

Q: So what's the square root of eight?

A: I don't think it's double.

Q: Well I don't know it either. Two point something. Here's an easier one: Kant is to the 18th century as Descartes is to the 17th—true or false?

A: "I think, therefore I am," and Kant was good with, he always had a good line or two.

Q: True or false, true or false?

A: Using my logic . . . *oh*, why not?—false.

Q: Well, who knows? I think their answer, whoever they are, would be true.

A: Well *I* think it's false.

Q: Okay, let's get serious: Why does Hollywood stink?

A: Because there is . . . *no room* for personality, uh, for human, for truth.

Q: So how do you feel about that?

A: It makes me cry.

The Author's Favorite Actress

Q: *Because?*

A: Because I will not give up myself and . . . so I don't have a voice.

Q: *Have there been times you might've given up yourself, uh, in order to . . .*

A: I *would* have, before I knew who I was, 'cause I was just looking for a piece of cloth to sit on, but now it's too hard because I finally have something to say. . . that no one wants to hear.

Q: *Apropos of who you are, are you a natural redhead?*

A: I am. A dark-haired redhead.

Q: *Well, moving right along to your most recent work, the role of Wendy Cassidy, a very challenging role . . .*

A: *I* thought so.

Q: *. . . that blue sweater you wore was really nice. Did you get to keep it?*

A: No, and I had the opportunity to buy it. You get to buy the clothes you wear for half the, for wholesale, and I thought of buying it because I liked it so much.

Q: *How much?*

A: I didn't ask, but I'm sure it was a pretty penny. The reason I chose not to was it had big sleeves.

Q: *You mean* wide *sleeves?*

A: It had very wide sleeves, and I generally with wide sleeves get it in my coffee.

Q: *That's 'cause you have skinny arms.*

A: I have skinny arms and also I'm not very good at managing, uh, so I decided not to buy it.

Q: *Did you sit on any interesting furniture as Wendy Cassidy?*

A: Um . . . I sat on two separate kinds of chairs, the classroom kind . . .

Q: *Uncomfortable?*

A: *I* was happy with it, because I could lean on it, and then the other was a cafeteria chair, which is always pleasant.

Q: *You* like *cafeteria chairs?!*

A: Well they gave me *food* to play with. Meatloaf, some horrible meatloaf, and bean salad with . . .

Q: *Is that what the cast gets to eat?*

A: No, it was prop food, but it was real food.

Q: *And some people eat it?*

A: Yeah, you can eat it. The other people in the cast were indeed eating it—'cause we were hungry, before lunch—but I didn't like it myself.

Q: What's the actual cast food?

A: You go to the commissary and you, if something's shot on the lot . . .

Q: You have to pay for it? Aren't they required to . . .

A: Only on location. If something's shot on the lot they're required to provide, y'know give you a *lunch hour . . .*

Q: That's not fair.

A: No, why should they feed you? If you work in a factory they don't feed you, they just give you a lunch hour. But on location they don't have facilities, so they cater food for you.

Q: You could bring a bag lunch to location.

A: Yeah but you don't.

Q: I think the union should demand . . .

A: They give you breakfast, you get . . .

Q: Why don't you get up at the next SAG meeting and complain?

A: Richard, I don't care about food. Besides, they give you free breakfast.

Q: What, coffee and donuts?

A: No, you order, you can have whatever you want.

Q: So why shouldn't lunch be the same?

A: Because . . . I don't care. This is a *side* issue, I don't care about this.

Q: Okay, let's get to the so-called meat *of the Hollywood issue: Have you ever fucked a director?*

A: Uhh! Richard, what a question!!

Q: Have you?

A: Um . . . for a part?

Q: Or any . . .

A: Or had a love thing with a director?

Q: Well, have you had a love thing with a director?

A: Let me see if I can remember. I don't think I ever actually fell in love with a director.

Q: Forget about love—have you fucked a director?

A: I don't *fuck* just for fucking.

Q: *So'd you do it to get a part?*

A: No, I don't think so, I mean *no*, I never fucked to *get* a part. But I'm trying to think if I ever was, there have been a couple of people who are directors that I have been *attracted* to, but nothing happened.

Q: *Yeah, well how was it working with the great Robbie Benson?*

A: . . . .

Q: *In* National Lampoon Goes to the Movies.

A: Oh, right, I forgot about that. I *liked* Robbie Benson. As a person he was . . .

Q: *Did you fuck him?*

A: Richard! Robbie Benson doesn't fuck!

Q: *So how was it working with such a great actor?*

A: I *liked* him, I *did*. He's a very sensitive person, we talked about things, and I'll tell you something—I even liked the way he looked. In real life.

Q: *Would you go out with him?*

A: He never asked me. If we had developed a *relationship*, uh . . .

Q: *Have you ever acted in Puerto Rico?*

A: I have been to Puerto Rico but I've never acted there.

Q: *Not even . . .*

A: Even in life?

Q: *. . . in your moment-to-moment . . .*

A: In my living, or in my theater, like my. . .

Q: *Okay, were you theatrical on any level while in Puerto Rico?*

A: In my life, *surely* . . . I must've had a sense of drama.

Q: *Can you recall what the drama could've been?*

A: Uh, I remember *situations* in Puerto Rico, for five seconds maybe.

Q: *Such as?*

A: Richard, I . . .

Q: *Well never mind. Have you ever acted in France?*

A: I've never been to France.

Q: *Oh. That takes care of that. Now I'm gonna read you something. This is from* Boulevards, *one of San Francisco's finest defunct rags. It's a comment about a certain type of actress such as Susan Tyrrell, Sandra*

L.A. Is the Capital of Kansas

Bernhard, in a certain sense Sandy Dennis it says here . . . and you. *This is from a few years ago, I'll read it and see what you think. "Their 'act,' as devoid of insulation as the wax/wane of their lives, teems with palpable anthropoid contradiction, conflicting stages of emotional development sticking out like exquisite* sore thumbs. *To be even partially appreciated by the neo-escapist hordes, they are generally required to 'normalize' that which in their personal makeup is unique, bizarre, and/or merely florid or excessive, and the ensuing struggle can make for jagged big-screen magic that is at once frightening and hilarious, poignant in the undefamed true sense of the word, and totally, wholly, universally* real, *although more often than not they are perceived as '60s/'70s/'80s clichés, for it is hardly easy for these same hordes to see them—or* admit *to seeing them—for what they indeed are: timeless, ageless. Often stuck with hyper-ordinary scripts, they're forced to call upon every nuance of their creative oompah just to spin out their mastery of ordinary-equals-special, which at the same time is their craftwise bread and butter, if not in fact a piece of cake, as this is precisely the calisthenic they've had to contort themselves to, literally on a first-principle basis, just to be wasting their time in such an uncooperative medium to begin with . . . etc., etc." This guy really lays it on, must be a friend of yours. So what do you, what's your* response *to that?*

A: You're including *me* in that?

Q: *This piece was* about *you. Didn't you read it?*

A: So you think of me in that way?

Q: *I didn't* write *it, this is what the* author *had to say. So what is your response to that as a description of your milieu, etc.?*

A: I would be overwhelmed if that were only true!

Q: *Well, c'mon, let's pretend it is. Forget about blushing and all* that *crap. What about just the terms it implies about your* task? *Your personal task, mission, etc., in order to endure this shit—gimme some comments, c'mon.*

A: Well . . . to endure it—or to *do* it?

Q: *Whatever.* You *know.*

A: . . . Okay. The first thing that triggers is this thing that I've been thinking about lately, which is . . . I can only talk about, forget all that highfalutin stuff, that one of the, okay, here you are, you're a person who's an actress and they write these words and there's like this role. And there's, then there's, there's the role on the paper which has to be the role in real life, in the context of the medium. And then there's you as a full person who for some reason or another are drawn to behave, to exhibiting, expressing *your*self as this pretend person in these pretend circumstances. Now one of the things that I've been thinking about is for me it used to be that when those things would, I'd have these like minor goals, minor peaks where I'd feel this enormous sense of accomplishment if I could have these moments in any given acting circumstance where I'd have, where it felt like it was happening in *real time*, y'know?

Q: *Yeah.*

A: Of the moment, a real sense of truth. Lately, coupled with that, I now want to... I never was able to perceive how most people would say this, y'know what in any given line, in any given scene let's say, what the *pattern* of the scene is, y'know? Like just the basic *analysis* of what that scene was, so this person's saying this in this kind of way. And, but whatever I came up with always felt like it was okay, y'know, but it wasn't ordinary. Lately I've been feeling very good 'cause I could tell, I could find the *normal* of the scene and *still* fill it with me.

Q: *Yeah, but what I'm wondering is these are issues that... isn't it true... most people, most* act*people, don't give a flying fuck about...*

A: I don't think that's true.

Q: *... and whether they do or they don't, they don't have it* honed *to a first-principle level where it means anything that they even* do *think about it. Because it's, y'know, people think about freedom and they vote for Reagan.*

A: Yes.

Q: *And by the same token, do you really think there are three people in Hollywood who, uh, look, I'm not gonna force it on* you *to be a representative of, uh, uh, a type of hardcore blah blah blah, but don't you think there are really not too many people who can actualize...*

A: I think there are a lot of puppets, yes.

Q: *Yeah. And how do you feel about that?*

A: I think there are puppets in every, um, y'know people who work for the phone company, there are people who, I mean everybody...

L.A. Is the Capital of Kansas

Q: *Yeah yeah. But where like once upon a time Dorothy Parker could say about Katharine Hepburn, uh, how she did the whole gamut of human something or other from A to B . . .*

A: Um hmm.

Q: *. . . and now, uh—like that was a pretty hip thing to say, and it's probably accurate—but are there people now who can even do A?*

A: Ha huh! Or where A is even something somebody wants! I know, Richard, it's very, I just think you're gonna make me say stuff that's very *bleak*.

Q: *Say it!*

A: I need a tissue.

Q: *Tissue?*

A: Um, I mean, okay so everybody's just in this straitjacket and told to *dance*, or to speak or whatever they're supposed to do within the context of the straitjacket. I know that and I, there's a part of me that the only way I can cope with all this, with the constant input of the *data*, is to just on the outside get more, uh, *idealistic* about this stuff, y'know? Just to keep thinking somehow my own will and my own sense of . . . cleverness, my own *ingenuineness*, honest ingenuineness, *true* ingenuineness as opposed to posed ingenuineness . . .

Q: *You mean ingenuousness?*

A: . . . ingenuine . . .

Q: *Ingenuity?*

A: . . . ingenuousness, will continue to ride above like a cloud or something, I don't know.

Q: *Yeah? 'Cause for instance one of the, what I notice about your performances is that a lot of the things you do gesturally, like just going from a smile to a frown or something, is the sort of stuff that if you looked at a mirror while doing it I don't think you could possibly, you could do it any differently. And it's not so much whether you do it in life—and you are doing it the way you would do it in life—as it is that, the case that because you're given parameters of what to do actingwise, transition-from-this-to-this-wise, that you, you're given such trite occasions for transit that whatever you do from an x to a y involves a lot of real, uh, quantum leap in the sense that you realize, I think, that neither x nor y are credible stations of any cross—and you have to* imagine *it being a part of a possible world.*

A: Yeah.

Q: *And what I'm saying is there is a lot of just pure* incredible *imagining that you have to undergo to believe x, to believe y, and to believe x-to-y, and that . . .*

A: Isn't that what an actor's supposed to do?

Q: *. . . and that you're playing it almost like a* Martian *because* only *a Martian could play it . . .*

A: You mean like an alien visitor to this world?

Q: *. . . 'cause with these stupid, dumb movies it's a totally Martian situation. The point is that no human being could possibly . . .*

A: You know what I *like* about that stuff is it's, okay you have this idea of normality, a standard of normality that is neither normal nor real, right? And that's the standard that's put on television shows and in quite a few movies, or *most* movies, and what *I* like about that is I have this thing where I, I like the time around twilight time which is dinner time, right, and you're walking down the street and they have all these people eating dinner in their houses and apartments and their windows are occasionally open and you peek in and you see families eating dinner?

Q: *Yeah?*

A: And it looks very nice? And warm and—I like that kind of, y'know, *voyeurism.* Where you can glimpse at pretend family warmth, I mean this is one *myth* that you see in, let's say on television, it's one that's always shown, and that's *normality,* that's supposed to be normality. Well to some extent this is like that, like a Martian looking in those little windows, in the sense that, ha— not in *my* world!—has it ever really been that way. So let's say you're an actress and they give you these ridiculous parts. What a long, hard journey it is to find that level of, y'know, complicated person and still be the kind of person that could just have a "lovely dinner" with your husband and children!

Q: *But what I'm trying to say is I think you have to have a* vivid *imagination to be able to . . .*

L.A. Is the Capital of Kansas

A: Be that banal?!

Q: ... *well, forget about "art as imitation," or "motivation"—any of the trite catchphrases of the profession—just to be able to, to, uh, be the person wearing the blue sweater.*

A: Yes! But you know something, Richard, the thing *you* don't understand, you think of it as being all sorts of hard work and labor. My feeling is that, just in terms of *my life*, it's like now I have this other person that is very close to me, you know Wendy Cassidy? Okay, she wasn't even on the show all that long, she was in like four scenes, very short amount of, I would say the *foolish* parent, y'know? I don't know *what* her role was within the series, but I would think that she was there to be made fun *of*.

Q: *You were the only comic character on the show.*

A: Yeah, but I think there was something that was, uh, the lovable foolish one, although what she represented to *me* was something I respected anyway, I think she really, I mean I liked her a lot. My point is that Wendy Cassidy *exists* in a way. For me this woman exists and I *know* her, and she is a combination of me and this strange person. That's not labor, but what I'm saying is that that's a real person, because a real . . .

Q: *But then again you were the only person on the entire show who bothered— not that one is required to, it's just a job—you were the only one who bothered to invent an actual entire person who had . . .*

A: I don't agree with that. Several others, I think other people did that too, I really do.

Q: *But these other people . . .*

A: The other *actors*.

Q: *. . . excuse me, the other* actors *played the lines to a certain hilt but they did not give to 'em a persona* beyond *the lines.*

A: Yeah, but you know something, I tell you the only reason that's . . . I think they *did* give them a persona beyond the lines, they just gave them a more obvious persona because they know what the normal, obvious, correct persona is. I *don't*, I just have this complicated version in my own head.

Q: *But the point is it's all from computer central. There is no humanly obvious, normal, y'know, you know, I mean forget about whether such a thing exists either demographically or in such and such suburban homes, what I'm saying is you're the only one who took a* whole *person, unless these other people are just conceiving characters so across-the-board* bland *that, uh, they played bland for bland sake to the hilt.*

A: I don't think they played bland or they're conceiving characters so bland, I think from their pool of resource, from who they are, they could perceive what it is they're supposed to be in this situation, and they give it and they gave it and I think in *fact*, I think the actors on that particular episode were extremely good—I *liked* them. None of them were . . .

Q: *I dunno, I don't wanna continue making fun of these working stiffs, I just believe that uh, I'll change the subject, it doesn't matter.*

A: You believe that they, there was a certain amount of, of what?

Q: *Well, I don't even wanna say supreme* caution *to what they did, just uh, like uh . . . they didn't deliver as much, from where* I *live and breathe, as you get when you buy a made-in-Hong Kong flannel shirt that shrinks two sizes every time you . . .*

A: Oh, I don't agree with you at all.

Q: *. . . wash it, but yet somebody sweated and died in the Philippines to make the shirt. My feeling is* yes *there was labor, effort, but there wasn't, y'know, much in the way of* qual, *I mean, you know what I'm saying? They earn their fee, they did exactly what they were called upon to do, but they were* not *called* upon *to do much more than make a shirt that's gonna shrink two sizes. Whereas* you, *but so they* didn't . . .

A: I don't think these people just hacked it *out*, though, is what you're saying, I don't think so at all.

Q: *Okay, let's change the subject. Do you have secretarial skills?*

A: I do.

Q: *Would you type this up for me?*

A: I can't type this up for you. No!! Do I get to edit while I type?

Q: *No, no.*

A: Then I won't do it.

BICENTENNIAL BOOTS AND BUTTER

Yup, you got it right: old Meltz the killjoy—overtaken by bicentennial fever.* 'S an ole town we got here, older even than Yukulpa, Minnesota (founded 1938), and age sure as heck is an overTAKER. On the SAME DAY for instance TWO PEOPLE had birthdays in their THIRTIES, J----h McB---e, 33, writer for the prestigious trade sheet *V-----y*, and this chunky babe he's known for a while who don't do much of anything but sit around and be rich named P----a. P----a is 30 and pissed about it, shouldn't be because age is just illusion, and even so she's been ACTIN' 50 since she was umpteen plus one. Dresses like she's maybe only 45, f'rinst this lavender "matron's gown" that don't really hide her belly, also hair like Marlo Thomas (born 1943). "Emotional age": 3 or 4. Stepdaughter of R----t W--e who directed the highly successful *S---d of M---c* and the old goat was conned into shelling out for a dual BIRTHDAY GATHERING

---

*L.A.'s bicentennial, 1981. Not that anyone particularly cared, but many an ad-hungry mag (in this case, New Age catbox-liner *Stuff*) published at least a bicentennial special.

62

featuring friends of her and friends of J----h at the West Beach Cafe (60 North Venice Boulevard, 399–2946).

West Beach is not on Main St. that chic st. that realtors're tryin' t' turn into ANOTHER GODDAM WESTWOOD, 's in the still funkee part o' Venice so the rich c'n ketch up on their quota of slumming. Half a block up from the seedy, sandy lot where you park if you're going to the BEACH, busted bottles and winos and sand, beatniks useta beat it here in '58. Spiffy neon outside, inside're four tables of FUN and as luck has it me and my companion (friends of the 33'er) are relegated to Table D. 30-yr-old's just been DI-VORCED or in the process and aside from grabbing people's metaphoric dicks all she wantsa do is make sure you sit in the prearranged SPOT. Name things next to your FORK. At our tabe are Pat McGilligan of *Playgirl* mag and his best gal Tina, Byron Reisel of the *L.A. Weeder* and his rib Carol, some jacuzzi salesman named Roger and his wife whatsername who's constantly givin' me the "eye." (Guys 'n' gals all around, if you're a one-on-one fan you couldn't of been more PLEASED.)

I check the menu for bicentennial relevance and find the going *rough*. Hafta resort to cryptography like in the appetizers there's clams with garlic & (B)as(I)l and (C)alamari with b(E)urre bla(N)c = b.i.c.e.n. w/out the tennial. Seven bucks per, gotta have both and am glad as heck SOMEONE ELSE is payin'. For additional bicen. flavor Capt. Jacuzzi who is actually a lawyer RAVES ON & ON 'bout how much he luvs L.A. for its SALTWATER. "I went to school in Cambridge (= Harvard or M.I.T., nobody's askin' which) and realized I was 3000 miles from the nearest ocean (hardy har)," this baldy tells us, a baldy who combs his remaining strands "over the bald" and could easily be played in the motion pics by the versatile JACK WESTON. Yes indeedy Roger, Pacific is my-t-swell, only objection *I* got is L.A.'s finest eau is sulfur not salt, CESSPOOL is my "scene" in this 200-yr-old scuzzbowl of an incorporated sprawl (I two-cents him to his amusement, mine and all the others—a *charming* fuck I'm quite capable of bein').

Calamari 're stuffed w/ orange stuff & onions, on a bed of yellowish sauce and plenty of tentacles NOT removed, three li'l squidlings that come to (he does his math) $2.33 a throw and sure are suc-cu-lent. Conversation switches to the *Times* and its half-blind sportswrite hack Jim Murray. I hate the guy like bubonic but Pat, in town all of t'ree wks., thinks he's boss, bicentennial spirit does not gotta be monolithic so I tell him 's cool, the jerkoff might have REDEEMING FEATURES, I don' write for the sports section of L.A.'s worst daily so who am eye to "complain"? Clams are clammy but "nice," whole *puddle* of spicy green wet stuff to gob up w/ your crusty bread product that you probably coulda got warmer on the inside w/out petrifyin' it outside if you did it in your own HOME. Home it turns out we all got *nearby* each other, all in the wonderful vicinity of the GORDON Theater. Double features for two bucks or a buck fifty (exact mem'ry fails us all). "We go there all the time," mr. lawyer person sez, "the ambience does not bother US." Cinema on our collective MIND, the S.A.G. strike is brought up. Only one of us bein' a picket-carrying unionist—my gal Xylene—'s only minimal skin off OUR ass as our *Weeder* friend has a chuckle re the non-union film he's PRODUCING in N. Carolina where they got right to WORK laws.

Back to our stomach, salad is cheese-y (has cheese taste on it) and main events are—without exception, except the whitefish—*saucy.* My "braised sweetbreads in dijon mustard" are also *in* something else, this brown stuff that IS NOT GRAVY. Half the plate is mustard colored and half the plate is brown, one sweetbread t' each @ ten bucks/2. Braised in wine and speaking of there is California vintage at all four TABLES. Not Almaden or Wente Bros., some other brand, white, brung in by the case for the occasion. Sweetbreads're sliced so thin you wouldn't know they're an animal's pancreas, *I* know but some might not. Bicentennial egalitarianism is rampant and we share the many dishes we have ordered: swordfish (thin); sea bass (fat) topped w/ scallops (thinnn); WHITEFISH IN PASTRY WITH 2 BUTTERS. Dunno which 2 but there was this fake eyeball made out of a peppercorn and no sauce, a welcome relief as most sauces tasted ALIKE. Brown, yellow, yellow ochre, it did not much matter (quite alike). TWO HUNNERD (= bicent. if it was yrs.)

CALORIES PER SPOONFUL. Bathroom was high tech meets Jim Dine, outa focus photo of a female torso (nipple visible).

We stuffed our goddam gut while R----t W--e sat at Table A and who knows what other bigwigs at B & C—no way to lay our insipid, asinine "trips" on the mogul who gave the world *T-e D-y t-e E---h S---d S---l* or even his buddies who mighta (for all we knew) gave us *Ice Station Zebra* or *Cat Women of the Moon*. They were there and we were here; rules are rules and who the fuck were WE t' ask for different? (Noblesse oblige—bi.cen.tenn.ial style.)

We are thankful for our meal including dessert featuring chocolate moussish thing w/ cream that ain't been whipped, blueberry ricotta cheesecake which tasted like vom, okay strawberry BROWN-BUTTER tart and praline ice cream that tasted like deodorant and gather our shoes & jackets and move along to a screening of OUR BIRTHDAY GIRL'S favorite FILM of all time, Billy Wilder's *Love in the Afternoon* which she insists we enjoy or she'll cry if she wants to. Known as "singing for yer supper" and we don't gotta sing, just move our ass to TONY BILL'S SCREENING RM. on Horizon Ct. or St. or whatever. Despite his busted wrist J----h who may or may not have f---ed P----a (they're very good friends) totes along the cheapo Almaden (this time) for our afterdinner sipping pleasure.

Capsule review of the pitcher—One o' them "sophisticated" Paris/France ooh la la l'amour fiascos that're *so* kyootsy pie & STOCKED TO THE GIZZARD with dooble intenders you gotta figure everybody hadda be in the 2nd grade when they made it (1957, bicentennial of the planet Uranus). Black & white. A pathetically miscast GARY COOPER of "watch me, I'm a hick" fame struggles like a sweaty chicken as the Cary Grant/Burt Reynolds suave debonair man about th' globe who slips his Oscar Mayer wiener to at least one different gal per night, sometimes also the afternoon as the title snidely "implies." Bags under the eyes make him, lessee, oh about 65-66 even tho the *Information Please Almanac* has him at only 56 which he sure don't look—obviously did a "lot of living" offscreen including the very famous porking of Patricia Neal that led directly to her first famous "nervous breakdown." Pat ain't in this one, they got Audrey Hepburn who is made to look like Julie Kavner of *Rhoda* (from the side) and (from the front) a female Carl "Alfalfa" Switzer. Verrry attractive (yuh). Anyway she luvs the creep tho all he's after is a quick dip in her Belgian sweetmeat (at first) and later the keys to her kingdom (of damp)—altho she 'ventually turns the tables and gets to ride off with him in a train not unlike the one from *The Lady Vanishes* while fake gypsies play the same song that's been giving you the creeping willies for TWO hours and TEN minutes. Her pop is greasy Vichy collaborator Maurice Chevalier (= man of horses). Hotel where they fuq is actually called the RITZ (I wouldn't kid ya). Y'never see anyone remove a garment or even put one on, just a little hairbrush action to tastefully indicate post-coital "disarray." Ending is *Gigi* meets *For Whom the Bell Tolls* and four yrs. later baggy-eyes was dead, inotherwords he couldn't act t' save his life (that's a joke). I don't care if he also directed *Lost Weekend*, if Billy Wilder is a director after this one then I'm Desiderius Erasmus (1466?–1536), I mean the guy's got a PROBLEM with this virgin-softens-the-heart-of-a-cad number that mebbe primal scream or Scientol could do somethin' *about*, him and the jerk who did the movie *10* oughta make the scream box scene TOGETHER.

7-teen years later when *Laughing Policeman* came out and hetero azzhole Bruce Dern sez to Walter Matthau "love in the afternoon" when this middle-aged leather guy they've been tailing is S&M'ing some guy from a bar up in his San Fran pad there is FINALLY sumpin' ironic enuff to laff about. Mr. & Mrs. W--e tho and all their lackeys were already laffin' at all the "appropriate" moments but not me who was cracking jokes all *thru* the shit and once when I got Xylene to éclat de rire in a "wrong" spot by cutting off the air to her nose by clamping down on it sideways in a parody of "kissing" Mrs. W turned around—she was in front of us—and looked kind of super ANNOYED.

The curtain goes down amid two hands clapping to the left, right, forward & back. Mr. W proclaims: "That's one film that certainly wears well with age"—I'd rather wear a rusty neck brace myself— "It's a pity they don't make them that romantic anymore." Everybody's thirsty from the shitty chablis and a beeline is made for the water cooler which ain't working so you gotta lift the jug up and pour it yourself. As I'm nothing if not a gent I perform the backbreaking honors (paying my dues).

Birthday broad is all aglow and, buoyed by the CONTENT of her favorite pic, she shoots us a coy "Let's all go to the you-know-what this Friday." U-know is a Hollywood o-r-g-y she has tole us about (A. Hepburn fans apparently *love* 'em). We nod her a yeah-sure (y'know?) and depart into Venice nightness still stuffed to shit from the so-so fare.

My tire is punctured by a busted Coors and I'm disappointed, it could at least of been a FALSTAFF BICENTENNIAL BEER left over from the USA's 200th and still sold some places but only in cans.

THE ARMENIAN SHOW (NOT TO BE MISSED)

Fred Astaire special on the occasion of the AFI folks figgered he's due to croak so let's honor him before the worms get their turn was real reet and a half from the wd. go—one of them Great Moments In Nothin'-type events that nothin' fans are fond of and will *kick themselves* for missing when they do (it happens). Me, I kicked the nothin' habit a longgg time ago but the guy does have the same birfday as me (May 10) so shoot if I did not watch. Watched and watched and watched—till my eyes were blue in the face—but did not find the answer I have long longed for, ans. to what is the goddam APPEAL of Frederick anyway?

Appeal COULD BE: he is harmless (cannot, will not HARM YOU). In mod-rin terms: not macho (won't stick his hand up your dress). Also possible: dances about as good as EVERYMAN (you remember *him*). And: sings no better than Dom DeLuise (so you don't get dazzled into heart attacks or anything). Plus: man is a SUAVE motherfuh (for all the suaveness fans). OTHER THAN THAT his qualifications for the coveted AFI whatsis were: dunno. Walked: not especially gimpy (considering).

The Armenian Show (Not to Be Missed)

From the 37th floor of 2029 Century Park East I look down on HUNDREDS OF TINY LITTLE ANTS partying, lunching & having a goodtime while *The Incredible Hulk* has been *canceled*. They are sitting at CUTE LITTLE TABLES OF YELLOW, PINK & GREEN out front of the Century Plaza celebrating their merry rumps off at the ABC Affiliates Convention while meanwhile *The Hulk* is *gone*. Hey I know it's on CBS and all that but FUGGA WUGGA you'd think networks *everywhere* would be mourning, instead of sunning themselves over frosty cold piña coladas and Long Island ice tea. *You'd think*—but the *is* is scarcely ever the *ought* so boo hoo hoo hoo hoo. A fanntasstic show—I watched it twice—is no mo' . . .

Commercial for Off! with the $100 bill in the bug tank is DIRTY, FILTHY, SMUTTY—dirtier than pee'd-on doo-doo on *Peyton Place*. Woman sticks her arm in a den of mosquitoes to *get the Ben Franklin* (i.e. hoor herself like a common garden-variety FIVE-DOLLAR TART) and then the Off! guy tells her "GET OFF!" (i.e. have a real major thunderhump of a-louder-than-life MULTIPLE ORGAZ). As this advert is just *loaded* with genuwine GOOD STUFF like you only find in torrid, stimulating, suggestive FRENCH MAGAZINES, I suggest you tell your friends to watch it real quick, before the Moral Maj. gets wind o'things and they turn it into *Lassie*. . .

Two on the Town temporarily ABANDONED THE TOWN for Ulster, and in so doing co-hosts Steve & Melody SHED MUCH LIGHT on the Northern Ireland QUESTION. "Life goes on," explained Steve, "as it has for centuries"—beautif'ly put. Furthermore, UNEMPLOYMENT is kinda high BUT (Steve again, he had all the good lines) "many *do* work, contributing *many things* to the world"—hey that's WONDAFUL. Thanx Steve, thanx Melody even tho you didn' say diddleypoot, WE SURE THANK YOU f'r takin' time out from your Brit Isle stay to 'splain us what we di'n't know about the IRISH PART. . .

"Pete Ellis Dodge, Long Beach Freeway, Firestone exit, Southgate" is a jingle that is *not half bad*. Very tuneful.

Sunday, 3:30 P.M., channel 22—*The Armenian Show*. Guy in a tan suit, brown plaidish tie, black shirt, conventional non-square haircut (black), black beard & moviestar specs with one of those horizontal THINGS over the nose, hands in front of him like a *gentleman*, intristing delivery in a non-anglo tongue that could be, yes, it could be ARMENIAN. Pale blue backdrop w/ dark blue rectangle in upper lefthand corner, ASBAREZ DAILY (213) 380-7646 in white letter-over toward the bottom. You will enjoy this enjoyable show—not to be missed.

SPEAKING OF foreign type UHF shows do not be a-scared of *Sumo Digest*, ch. 18, 9:30 P.M., three Mondays every other month. Have no fear as the voice-over of Gordon Berger (this word jockey's fave UHF'er of all time) supplies commentary in queen's eng. over jap-o-nese from the original tapes so if you're one or t'other you'll get plenty o' verbal drift to accompany your sumo entrancement. Last month it was Chiyonofuji losing to Kitanoumi on senshuraku by tsuridashi, and the whole shebang'll be back next with the NATSU BASHO which if y'don't watch hang your head as it is the GREATEST SHOW IN ALL OF L.A. (true).

Brenda Vaccaro for Playtex tampons is one big face filling THE ENTIRE SCREEN. She is wearing lipstick. "Double-layered design" is what she prefers. Fine, ok, rooty toot. But then a kind wart is given to Playtex DEODORANT tampons, at which time you kind of gotta take INVENTORY on her credibility and not even waste your time on Playtex *regular*: WHO WITH THE INTELL. & TOLERANCE OF MS. VACCARO WOULD WANNA DEODORIZE THE FINE BOUQUET OF FRESH MENSTRUE?????

Moving from tampies to nappies the ANTI-MOISTURE BRIGADE must be stopped. Ad for Light Days sez make 'em part of your "morning routine." Inotherwords keep yer region DRY even when the droplets ARE NOT red. Tell me this: whose wool're they tryin' to pull with that one?!?!

Doing some good . . . channel 9 went & did some rilly fine GOOD with *Just Like All of Us*, wherein it was showed—for the whole-wide-whirl to see—that RETARDS CAN ANSWER PHONES, write down (if you spell it out for them) names like Smith and Jones, load machinery on a truck, make amorous physical whoopy w/ others of their KIND, get a degree from jr. college, and (even) be neurotic like everybody else! (Another 10-11 stereotypes bite the dust . . .)

Don Wilson—it turns out—IS NOT DEAD AFTER ALL. No Candy-Gram ads for the last three yrs. had us imagining otherwise, but now he's back pushing various prod with that special flair for touching over-the-hilless that is HIS & HIS ALONE. Appears he's lost a couple lbs. in the interim as well. WELCOME BACK, y'old dogface!

WISH-I'D-SAID-THAT DEPT.—"When the day comes that there's no sportsmanship in golf, there'll be no sportsmanship left." (Stu Nahan at the L.A. Open.)

A SICK SHOW AND GOOD THING IT'S NO LONGER ON—*Private Benjamin*. Grownup boys and girls calling each other "sir" is sick sick SICK, that went out with the '49 Studebaker. Not quite as sick but certainly UP THERE is this drink they invented for the final show: a "pinky suprise" (lots of fizz or foam on top which Eileen Brennan fingers out with her pinky & says *mmm mmm good*). Sicker than the rest of it put together: "Liebestraum" or something playing in the background as she "puts on something a little more comfortable" in her PRIVATE SUITE . . .

Mrs. Salvador Boapadoap writes: "I would like to know if any stars of local televicion [sic] are of the Roman Catholic faith. Please tell me because I must got to know." To tell you the truth Mrs. B, none of my many contacts inside the industry have been able to come up with such admittedly essential info, altho it is RUMORED on the network front that Robert Walden of *Lou Grant* once attended Mass on an occasional basis. ANYONE WHO KNOWS MORE'N THAT PLEASE DROP US A CARD . . .

What's green and skates (and sez "Trident is recommended by moms like me")? PEGGY PHLEGM.

Newly unearthed anagrams for television: EVIL ON SITE; I STONE LIVE. Newer still (just did 'em this sec): VILE ION SET; LEVI TESION (y'know, the *big jean tease* on account there's no designer type ads for Levis but probably *some day soon*); TENSIO. "E" I.V. ("E" type *tension* that you get *intravenous*); STENO VEIL I (the *world's first* thing for stenos to wear over their face so the x-citement of daytime shows won't distract them from their *work*); NO ELEV. IS IT (teevee explained in terms of sea level); NITE IS LOVE (that's true); NO LITE SIEV. (a sieve has *not been developed* that'll skim off *all remaining calories* in Miller Lite); LE VIN 'TIS O.E. (the wine is *only ethyl*, i.e., ethyl alc. is *why you drink it*—Orson Welles is *not the reason*); SEE, VOIT NIL (= do not buy a football from the principal sponsor of *Pro Bowlers Tour*). Fun with spelling & letters!

Speaking of fun, the author's only regret, now that Cyndy Garvey's flown the coop at *AM Los Angeles*, is she never showed us (at least a foto of) her CLITORIS.

If you can read this sentence you can read a book. GO READ *Richard Dawson and Family Feud* by Mary Ann Norbom (Signet, 150 pp., $1.95), the type will not rub off on yer hands nor the nifty pixture of R.D. with former mirage partner DIANA DORS and their ugly offspring GARY...

A number to reckon with: 186 HMR. License # on a powder blue VW being driv by a bearded fellow with "ABC–TV" plastered on the rear. Could THIS HIPPIE be the ex-mastermind behind *Battlestar Galactica*?

Steve Allen, Friday nite, NBC. What I wanna know is izzit a SPECIAL or izzit a SHOW? Not on every week and t' make things rough *TV Guide* duz not say SPECIAL under the HEADING. So it must be a SHOW. A truly HORRIBLE show. One of the POORER shows in the HISTORY OF MAN and his kind. He sends out Billy Crystal and his new lame PUNCHDRUNK BOXING routine and tells you "No, this is not really comedy but a *plaintive portrayal* of an ex-pug." He—no that's all I watched, 10 seconds of Steverino and 15 of Billy C—I turned it off it was just too NAUSEATING. So all I wanna know is whud they do with Steve-o's JOWLS and SENIL-ITY, both of which he sure as fug HAD for it musta been 10-15 years so really WHUD THEY *DO* WITH 'EM???????

They finally got something RIGHT—Host Larry Carroll of *Where Were You?*, on the controversial subject of 1974. "In all, it was a pretty good year" and that's no lie: The annum that gave us the abolition of pneumonia, the death of Eisenhower, the Plymouth Bobcat and the election of Buddy Hackett as mayor of Hartford could not be *all bad.*

1, 2, 3, 4, 5, 6, 7, 8, 9, 11, sorry, 10, 11, 12, 13, 14, 16, oops, 15, 16, 17, 18, 19, 20, 21, 22, 23, 24, 25, 26, 27, 28, 29, 210, that's wrong, 30, 31, 32, 33, 34, 35, 36, 37, 38, 39, 40, 41, 42, 43, 44, 54, no, 45, 46, 47, 48, 49, 50, 51, 512, wait I got it, 52, 53, 54, 55, 56, 57, 58, 59, 60, 61, 62, 63, 64, 65, 66, 67, 68, 69, 70, 71, 72, 73, 74, 75, 76, 77, 78, 79, 80, 81, 82, 28, no, 83, 84, 85, 86, 87, 88, 89, 90, 91, 92, 93, 94, 95, 96, 97, 98, 99, 100, 1001, 1002 . . . (Proof that TV does *not* impair your ability to count!)

WHO'LL STOP
THE WAYNE?

THINGS YOU CAN ONLY LEARN BY TRAVELING—In case you thought L.A. has the monopoly on Raleigh Hills execu-drunk tanks, they also got one in Vegas (so who knows where else) and they even got Gale Storm. Yes I was in L.V. (on business), saw MUCH GOOD TELEVISED SHIT (the business of watching teevee), really fine upchuck I will share with you in the hope that you'll watch it too (next time you're in Puke City yourself).

CHANNEL 3: Ample Duds commercial featuring STILL PHOTOS of fatties in the latest up to date blimp attire. "Big, beautiful women, when you're in Vegas come to Ample Duds." (Sizes 36–60.) "You get more of the things you *love* . . . at Pizza Inn." (I LOVE A DONUT, but did not have time to check what flavors they got.)

CHANNEL 5: Every ten minutes they plug EVERY SHOW THAT'S ON SAT. & SUN. ShaNaNaCharliesAngelsLaverne&ShirleyBurns&AllenCrummyCartoonsMoviesYouveSeenSixTimes—2 seconds of everything. Governor Lisk of Nev. as Smokey the Bear: "Our forests are tinder-dry," he warns.

CHANNEL 8: Jack Concannon (3rd rate QB with the Eagles and

Bears, '64–71) does the sports at 11, interviewing the only black faces you'll see in town (besides Redd Foxx and Bill Cosby), those amazing athletes of UNLV.

CHANNEL 10: Crash course in the high cost of entertainment, the making of a "must-see" Vegas show. "You've gotta be a T.V. STAR, lotta television exposure, *maybe* some hit records. Wayne Newton on the other hand is *more than* an enigma, he's a Vegas institution. He worked his way up thru the boondocks, his feel for an audience is *phenomenal*. But he may be a VANISHING BREED."

CHANNEL 13: "Family Shoes is *going out of business forever*," spoken with a certain *affirmative joy*, the kind of a.j. you're bound to have with a great catchy name like Family Shoes. Ben Stepman Dodge (in Henderson): "We're the *other* Dodge dealer." Whoever the *other* other might be it's no big sweat t' guess why (duller than a CARPET COMMERCIAL). 11:30 sign-off editorial: "What percent of auto accidents in Clark County involve at least one driver who has been drinking?" Ans.: 65. Tho no actual *opinion* is given they welcome your response.

Capsule summary of the sheer greatness of LVTV: Three steps "down" from L.A. (if that's possible), probably on a par with Fargo or Sarasota. The town that TV (i.e., Johnny Carson) put on the map has certainly got its TV "act" together, consistently delivering the Buddhist/Hindu/LSD massage that LIFE IS LOSS—of small-biz staying power, mind-set tenacity, aesthetic acuity, and the integrity of actual needs (as well, of course, as wages)—and who're WE to grumble when it could be "worse"? We could be living in Mormon Penis, Utah (for inst) or Mumps, Tennessee.

Everything in Vegas feels like (and ultimately *is*) TV and I'm not talking *Let's Make a Deal* or *Joker's Wild*. The casinos now have slot machines with *electronic images* of oranges & cherries in lieu of the customary stamped or painted whatsems. You go to jai alai at the MGM Grand and the chain-link grid between you and the players, coupled with the colors and lighting, makes the whole thing look like TV dots blown up *too many times*—jolting your eyes and making you "doubt" what you're seeing. There isn't *one* cocktail waitress who couldn't be a regular on *Three's Company* or *Flamingo Road*. The whores all resemble Phyllis George. The best food in town is (believe it) Denny's. IHOP is second.

So after two days of gambling/losing, eating/drinking and digging the tube-writ-small, I figured it was time for a mega-dose of the REAL THING, a hefty tune-in on TV per se at its most ersatz, grandiose and fucked—the sort of BOGO-SIMULATION-OF-LIFE you can only get LIVE at any of the town's fabulous "rooms." Quick perusal of the entire Strip offered 16,000,000 TONS of hot worthless pathetic ugh—Liberace, Mac Davis, Charo w/ David Brenner, Ann-Margret, the Royal Lippizan Stallions (in their worldwide debut anywhere other 'n turf), Neil Sedaka w/ Fred Travalino, etcet. But none of these jerks, be they equine or human, had the goods on y'already know who I'm talkin' about: the one the only mr. entertainment himself WAYNE NEWTON. At the Aladdin which he owns. If TV sez he's the man he's the man.

At 30 bucks a pop (plus 15 ¾ % "entertainment tax") for 2 drinks and a show, it's got to mean I take my work seriously. Seen the guy on Johnny and a telethon, and already know he's gotta be the biggest no-talent dork ever to simultaneously be the biggest thing in contempo-squaresville make-believe, but still I ain't seen the TO-TAL DIMENSION(S) of the thing and fuck if I'm gonna pass up the chance. Besides, Liberace (second choice) is only $17.50 so that must mean the poor bastard's over the hill, and what I'm lookin' for in worthlessness is MR. NOW. The Dadaist in me sez go with Wayne and lemme tell ya DADA NEVER HAD IT SO GOOD.

For starters consider this: *The* first Elvis medley (anywhere ever) comprised SOLELY OF BALLAD SWILL—"Are You Lonesome Tonight?," "Love Me Tender," "Can't Help Falling in Love with You." It's dedicated, naturally, to the man Himself, "a giant of the entertainment industry I had the good fortune to call a close personal friend during his final days on earth"—which is prob'ly even true, and prob'ly says more about CULTURAL ENTROPY than umpteen *This Is Elvis*es. Speaking of which, even after he'd turned to shit himself, Elvis still had the pipes to at least sonically distract you from an obvious retrograde lyric; this was therefore the first time I actually managed to catch the *words* to "Lonesome" and Wayne's

TOTAL NON-MASTERY OF SINGERLY NUANCE has gotta be why. Even some demi-quasi-*semi*-pro like let's say Diane Keaton could probably've dredged *something* out of the tune, while this boy comes up empty 'cept for I-miss-you-do-you-miss-me you could cut with a butter knife. Which has gotta be the dandiest OUT-OF-CONTEXT FORCED-ATTENTION TRIP in yrs., the sheer inadvertency of which (not to mention its in-the-cards *inevitability*) hasta put him one up on Marcel Duchamp getting the bumpkins of his day to ogle a urinal.

But don't let ballads fool you, Wayne's a rocker from *way* back, as his hobbling, bobbling renditions of the Elks Lodge R&R Songbook adequately proved to all outpatient "geris" in from Cripple Creek. Average age hadda be somewhere around 67 or 68, and these folks were ALL SMILES as the puffboy in the Slim Whitman 'stache yanked 'em, by the numbers, from "Good Hearted Woman" to "Polk Salad Annie" to that guaranteed showstopper "Johnny B. Goode." And by showstop I ain't kidding, twice the band lurched into "J.B.G." overtime when Wayne insisted on ROCKIN' SOME MORE and each time the show just dead fucking STOPPED. And by smiles I'm saying that's all there was, *the ecstasy was minimal*; was more like these slap-happy sexagenarians were pleased as punch seein' the NICE YOUNG MAN—who could eas'ly be their bouncy beloved GRANDSON—be oh so tasteful & harmless WITH THE MUSIC OF NIGGRAS & REDNECK BEASTS. If he'd done "Midnight Hour" (some sets maybe he does) it wouldn'ta raised a hackle.

Which is not t' say the customers did not at times get *carried away*. They got carried away exactly TWICE. One, a standing ovation for Wayne's stirring (lame & literal) reading of "MacArthur Park"—Tommy Velour could not of read it better—accompanied by frighteningly authentic fake lightning, fake thunder and FAKE RAIN. Two, "God Bless America" (slide show of clouds and a *heap* of unintentional wrong wds.—if they'd been on purpose *somebody* woulda chose 'em a mote less dumb) had 'em on the edge of their seat in silent googoo-eyed communion with their LORD (prob'ly ashamed they couldn't kneel), an appropriate response to what had to be the apex—the acme!—of the show; if L.A. is the cultural capital of the republic (for which it stands) then Vegas is the RELIGIOUS CAPI-TAL, the capital of capital.ism, a truism if there ever was one (and truism is the hick version of irony).

But hicks in Vegas also need DIRT, a passel of smut to give 'em a guilty "thrill" that would only embarrass them and make th'm fear for the social order back in _____ (tired of making up silly hometown names). With his "phenomenal rapport" w/ an audience on the line, Wayne *had the smut*; told this utterly *bizarre* sexist joke that filled their quota and more. "Has anyone out there ever had a COYOTE DATE?" Members of the band say me-me-me. "No, *you* guys don't count. Oh excuse me, you don' know what a coyote date is? Well first lemme assure you this *does not apply* to any ladies in attendance tonight. Let's say you're at a bar. . ." He then goes thru this whole routine of after you've had a few the uggle at the end of the counter is finally not too bad. "So you take her to a motel, I won't even say what the two of you *do* but you wake up in the morning with a head-splitting hangover and this *weight* on your arm. You're afraid to open your eyes and *look*, finally you muster the courage and she's WORSE THAN YOUR WILDEST NIGHTMARE. You've got to get *out of there* before she wakes up, but if you remove your arm that's exactly what she'll do. So you do what coyotes do when caught in a trap. . . YOU CHEW YOUR ARM OFF!" Haw haw hoo as the aforementioned bandboys wave empty sleeves of their tux.

Yes, the rapport is phenom'nal, for a guy with *no discernible charisma* he sure knows how to occasionally get a rise. (Could be he's learned the skill by doing "time" with encounter groups brought in just for him.) At other times tho he falls flat on his nose with self-deprecating INDIAN JOKES (claims now he's part Native-Am., wears feathers on his silver buckle: niftiest way IMAGINABLE to get you t' stop thinking *Mafia*) which expose an itchy inability to even be overtly *in*sincere. (He is not your garden-variety "Vegas phony.") Obviously he knows (to some extent) he ain't got nothin' but success (like nobody's *that* stupid), question remains to what extent he maybe fancies himself as a *charlatan* behind it all—how much actually boils down to (what could pass for conscious) "manipulation." In any event, the setup seems to be for everyone (8 million L.V. tourists a year) to see Wayne ONCE—and once is sure as heck sufficient.

But I haven't even mentioned (& I'm sure you'd like to KNOW) the final segment of th' show, the part where he PROVES BEYOND A SHADOW OF A DUCK he is one helluva competent practiced Musician. Earlier, on "Johnny B. Goode," he toyed with a guitar, *possibly* the playing was his, a mere TEASER for his hogwild romp thru the wonderful world of strings-other-than-bass. With malice aforethought he flaunts his virtuosity on BANJO (bandleader holds up the sagging mike), documents it on amplified VIOLIN. For the rousing grand finale ("Saints Go Marchin'") he even grabs a TRUMPET, hits four-five notes before laying it down, geez this cat can play 'em! . . . nice t' know what it was *about* was MUSIC.

Bravo, bravo, halfassed applause (no encore tonight) and then we're herded out to this stack o' discs. On the Wayneco label— natch—for the bargain price of six bucks (hold the tax) a throw; still plenty time to throw away even more on blackjack, roulette. At this point I can't see ANY WAY I will wager a wooden quoit, not after the total-loss farm of 90 minutes of Wayne. Formula for all this must take into account how much the idiots're likely to bet & lose B.W.— before Wayne—'cause after Wayne it's bound to noticeably diminish . . .

Okay, I did my bit for world TV knowledge, live version of TV has gotta be 50 times more noxious than the basic small-screen gig; please don't 'spect me to do it again—soon or otherwise. Only personal "benefit" from my Vegas stay is after Vegas EVEN MELROSE LOOKS FUNKY. (If you're planning to somehow *vacate* L.A., y'oughta take a quick one to Vegas and L.A.'ll look like San Francisco.)

A LONG
GODDAM DRIVE
THROUGH
THE NIGHT

In a place with 1.2 seasons—a few weeks of rain, or the possibility of rain, and 52-minus-the-few of tinder-dry white-sky summer—the key to time, to the passage of time, is superhuman patience. In *this* patience-trying earthpost of whuh, the key to space, thankgod, is only a car. And cars, thanksomeothergod, used to be cheap. At the wretchedest depths of my first few months as a post-New Yorker, my one ace in the hole (aside from my wits) was a new-bought CAR.

One of which I hadn't used, or had reason to use, on a regular basis since college, the mid-sixties, out on Long Island. My final attempt at keeping one in Manhattan had lasted only a week, during which it had taken me five times as long to get anywhere as it would've by subway—or on foot—and my *minimum* parking distance from home had been something like nine and a half blocks. In L.A., with no rapid transit, and where nobody walks, not even to the nearest mailbox, I parked on my own street and drove anywhere and everywhere with astonishingly minimum grief.

Well, individual *places* sometimes griefed me, but rarely the drive itself, the process. In those days, up 'til just after the '84 Olympics (when the *world* started moving in), there was basically *no* non-rush hour traffic. Nor were there traffic-originated reasons to avoid this/ that end of town, or this route to it, or that. Everywhere, in terms of simply the drive, was generally cool, and I generally drove every-where.

L.A. Is the Capital of Kansas

And *out there*, on and along the road, from neighborhood to neighborhood, thoroughfare to thoroughfare, building to building, tree to tree, there'd be these amazing dualistic juxtapositings: old/new, rich/poor, natural/artificial, genu-wine/ersatz, whitebread/ethnic, manifold/monotonous, unique/modular, benign/lethal, ugly/attractive—anything and its quasi-opposite in the same extended geo-transit breath. As long as you just kept moving, as long as the whole flashy thing whooshed past your windows, you'd at least get the *illusion* of multiplicity—of "big city" cornucopial to-do—as suspension-of-disbeliefably *viable* an illusion as any this fairyland has, in my tenure, served up.

But it didn't last forever. Not for me. Aside from inevitably running out of places to drive and ways to drive there, aside from the quantum leap in traffic, there's been an incredible nosedive in basic Look. Since well before the Olympics, even cruising for burgers, I've needed a *target* when I drive, an approximate destination. Moving or still, I can't fugging *look* at the dump.

Case in point: the modular proliferation of ersatz. Malls. Malls. Malls. And mini-malls. And Melrose, the New Age black hole of the Western Hem (a non-mall "community").

Case in point: highrises. As recently as, oh, 1980 you could stop at a light, any light, and see infinite vistas in four directions. One direction might have a hill, say, but even *semi*-infinite is cool with a hill in the picture. Life could suck, L.A. could suck, but you'd always have three infinite, one semi- with a hill, for symptomatic relief.

So what'd they do, they started building high, ugly, nothing but ugly and high. Everywhere you drove, in three sightlines, four, there'd be rivals of Century City. You'd be driving and thinking, well, it can't be to house the homeless, no, and it can't be some wiseass saying let's go urban (catch up with N.Y./Chicago/Detroit), and it can't simply be a fault-line deathwish or a sudden outbreak of Vertical Manifest Destiny. It can't be those and it can't be . . . and as you'd be thinking, your sightlines were raped in the goddam NOSE.

So where—on a clear day—you once had three, three and a half decent lines on whatever, you were suddenly, scarily, down to two, one, *none*. And suddenly, what a joke, everybody was less concerned about the *previous* line-raper, smog, which, truly, really always bothered 'em more re visual aesthetics than pulmonary health. Now, with all the highrising, you hardly ever see smog. And if you did—so? Highrises're every hour, every day; smog is at worst two rainless days out of three.

And people get HEADACHES from these highfucks, headaches *not caused by smog*, they get bouts of the running, flying heebie jeebies. They even, well, between the highshit and all the ground-level mod/ersatz yug, where's to look anymore *without* headaches? Up, down, 45°, stuck in neo-traffic, 's all one story: WALLS CLOSING IN! In New York there's no more *in*, they've *been* closed since when, 1880?

Tight quarters, if y'ain't used to 'em, can drive you *bats*. There's been a sharp increase lately in guys shooting each other on freeways. In cars, dig, they're whacked-out urbanites. On the road they're bats in a cage. (And still no one walks.) Ain't that cute?

It's a good thing I already know where the good burgers *are*.

HOW ABOUT
A LITTLE TRIP
TO WATTS?

For a town with so many people driving so many vehicles so many places nine days a week, L.A. is still basically mired in a zero sense of automotive adventure. Everybody and his/her aunt/uncle's always taking the customary spin to job x, restaurant y and party z—with, of course, the occasional longer spin to Palm Springs or Santa Barbara—but just about nobody's willing to follow his/her nose and/ or instincts or just pick up a Triple-A map and say, "Today I'm driving to Hawaiian Gardens—wherever (and whatever) in hell that may be."

Which is pretty much a pity since 99 per cent of So-Cal's true tenor-and-import worthy of the name is Out There Somewhere just begging to be seen by mainstream eyes, 5-10-20-30 minutes off any given beaten path, geo-coded hotstuff that really shouldn't need an annual Something-or-Other Festival to be frontally experienced. The incorporated township of Cudahy, for instance, certainly within that time radius from Sunset & Western, is as worth visiting as the principality of Liechtenstein (or Andorra), if only because the whole silly thing is three blocks by five blocks *in toto*.

How About a Little Trip to Watts?

And like how many jaded standard-issue white sophisticates have ever been to the Watts Towers for gosh sakes? Here's an "art treasure" greater by far than anything you'll ever see at the L.A. County Museum (including for sure the current Tut show), but the very idea of Watts seems to daunt even the most committed of blue-eyed high culture hepcats. In New York everybody's been to 125th Street in Harlem at least once, even if only by mistake (subway codings *can* be confusing), and even stockbrokers en route to work in the morning are forced to confront a multi-ethnic urban gestalt, but to most whitebread motorists Watts is just this shadowy whatsis off the Harbor Freeway with street numbers in the mysterious 100s, and who in heck's even *curious* enough to just once take a random exit and (at "worst"!) end up cruising in abject short-term fear 'til the fabulous *way back* is ultimately, miraculously unearthed? Simps, wimps, call 'em what you will . . .

Well anyway, me and a pal navigated our way to the Towers with nothing to assist us last week but page 62 of *Gousha's New Revised Street Atlas of Greater Los Angeles and Orange Counties*, on which the "Simon Rodia Towers" are but a dot beside the intersection of 107th St. and Graham Ave. As always, the block was functionally immaculate, upkept to the gills, more so than any equivalent venue in Hollywood, let's say, or Venice; a lot more "residential looking" than its closest ethnic counterpart in New York, one of your "better streets" in Jamaica, Queens. People live at 107th and Graham the way they do at the non-commercial crossings of almost *any* So-Cal community: calmly, suburbanly, antiseptically. L.A. is, after all, the world's largest, and slickest, hick suburbia from top to bottom, so why should its major black enclave be less slickly, hickly livable than its whiter, wealthier suburban-hick locales?

A gem of a street but—darn—the Towers were "closed for renovation," they've gotta reinforce the supports or something in time for next winter's rainslaught. Closed, ha—you *knew* there was a reason you avoided spinning down last weekend! Still, the outer environs are inspectable, all those fancy china tea set, seashell and 7-Up bottle fragments embedded in cement by Simon the driven Italian-immigrant candymaker or candlemaker (details vary—tilemaker?

shoemaker?) half a century ago. Weeds in abundance—a *natural* approach to suburban gardening for a change. But almost no graffiti and not one sign of structural desecration—this is *not* the South Bronx or whatever the latest geo-ethnic (racist at heart) media metaphor might be.

Even a quick peek is cool, and we split for Central Avenue—once bebop capital of west of the Rockies and setting for Florian's, the "dinge bar" which figured prominently in *Farewell, My Lovely*—our chosen north-south thoroughfare and pitstop for a much-needed sixpack. We cop at a grocery, plus a couple cheap cigars, and spend the next half-hour quenching our heatwave thirst right where God intended, in the open, in the car, right out on Central Ave., a "charming," quaint-as-all-getout "older part of town." As there's something brazen about our action—this after all being the repression capital of America, at least in regards to vehicular beer—it isn't long before an impressively bold teenage local bops by to make an inquiry. "Are you guys cops?" he asks, cordially.

Huh, what could make him *think* such a thing? "You're drinkin' beer, right? You *must* be cops." Friendly, fearless little guy: is that any way to talk to Eulia Love's executioners?!* "Hey, but we're smoking cigars. Cops don't smoke cigars." He has no answer for this and abruptly reverses his field. "Well, how'd you like to buy some reefer? I got a, uh, *cousin* I could call." Thanks but no thanks, buddy—what a gracious, brave, generous gent-and-a-half!

And you with-its tell me you're *afraid of Watts?!* Geez, it's about time not only you but this town's squaresville media just started going out, meeting and *greeting* a normal healthy dose of race-related copy—'stead of sending in the usual pack of clowns with the usual tedious questions, the answers to which can only reinforce clichés no more viable on a basic reality front than your customary diet of

*On January 3, 1979, two uniformed officers of the LAPD, responding to a utility-company employee's complaint of interference in his attempt to shut off a household's gas, opened fire on recently widowed black housewife Eulia Love, unarmed except for a kitchen knife, fatally piercing her flesh with eight .38-caliber slugs (on 11 shots).

made-for-TV. In oth'words: you wanna know about real genu-wine true-life *life* in this here burg, you'll need to scrutinize it firsthand yourself. Personally. (And semi-regularly.) Gas isn't cheap anymore, but neither is the *Times* (or *TV Guide*).

NO SAVING WHALES IN POMONA

ALL ROADS LEAD TO POMONA. 101, 60, 210, 57 and even 71, each of which'll put you on #10, the San Bernardino Freeway, which can't help but dump you on the doorstep of the L.A. County Fair and I do mean COWnty. 'S got cows (one guesses) and even if it don't actually *have* 'em it's at least got cowboys, farmers, ranchers, ranch hands and imported indentured "wetbacks" (their backs're wet). 'S got all that & more so why not celebrate L.A.'s AGRARIAN HERITAGE the way you if so inclined celebrate its celluloid tradish? Makes sense.

Buck to park and two-fifty admission sure beats heck on Disneyland and beats that dump in 2 additional depts. as well: 1. they sell beer (indicating they ain't worried about you behaving in an "unchristian" or pro-life manner); 2. nobody's wearin' hideous mouse outfits or uniforms strictly from cubesville. They're wearing nongaudy street and/or work duds, cowboy hats and an occasional boot; teens in pre-punk short hair and the customary Cheap Trick t-shirt. Likewise there is NO CAMOUFLAGE WHATEVER on the occasional albino, cripple and gimpster in attendance so you get a sideshow at no extra cost even if "contemporary goodtaste" has banished hardcore geeks and deformos to who knows where.

As bad as Disneyland however is 75¢ a ride and lemme tell ya these rides're the *pits*. Fake spaceship where you sit inside and watch a laser attack on a blurry screen while they shake you around a couple times to simulate interstellar whatsis. Dayglo funhouse with ersatz werewolf mannequins and a clown who grabs you by the neck. Various smudged-up halls o' mirrors. Ordinary ferris wheel (closed for repairs). An upside down thing with fake screams amplified so bad they sound like laughter (ha ha ha). Merry-go-round (big deal). Each for three-fourths of a buck except this slide where on one ticket you go down a chute on a burlap bag *twice* so it's really 37½¢ per fabulous RIDE.

Just as hep is the knock-something-over-with-a-ball part o' the fair where you can win stuff y'always wanted like inflatable Pink Panthers, a LARGE STUFFED VERSION OF DINO FROM THE FLINTSTONES, plastic whistles worth at least 4 cents, goldfish in blue water, a box of melted candy (it's been hot), ugly horse and dog plaques. Carnywise it's all pretty low key and non-intense—this is *L.A.* County after all, not Pascagoula—no pitchmen busting your ass to spend yer coins on balls *right now motherfucker*, so I freely spend mine on darts. For two bits you get three of 'em to throw at seven hundred red balloons, my aim is true on #3 and I win me one of those antiquish metal-clicker things you don't hardly see no more with the face of a cat worth at least a DIME.

Cat/horse/panther seems to be tellin' us something—hmm, lessee—duh...uh... Got it! We're here to see LIVESTOCK so let's git with it!! En route we inspect: boring rec vehicle display, dull model living rm., quilt show that is already closed. 'S late and quilters must SLEEP...but not too late to see SHEEP.

Baa-ing their pipes off and looking V. STUPID IN THEIR PEN while they pee in the sawdust. As one large sumbitch has this big fucking ribbon indicating prizewinner of some sort we peruse a bit to figger out why *this* one. We check the face. Stupid stoopit, eyes like a butcher shop only this one's living, couldn't't've been the face. Fetlocks? No. Bulk? Dunno. Wool? Nah, but speaking of there is wool by the bucket all over. Shearers shearing like krazy (a/k/a/ "grooming" like if you gave Frank Sinatra a haircut) but no wads large enough for a sweater that'd possibly IMPRESS folks at the local ski lodge, just tons of minimal snippets down and around the future lambchop's feet. Feet! Must be it: the champeen has MAG-NIFICENT FEET, the only logical reason for how come he won.

He? No, it's a she as one notes upon inspecting the male-ish enormities dangling from a nearby neighbor: big'uns! Biggest set of gabongas this frequenter of zoos has ever eyeballed on a known variety of captured animule. Or are they udders? No such problem in genderizing the rams, i.e. sheep w/ horns. Or do they *all* have horns only somebody cut them off? HOW LITTLE WE KNOW ABOUT OUR FRIENDLY BARNYARD BRETHREN. The "schools" we attend teach us whole lots more about frogs and hamsters.

You want horns tho this fair has got 'em in spades: goats. Smaller all around including sex orgs, therefore more of 'em per stall. And where you got more you've also got: fights. Goats butting goats! Entertaining to say the least! Primitive biological hoop-dee-doo! Or maybe they're just bored standing/sitting/lying waiting to be milked 'cause they sure as heck won't be slaughtered for anyone's chili goatburger (hold the mustard). Not enough meat on the unit goat so they luck out and live long productive lives as lowbrow rural comic relief. We purchase a goat milk at the convenient nearby goat milk stand to see if it's any diff'rent from the usual bovine variety: gamier (whatever that means).

Next come the cows. We moo at them, they moo at us. COWS ARE NOT VERY INTERESTING. They're big and cowlike. They chew on hay or whatever it is they chew before it becomes cud at stage two of the process whereby they GIVE mankind its pistachio ice cream. Some tho have muzzles and cannot chew, a cruel & inhuman deprivation with only two possible explanations: 1. they're too fat already (adipose is adipose, even in the world of beef); 2. feed, like everything else in today's day and age, is expen$ive so why waste it on bossy when the nearsighted judges will hardly know the diff? A pair of muzzlers manage to sneak a hayish morsel between the mesh: god bless 'em, they're as sharp as their dieting counterparts among the homo saps. It's a life!

Lest we forget what cattle are HERE FOR pamphlets abound on the ultimate USES of these humble dumbos' fleshier parts. "Do It With Beef." "Cut a Little—Save a Lot." "Retail Cuts in California" which delineates your chuck from your rib from your round from your rump. Valuable info I never knew: loin is from somewhere along the BACK of the beast, NOT the groin region (I never knew!). Did know (of course) that it's only the bull of the species that gets carved & sliced but wish the hell I knew what they DO with non-bulls beyond parenting age. (For the record: barnyarders of all species were segregated by sex, and only one instance of lavender behavior was observed—a EWE couple having at each other's pudding in graphic oral fashion.)

Finally, my pre-fair faves, the piggies—and I'm not disappointed. Lazier, dirtier squealers you are not likely to see. Covered with sawdust, lying almost to a man/woman on their lazy swinish sides, these fatties behaved like life was one long bedtime. Brown, pink, whatever, curly-cue tails curled against the dewy night, these generous suppliers of bacon bits for the salads of America rarely got animated enough to even lick the salt block which dotted each & every—for want of a better wd.—STY. Porcine literature revealed just how much they *normally* dig the sodium: in "Durocs on Parade" every last hoglet is posed sideways with tongue on NaCl—oink equivalent of watch the birdie!

'Scuse me if it sounds like I'm funning at the porkers' expense, I know goddam well that pigs are the MOST INTELLIGENT FAUNA we insatiable carnivores normally ingest. They have a damn good idea what's on the agenda in terms of non-scientific vivisection and wallow day in day out in a miasma of cynical gloom, exposing their unattractive multiple nipples to the yuks of callow onlookers thru no fault of their own. The bible knew surely of what it spoke with its frequent snide references to "lying down with hogs": no horror-show one-nighter with neurotic human stranger X could ever be so sullen, so glimpse-of-deathish. STILL: win a ribbon and you just might get to spend your remaining pigtime with the Porky or

Petunia of some hogbreeder's choice—propagate those hamhocks!

Speaking of which we were hungry by then from observing all the succulent, smelly hindquarters and took leave for refreshment at a barbecue facility. Three choices—beef, pork, turkey—and who in his right mind wants b-b-q TURKEY, which narrows it to stiff gristly steermeat or what TENDS TO BE TENDER (unsolicited testimonial), namely p-o-r-k. Surprise: remains of an anonymous besnouted pal who did not make it to the blue, green, purple or any color ribbon STINK. Bad sandwich, chewy and sinewy, tastes like fish or something—could they have pulled a fast one?

And fish, while we're on fish, the sadness & sorrow which had fortunately avoided us on our journey thru stytown descended whole hog as we sped for an exit thru a boring, enormous truckers' expo. There, within the body of a truck no longer than a double-length mobile home, was ensconced what was claimed to be a LIVING WHALE. "Closed" read the sign—closed for the night with no one to tuck the poor leviathan in. If it squirms and turns in the middle of a whalish nightmare (or pleasure-filled "wet one") it will bang its spout, fin, whale organs and ambergris. Sickest use of an edible mammal at the whole damn fair, and no redeeming booklets on the virtues of cetacean dogfood. Sick I tell you, SICK!

We did not get to see horseshoe pitching or Freddy Fender or the Miss Appaloosa finals. Maybe next year.

NAPALM NEWPORT BEACH!

Orange County, CA. You know it. Disneyland, Knotts Berry Farm, the J. Birch Society. Per capita income $11 billion per annum except for a couple towns where there's enough Vietnamese and illegal Mexicans to drive it down to maybe 9.7. One county down from L.A. Horrible, worthless, awful, disgusting, miserable, ugly, horrible, heinous, despicable, awful, miserable, worthless PLACE. Even worse than Marin.

Did they ever have oranges? Dunno and don't care. All I know's they got the ugliest beach I have EVER SEEN on any Coast including Gulf and that beach is: Newport Bch. Hadda go there on the 4th for some former editor person I used to get along with was in town. Didn't actually hafta but I did. Long fucking ride. In somebody else's car (more on which later) to this ugly decrepit excuse for a beach house which couldn'ta been too old but it sure looked BEAT. And grey. Even tho it was brown. Or olive. Or something. Anyway it was ugggly. Rented for the week by a publisher friend of the former ed. How much to rent? "Don't ask." Party (so-called) was in ed's "honor." Not much of a so-called party.

L.A. Is the Capital of Kansas

Ugly dumb relatives of the renter. Sun-bleached sons who surf. Cousins. Uncles. Billy Joel LPs. Nitrite meats on stale buns. Staler conversation. Nothing to do but hit the beach. Millions of ugly WHITE PEOPLE. Under an ugly WHITE SKY. White sand, white sky, white folks. Buns were white too. Celebration of whiteness. As it were.

Imagine Beverly Hills as Coney Island. Not the residential part; Rodeo Drive. Imagine it's a crowded, unsecluded mecca of summertime frolic. Only the frolickers are all blond-haired ASPS (W is all too obvious so let us *delete* for economy sake). Blue eyes? Hard to tell thru all the tan. Saccharine "this is paradise" smiles focused two inches max beyond their nose. Radios playing Jackson Browne and the Eagles. Playing, not blasting. These folks have decorum. They walk a hundred miles outa their way to deposit the trash. Burns your feet but things must be CLEAN. No dogs. No baseballs, footballs or frisbees. Objects in flight are just too busy, too rowdy. But surfing is cool. As is swimming. Aquatic excitement can't be beat. Wholesome. Please pass the velveeta w/ miracle whip. Is there any Pepsi left in the cooler? No alcohol is drunk from brown bag or otherwise. Good enough to be banned by Disney, good enough to be banned by us. Plane overhead announcing Bob Hope's latest gig. Fun in the sun on our nation's date-o-birth.

Too much fun for me, I return to the house. Too much too for my partners in visit so they head back as well. To the house. Which is even uglier from behind and from there you can see all these other uglies as well. All built in a day and a half, all *ugly*. Not exactly w i d e to begin with, on top of which they're slammed so tight there's maybe a person and a half distance between them at most. Crammed in. Contractors and realtors had a field day. Where there ain't houses there's concrete. And crummy plastic chair things and a water thing for stepping the sand off your blisters, your feet, 'cause who'd wanna ruin the rented LUXURY by tracking filthy grit onto the puke-green carpet or the doody-brown couch? Actually, no room on the couch—crowded with festive, uh, 4th'ers—but carpet and couch ain't *that* big a draw (seeing's sufficient) so I'll stick with the concrete. On which heat's up, grill's on. Meat/cooked being churned out in a jiff over quick-light coals. No adjustments on the thing, just one height, so it comes out burned on the outside, raw on the in. Or if you wait a bit: charred to living shit out, medium-rare in.

No more than 18 inches from the grill an emotionally defeated uncle with about 35 minutes to live sits enjoying his oxidized meatstuff in an equally enjoyable chaise longue. Reminding the author of the opening shot in *The Pawnbroker.* You saw it. Rod Steiger as an old guy enjoying life likewise, or *seeming* to (in closeup). Wide angle then reveals the suffocatingly fenced-in "tomb" of a suburban backyard in which he, Rod, is in fact suffocating to be but ONE AMONG MANY identical "living spaces"—all o' them bleak. But no fences here. To the side: no room. And in back: view of fabulous expanse of loathsome disgusting beach is just too fab to interfere with. A good hearty choke at the "stench of non-life" has been stifled so long by Uncle Ezra that it's just one more part (& parcel) of his brittle, weary bones.

Thirty-forty seconds of this fine concrete fun is a-plenty, especially when news comes back that two guests' cars have been towed from the cheezy outdoor mini-mall where I and my cohorts are also parked. Nowhere to park on the street unless you live there or get there at 4 a.m. So you use the mini-mart. No public parking within a lightyear or two, public parking would only bring in greaseballs and niggers. Whudda ya think this is, Santa Monica?! 'S Orange County and don't ferget it. So much BEAUTY TO PROTECT, to protect from L.A. scum and the likes of YOU. Meaning us.

Mary the driver splits for mart-town a block away to discover she ain't been towed. Only been about 15 minutes so evidently they ain't *that* mean. Has a coffee at the coffee shop and while she's coffeeing (5 more mins.) they tow. "Hey wait a minute," she protests, "I was right here sipping a cup." Turns out they have a permanently employed "spotter" up in some crow's nest taking note of vehicles as they enter; depart the lot with your vehicle behind and the call goes out. To tow. Come back don't make no diff, your losing hand's already been played. Kinda like getting a jaywalk ticket the second you step off the curb. Great towns have great policies. (Go to hell for coveting your neighbor's poodle.)

L.A. Is the Capital of Kansas

She returns to tell us of all the fun in store. Fun of digging into our pockets for the fifty-buck ransom. Luck has it the long weekend forced each of us into withdrawing our savings to make it to Monday so we've got it with 90 cents to spare. Happy day. To get our full fifty's worth we split 4603 Seashore Drive (rent at your own risk) and "take in the town." Block after block of which features commemorators of the sacred holiday—this is true— snarling at our *unconventional appearance*. None of us are blond, none of us come close to resembling any ASP archetype. Mary's got SHORT HAIR (on a girl???). No beach togs or Hawaiian shirts. They snarl and hoot from porches, verandas, motor vehicles, bicycles, etc. Not everyone, just maybe twelve separate occasions. First time I've encountered this sort of shit in let's see, 15 maybe 16 years. Back when I was the first actual male longhaired creep at the local college back east. After the seventh or eighth taste of Newport tolerance on parade Mary asks a bicycler at a light WHAT *GIVES* WITH THIS PLACE?

"Oh, it's just crazy down here by the beach. I live up on the hill." Which is where the car's been pirated to so we'll soon find out. Find out what? We'll soon find out.

Meantime we take in the local SIGHTS. Exclusive venues have exclusive attractions and this one's no exception: local Carl's Jr., local Baskin-Robbins (under construction), local weight-loss salon, another park-trap shopping mall where the friendly local tow-boys can be seen plying their trade, a phony "ports o' call" type fake cobblestone (molded concrete) harborside dump for ogling real yachts with one eye towards purchase. Available yachts include: 42′ Westsail 1975 ($113,900); 57′ Custom Stell FDMY 1970 ($285,000). (For bargain hunters only.)

We circle back and opt for the further fun of all of us confronting the wonderfully cheerful scuzzhead who had us towed. Back at the mini-mall. An assflame with veins on his nose, he orders us off his PROPERTY or he'll call a cop. Cops're all over the place (as mentioned, *much* to protect), wider at the shoulder than your average LAPD and mustached to the last manjack. Their beady eyes dart around searching down trouble: maybe someone's about to spit out their gum. Daring to dare, we ask one what's with this tow biz. "Private property" is the not unexpected reply, property qua land means you can ransom people's property qua wheels. Proof that land is still a meaty investment, gotta hand it to these shrewdies of terminal capitalist pus-suck, they certainly know their biz. PROPERTY-IS-THEFT IN ACTION: erect a mall or plaza that no one will actually wanna *use* (no one was using), make your bucks on a tie-in with the tow-folks. "But they sometimes make mistakes," our officer assures us. "You can sue for your money in small claims court." You bet, Jack, all we wanna do is *return* to this piss-mo of a bch!

Uphill we march, burned to shitsville by the cancerous sun. Up upon the hill we discover what Good Life hill-style is all about. A 100 million ugly condos, give or take five or six. Uglier times ten than the worst L.A. proper has yet developed.* Pot-o-gold at the end of Newport's rainbow except for whatever hypothetically "classier" digs superstar residents like H. R. Haldeman have conceivably got, not to mention the late Duke Wayne whose concept of frontier justice we now understand ('s called rule w/ impunity by the rich, powerful and above all CONSTIPATED).

Speaking of pots tho ours is yet to come. Comes when we bail out the car from lackeys employed to take bucks rather than tow, cute little song and dance by the NASTIEST FUCKS I've ever done biz with. They treat you better when you bail out a criminal (done it so I know). With these sleazy bastards it ain't enough to snatch your money, they gotta rub it in ("Didn't you *read the signs*, hey you *blind* or something?"). Like we're kids and they're mommy/daddy. Finally after threatening, challenging *us* to act real nice or we don't get our machine this prick relents 'cause he hasta go supervise the arrival of more newly towed.

We get it, it's been busted into and Mary's wallet is gone. We cuss and holler; the prick laughs. No, here it is, it has just been gone *thru*

---

*This was 1980. 'Tain't so no mo'! (L.A., both city and county, has *quite* caught up.)

(lying on the floor). The sanctity of property has not been too heinously fucked with after all—"*Funny* how these things show up," he chuckles (a reg'lar two-eyed Captain Hook).

A travel tip: next time you go to Mexico y'oughta take *Riverside* County. Boycott Orange, lemme tell ya.

THE UGLY, THE UGLY, AND THE UGLY

Three premises:

1. manmade L.A. has been one visually unpalatable cesspool since God (for instance) knows when;

2. the San Fernando Valley, almost by definition, and certainly by conventional acclamation, has since *its* inception been the cesspool's ugliest, most conspicuously blighted sector-o-shit; however,

3. in fairly recent times, say the last two years, the rest of the 'pool has been taking enormous strides in the direction of finally and forever catching up.

Which leads, I'm talking number 3, to new problems, not insurmountable but problems nonetheless, in the qualitative/quantitative EVALUATION of specific units, modules, exemplars of Valley Ugliness Incarnate—both in and out of context. The old problem, which certainly hasn't left us, was and is simply *too much ugly*. Ventura Boulevard, for inst, has been at 100% ug-saturation (*no* units, anywhere, that fail to make the human mind/heart/spirit wince, cry, shrivel like a grape in the sun) for a good half decade now. So you're forced to *select*—let's say you're cruising for *serious* ug—

you've gotta actually look at all this monumental shitpissdoodoo-vomit block after block, no letup, in order to come up with even a handful of examples of genuinely outstanding ug, ug-that-transcendeth-the-rest-of-the-ug, ug-you-would-really-and-truly-write-home-to-mom-about. Which, lemme tell you, is hard fugging work. 'Cause plethora has both trivialized the concept and short-circuited any sensory capacities you or I might've had for e-z recognition of the empirical FACT of contextual ug. You've gotta see 50, 100, 1000, 5000 just to catch *one*, one truly major eyesore that makes the others, in context, resemble benevolent *gifts* from the USC/UCLA architecture foundry, fourth only behind the war, film and record mills in wishing us dead. I mean they're *there*, the majors, but after the first 200-300 standard state-of-the-art (merely medio-cre) ugwugs you'll encounter on a given cruise, who's in any condition to continue the search? That's the *old* problem.

The new one is now it's everywhere. Blight unto plethora. Multiply the plethora and you multiply the critical hardships, obsta-cles in the way of your any longer concretely *finding*, specifically in the Valley, passable manifestations of the One True Spectacular Ug. First of all, just from driving around *non*-Valley L.A. you're already—critically speaking—all ugged out. By the time you make it over Cahuenga Pass your nose for the stuff is diagnostically unsound (to say the least). But more important, if you're filling your ug quotient *without* the Valley, filling it up the old wazoo, why even *go* there anymore just to groove on its no-longer-unique brand of ug? Sad but true: trans-local homogeneity makes the Valley irrelevant. *Requiescat in pace.*

Well, yeah. But for us folks who ug-critique for a living, a trip to the Valley, especially when it's 112 in the shade—and there ain't no shade—is still a blightfest for sore eyes. Still? More than ever. It used to be fast food, back when it was e-z; now it's a many-course banquet. The hors d'oeuvres stink—yuk—and ditto the soup, salad, vegetables, beverage, dessert. But main course—voilà! For main dish, à la carte, the Valley still holds its own. I share with you ug manna from San Fernando heaven: five fantastic plats du jour from my most recent Valley ug-spedition.

COAST SAVINGS/EGGHEAD DISCOUNT SOFTWARE, 14651 Ventura Blvd.

I guess your money's supposed to feel real safe beneath the tiled window level protruding like a fortress in a Foreign Legion film; maybe in fact that's the building's "theme." But on closer inspection the tiles themselves are so thin, so flimsy—thinner and flimsier than even your standard *fake* tile—that tile-pattern contact paper would've worked just as well in fostering the illusion. As it stands, it all just looks like a topheavy movie exterior with no insides, a reverse illusion heightened by the opacity of the tinted glass at street level. In certain lights you also get this sort of rainbow reflection off some glass panels but not others—so much for Valley eyes and/or glazierly consistency.

VALLEY BETH SHALOM, 15739 Ventura Blvd.

Unlike most gratuitous stained-glass monstrosities, which take their stab at design and composition with unicolored shards in visually pointless and/or thematically banal juxtapositions, this beast features design and comp *within* the boundaries of the majority of its monads. Walk up real close, especially at night when they've backlit it, and you'll notice birds, castles, torahs, menorahs, and this one whatsit that looks like either the opening of a cave or a ripoff of Edvard Munch's *The Scream.* It all seems stenciled on, spray-painted; imagine having to *construct* a menorah from individual pieces of I dunno, what are they—glass? plastic? Without actually touching 'em you would probably bet the latter. But no: 'tis glass *imitating plastic*! (Ain't life funny?)

ENCINO TERRACE CENTER, 15821 Ventura Blvd.

As huge as the Queen Mary, with at least as many yards (miles?) of nautical-style railing, this who-folded-the-blueprint? special takes up the entire north side of Ventura between Densmore and Gloria Aves., but a sea cruise to Tarzana seems hardly its mission. Not Tarzana, nor even Woodland Hills . . . how about Devil's Island? So formidable is the muhfucker's gestalt, so life-threateningly *fearsome*, that even the most innoxious of features can't help but be drafted into significant subsidiary scare-roles. The railing, for inst, on its own somewhat ugly/benign, is in some places doubled, tripled, even quadrupled, giving the impression of horizontal PRISON BARS. Be forewarned: to enter the premises is to do time—*serious* time.

PLAZA DE ORO FASHION CENTER, 17157–17253 Ventura Blvd.

Here's one cross-cultural hodgepodge that beats all non-Valley competition going away: a Spanish-named, Japanese-concept shopping center housing, among others, Hatsuhana Sushi, Bagel Nosh, The Nail Dressing, Bao Wow Dim Sum, Artistry in Eyewear. Mexican tile roof; lots of ugly wood, chocolate brown (bee-em brown?) and pink; gratuitous mirror panels on the upper tier; a low-rent tiled fountain with ridges that attempt (and fail) to generate artificial waves. The whole thing is one amazing multiplex marvel, but the standout feature, sushi above bagels, kind of puts it on a whole 'nother plane.

THE SHOE & CLOTHING CONNECTIONS, 17404 Ventura Blvd.

Many aspects of mundane standard ugly, combined. Sloping reflector panels; ugly vinyl awnings; painted and unpainted cement; 1972 lettering and graphics; sloping "lawn" on which nothing but death is currently in season; a single (seemingly funtional) cylindrical pillar versus several mock-cylindrical (facades flattened) mock-pillars that support zilch; nonfunctional nautical railing above functional (and rusting) metal strips intended, one guesses, to keep kids and dogs from falling to their death on the killer lawn. Note the plural name: it even *sounds* ugly. And aren't shoes "clothing"?

SOME LOCAL "BURGERS" I'VE RECENTLY ET

Geography cracks me up.
　　　　　—George Bernard Shaw

Me too. In Pittsburgh, for instance, they're called *tobos*, often with an e: *toboes*. Residents of Hartford, on the other hand, know them as *sarsaps*, possibly short for sarsaparilla, that New England sody fountain treat—and what's a fountain without a grill? You want one in Houston, meanwhile, a town with a hefty Croatian-American populace, you'll call for a *zagreb* . . . and like it. In Akron—Ohioans are strange!—they're fondly dubbed *wee wollies*. Can you imagine ordering a bacon-chili-cheese wee wolly? (*I* can't.) Stranger still is Portland, home of the *bunstuffer*, where beef is but one kind of "stuffin'," and popular combinations include: double beef; mixed beef & tuna; (a triple—the "bunstuffer deluxe") beef, herring & sweet pea.

At the outskirts of Denver reads a sign which sez: "Welcome—Try our famous *ground batblow sandwich*—A treat." Asbury Park hosts the *catjack*—these are all 'generic' terms, by the way—hence the expression "cruisin' for catjacks." Continuing the animal theme, we come to New York, N.Y., the fabled Big Apple, where they're known, quaintly enough, as *hot dogs*. Not to be outdone is Louise's Health Capital of the World (Racine, Wis.), where they're colorfully referred to as *murdered mammal patties*. In Boise they're *falphadallies*. Muscle Shoals: *corn-on-the-cob*. When in Cedar Rapids, make that *East* Cedar Rapids, ask for a *bordello*, while yonder in West Cedar Rapids be sure to smack down some *fairycakes à go-go*.

And so on and on, till we reach the safe, sunny harbor of our own sacred shore: Los Angeles—L!A!—home of the one and only *hamburger*. So named for our fair sister township, Hamburg, Germany— and proud of it! Yes, as the man said, geography is surely a gas—a horizon broadener if ever there was one—but those of us who love L.A. for a living (and I'm sure you'll agree) firmly believe that what we call them is best. "Burgers" for short. And our favorite beer: Burgermeister. Yes, *indeed*, it's a wonderful place, and a wonderful time, to be alive—to eat burgers and be happy as the livelong day!

And yet there are mockers . . . naysayers . . . killjoys. Those that would claim (as if we do not know) that burgers are poison, they're cancer, they are pimples, phlegm, cholesterol—not to mention the dread constipation!—but yet you will eat them 'cause they taste like meat. More to the point: Would you rather die from (1) burgers or— God forbid—bike spokes straight through the neck?

> Here in the 5-ish 6:30s, 7s . . .
> We begin grim encounters with 8:30-ish
> 6:30s of the heart.
>
> —James Fenimore Cooper

Replace 'grim' with 'bright' and you're talking Burger Time. Which the mockers—call them "doctors"—took, grimly, from me. That hour when suns of the day descend, daily, beyond steeples and wires, and nothing goes with nothing like a ground hunk o' cowmeat—it's the grinding that does it—& catsup. Mmmm yum, I can almost taste it! . . . but the docs told me *no, kid*, they got six kinds of personal and said *blood*, there's *pressure* and it's *high*, meaning no salt, no sugar, no starch, no fat, no oil, and no meat—the "red" kind. And no caffeine. But red fish: o.k., recommended (if broiled). So I did.

Question: What's worse than red snapper (broiled)?

Answer: Red snapper in Mussolini's weewee and red paint from the Civil War.

So I stopped. But not before finny friends galore had been slaughtered by hook or by crook (get it?) so that I might live to compulsory retirement. And not before 10 . . . 20 . . . *thirty* pounds had been shed from my girth—I was a "fatso"!—by fish, vegetables, fruit, salad, and dieting. So I look and I say—this is me talking—*who's that?*—the face in the mirror. Do not know him; should; this is bad, very bad, for 'interior' dialogue. So I say—me again—*I will gain five lbs.* (To recognize who I am addressing.) But then, says a person, *you look sick*, so I 'say'—in my head—*make that ten.* 'Cause my pants don't fit.

SO LEZ HAVE SOME BURGERS!!

So I et one, I et two, I et three burgers and four burgers and more. I ate many burgers, some excellent, some tasty, some squishy and repellent and soggy and horrible and bad, and I share with you my journey. And my notes. About the burgers. And also, so that (weather permitting) you may dine to the best of your pocketbook, my highly authorative burger ratings—the ratings that "jingle, jangle, jingle"—to separate the burger 'wheat' from the burger 'chaff.' [*Key*—The burger system herein used replaces the widely respected, if somewhat antiquated, "B-U-R-G-E-R-!" scale (B-U-R-G-E-R-! = "top of the slop," B-U-R-G = "not half bad," etc.) with the handy, convenient, as well as operational 0–7 scale employed by both the *Valley News* and the *L.A. Weekly*. In this era of digits we believe you will find it simple, convenient, and far less cumbersome.—*Ed.*]

Where better to start, after so long away, than **ASTRO BURGER**, 7475 Santa Monica Blvd., across from Danny's Oki Dog? A 'lowlife' hangout *years* before Danny's 'reeked' the 'ambience,' pulled in the 'scum'—many was the time I saw 'johns' treat their 'whores' to a snack after f---ing, or getting b---n, as the case might be—Astro's culinary pleasure is surpassed by few, and ditto for its fare. Case in point—the double cheeseburger. Two dollars sixty cents, and worth every penny. Shredded lettuce & onion form the springy bedrock of this treat sensation. Topped by a juicy, tasty tomato, fortunately sliced *thin* as they are bad for arthritis, and in turn by some wonderful delicious *meat*, prepared the way U-like-it—black lines, parallel, indicating flames! fire!—a far cry from the frying of 'spaniel' across the street. And of course buns. (And don't forget the cheese.) And some kind of mayo or something, and relish stuff down 'tween the meats. Ketchup: *none*. So it's not too wet. You'll be proud to be a carnivore at Astro Burger! (On a scale of 0 to 7: 4.9.)

Before we split: a word about "fries." The v. best *thin fries* are at Astro; the finest *fat fries*, at Oki's. Hats off to neighborhood planning—and Mr. and Mrs. Sprat!

Onward to the world of plastic; no, not the bad kind. The kind it was originally invented for—to serve Man—and, after all, who serves Him better than **TAIL OF THE PUP**, 311 N. La Cienega? That was of course a rhetorical query—*no one* does, not in the dual fields of customer comfort and burgers. To wit, their 'see-thru' plastic sheet, newly dangling out by the garbage, shielding you while-U-eat from rain, wind—is there *anything* sadder than a column of air spiriting your burger (gosh) away??—and armies of flies. That's flies—not fries—speaking of which, you would have to walk long, far and wide to find better *cold* fries than T of the P's: they're superior. But when superiority is discussed, y'know seriously, talk must begin, and end, with consideration of Tail of the Pup's extremely excellent #4, a/k/a "The Works." Chili, onion, grated cheese. Lettuce, tomato, bun. Rare—no need t' ask—is how it comes. The "smart set," however, axe 'em to please *grill* the onions—makes for a much better "mush." And a tangy mush it is, thanx to the grated Eyetalian. Plus, at no extra cost (a buck eighty-five): grease-absorbent paper plate; thirst-quenching long, skinny pickle. (6.)

Good things are worth waiting for, and the tempty, tasty Double Cheese at **JOE'S BIG BURGER**, 8001 West 3rd St., is no exception. You plunk down your $2.20 and receive your Double—but the wait is not over yet. First bite is the taste of lettuce—still waiting. Greasy but dry, lots of grease drip—waiting waiting. Rubbery patty— waitin' some more. Then the grease, the mayo, the tomato goosh all combine to wetten things up . . . now we're getting somewhere. *Finally*, when the meat & cheese have been given time to properly *congeal*, voilà! The savory, tasty taste of *a better grade* of greasemeat! (4.1)

> WHO needs pork pies? YOU need pork pies.
> —William Randolph Hearst

He's nuts. *Nobody* needs pork pies. Certainly not **GOOEY LOU-IE'S**, 12630½ Washington Pl., where the westerly toe of Washington Place nudges the rib of Washington Blvd., and where the beef is so *beau* you'll be tempted to call it *boeuf*. In any language, tho—and in any land—their Ortega Burger ($1.88) is clearly "the best in the House." The 'house' being, of course, our cozy little Planet Ship Earth—as there is no finer. No, I take that back, finer still are the (nominally x-priced) Ortega variations, some "customized" Ortegas you will know and love. Ortega with onions!—only a dime—w/ two strips bacon (one half a buck)!—ortega & avocado (same)! Ortega this, ortega that: How does Gooey's do it? I tell you truly I do not know. All I do know, as far as knowing is knowable, is that someday, hopefully soon, the incredible Ortega w/ Onions will be hailed, rightfully, as undisputed King—in the "good" sense of royalty—of Lettuce-less Charbroiled Wonders, and I don't care if you're talkin' "burgers," "falphadallies," "beanbops" (Detroit), or "hot fudge sundaes" (Oaxaca). 'Tis like chomping on a *cloud*, make that a cloud with onions: a unique, uncommon experience in the world of main-course cuisine, make that the whole, entire meal . . . holds its own with side dish, dessert, cheese puffs, and soup du jour. (6.8.)

But for every king crowned there is another one either dead, brain-damaged, or in exile "pretending." While not yet banished, de-ported, expelled, or even ostracized, **TOMMY'S**, the once-great *original* Tommy's, still to be found (if you know how to look) at 2275 Beverly Bl., would well be advised to look for its crown in the sewer;

it has fallen that far. Once, more recently perhaps than half a decade past, back when they *really* slopped on the Slop, there was a time when we (those who eat) would say *mind we the veins, hooves, snouts and even bellies that comprise this here patty? No, mind we not, as the burger* [taken in toto] *is yummy.* And it was. 'Qual' sometimes varied, but with Slop heaped high, wide and about, a Tommy's double cheese was your damn surest meat bet in town; an *average* showing of 6.5 was about average. But today's Slop (i.e., that chili-oriented substance, halfway between dog diarrhea and cement, that has for so many years covered the veins/hooves/bellies quite well, so well, weller even than Reagan's lies cover Christian nightmares of ugly dark rapers of their daughter) is hardly heaped at all—*dabbed* might be the word—leaving today's double cheese ($1.70) hardly a match for a turd. What?—unhh!!—sacrilege?!? No: truth. 'Cause wherever it ain't been dabbed: *bare*, dry, *mustardy*—and mustard is no match for meat. Not this meat, a tad (or am I imagining?) greyer than used to be, but let us not quibble. I beg to quibble, howev, with Tommy's tomato as thick as a THUMB... and the wind...cries...*greezy.* (2.2.)

BURGERS
I'VE ET,
PART 2

see Spot run
I mean really *run*
—William Carlos Williams

Last time we defined "meat" as *semi-porous edible matter, esp. as derived from the fleshy tissues of flora or fauna as distinguished from their shell, husk, teeth or hair* and "burger," specifically *animal*-meat burger, as *delicious, nutritious sandwich, either closed- or open-faced, utilizing as its filler the chopped, shaped and subsequently broiled, steamed or fried meat of the squirrel, parrot, bovine, mackerel or squid.* While it is comforting to know that steamed parrot burgers do in fact exist—variety, they say, is indeed the spice of life—I would not advise a neophyte "meat and potaters" gourmet a steady diet of same. Et a few myself once in Perth, Tasmania, and found it too (I hate the word) insubstantial— sort of a cross between duck seviche and a *soft* pigeon tostada. Ditto for mackerel, squid, and for that matter eel, hamster, and sea slug— trifles all, burgatorially—and even the brawnier squirrel, and I speak here not of steaks (nor of chops) but of *ground* acorn-gatherer, is

111

a taste for which, try as I may!, I have never acquired. Which is hardly to say—far, indeed, from it—that I am, or wish to serve, as a hoity-toity Universal Palate. I was born, as they say, with a "wooden tongue" and thus speak solely for "number one" when I bandy for bovine as the burger meat of preference, preferably broiled (tho grilled or poached will do), and beg your kind indulgence as I limit our scope to *beef burgers* of Los Angeles County.

SUNSET GRILL, 7439 Sunset Blvd., is, as the name implies, not a broiler but a griller. They grill meat until it's done. On a hot metal bottom-heated slab of dark shiny steel—it would burn your "buns" but good. Instead it burns, make that *toasts*, the kaisers. Rolls—whew!—not rulers: there is no human meat on the premise. Once toasted, these kaisers are crunchy, see, so the meat itself need no longer provide us that roll, er, role. It's enough work for meat to be meat. Tho sometimes—good ol' meat!—it does more. Like get all singed & crunchy. But not on a grill, no. Well the flame kind, yeah, with the grid, but this is the flat flameless flat kind. So it never gets crunchy, just *done*. But that's okay 'cause the roll does, making Sunset's Double Chili-Cheese on Kaiser Bun—two bucks & a dime—double deelishus but not singlehanded. No: pulling loads are also the cheese—plainwrap velveeta, v/v gooey (as petroleum "by-products" are wont)—the chili—sloppy, gloppy, moppy (an 8-napkin "mess")—and don't forget the beef... remembered! (On a 7-scale, a respectable *5.5*.)

Would that it were possible to choose your "C" (cancer) as easy as "A" (art pix) or "B" (burgers). Science has said—but never proved—the link between cancer and grilling. But what kind of cancer? Throat? Liver? Esophagus? And then—half of one & a dozen of another—there is c from c: cancer from charcoal (again unproven). And again: nose cancer? dick cancer? "c" of the kidney? It's far from clear. **ME & ME**, meantime, 465 N. Fairfax, clearly knows its charbroil; it knows it well. Would that this "Little Tel-Aviv" eatery also knew its meat. Scorched to a rare run of rubber, seared to a choice chunk o' chew, the Kabob Burger ($1.88) tastes like, tastes like—what's it taste like?—the *corned beef hash at Art's Deli on Ventura Boulevard.* And something is missing. Two things are missing. Served in a pita with a shitload of salad, the falafel eater's "delight," it is *not* a salad, not a true salad: contains no onions! And, tell me this if you can, if falafels have grease, why can't kabobs have it too?—A fair question. (2.4.)

And the grease prize—let's talk prizes—goes to **CARNEY'S**, y'know in the railroad car, 8351 Sunset. Grease...to pour over expensive library books. Grease...to light the lamps of China. Grease...to recycle in your fine French nouvelle cuisine. Yes, enough for all three in but one Carney's double cheese ($2.30), or should I say *on?* It's on the, well actually it's *in* the stuff that's *on* the gagmeat—meat that makes you "gag"—in the, uh, chili. (7 for grease, .6 for barf, er, beef: average of 3.8.)

A stiff piece of
american cheese
may be used
as a lever,
but it ain't
bein' used
that way
here!
—Frank Lloyd Wright

There is nothing stiff about **MEATTY MEAT BURGERS**, 5855 W. Pico, nor their cheese, nor their burgers, nor their lip-slappy, taste-tempty Chili-Cheese ($2.70). Just one big goopy goo-ball (nummy *nums!*), this two-handed tempt-tasty wonderoo delivers *much* in the way of meatty eatty—and I don't mean drinkky—satisfaction, tho it's so "moist" you'll be tempted to use a straw. Which would (pardon my Polish) screw up the eattin'...screw it up good. 'Cause the chili is *not* liquid (must be the mayo, the mustard, the meatblood, the goop-goo); it is solid, Jack, like an armed and floating beefboat. *Shards* of beef, *lumps* of it, mini-asteroids from off the rings of Saturn (the "Beef Planet"): so burgery is this primalest of ooze you'll be threatened to call it *the burger's own burger.* So eatt quick—before the burgers eatt you! (4.)

FATBURGER varies. From gristle in every bite (450 S. La Cienega) to every 4th (10955 Kinross) to every 7th (8500 Santa Monica). About what you'd expec' from a burger joint listed as a "restaurant" in the yellow pages. (Average showing: 2.)

NAUGLE'S, 6768 Santa Monica, on the other hand—speaking 24-hour joints—delivers. Well not to your home, nor even your car; Naugle's delivers *consistency.* From Naugleburger ($2.19) to Naugle-burger ($2.19)—the price never varies. Nor the burger. From shredded vegetable crap that is amazingly *homogeneous* (pickle, let-us, onion all treated equal re size, shape, locale) to meat that is at all times (and by all means) *bearable* to buns that are strictly (speaking) *awful*, falling apart in your hands in the car so you're *bare*handing meat/shreds/bun/mayo, it is *the* perfect 3 a.m. burger after they've closed up the inside & you're out in the dark gulping *blindly* . . . by sense *memory* . . . the miraculous sense of *touch.* (If you drove it home first, it would freeze like a freezeball.) A functional niteburger—is nothing to sneeze at. (3.)

> Any god whose NAME cannot even be
> damned can go right out &   Fuck
>   Him
>   Self.
>   —Ralph Waldo Emerson

The gods eat no burgers—for very good reason. They stem the sphincter, clog the colon, dam the door; in a word, burgers *bind.* Some more, some less—c'est la universe—but in no possible world has burgermeat been a morning plopper's best and dearest friend. With even the kindest of burgers you'll be "doing your duty" no earlier than coffee break—don't take too long or they'll taunt you with "shit" jokes the rest of the day!—and most likely lunchtime, when you'll need all your time . . . to eat burgers!! One burger, tho, is a guaran-fucking-tee you will b.m. in the p.m.—if at all: the Cheesy-

Cheesy-Cheeseburger (its true & honest name!), as served hot, warm, and above all bulky at **LOVE'S WOOD PIT BARBECUE**, 6633 Hollywood Bl. For the low-low price of $4.65 you get: half lb. chopmeat, cooked like (similar to) brick; three kinds cheese ("American," "Cheddar," "Jack") as yummy as the day is wrong. Cheese— I'm sure you know—turns already hardening excrement into *granite*, so snatch yourself a spoon—you'll need it for some subsequent "digging"! (1.5.)

Number two in the bulk parade is the mighty Slam Dunker ($4.95), available seven days a week at **HAMBURGER HAMLET**, 3303 Wilshire and selected malls. Grilled onions, raw onion, jack cheese, peppers, tomato, lettuce. Fine, fine, fine, fine, fine, fine. But the sauce—in this little *dish* where you "dunk" it like Bob McAdoo or (before your time) Win Wilfong—seems embezzled from the vat where Love's gets its b-b-q pus juice, docking us down a couple-three fines. Fortunately the meat—the good meat!—the pure meat!—meat unspiced by human hands that is so . . . meaty I must warn you against slomping down one of these humdaddies *too often* lest you suffer (in the process) from *hemorrhoidal symptoms*—it has happened to me so I know. (3.3.)

And while I'm no consumer advocate, I do advocate **PAZO** (24 suppositories, $5.98) for temporary relief of itching due to 'rhoids. Caused—I hate to harp on this (but how else to instruct?)—by pressure on the inner butt from difficult stools. Themselves the direct result of diet (for instance *burgers*, but also—let's be fair— donuts, vitamin-enriched udder juice, etc.). So if you must eat burgers I suggest, nay, I *implore* you, do not waste your precious little a-hole—your one and only!—on a steady dose of **CARL'S JR.** ⅓-Pound Super Stars w/ Cheese which taste like *yicky* sweet hors d'oeuvres in a dream that you hate (but ate) @ $2.19 per intake. (Various locations; 0.3.)

Which brings us to our penultimate category: burgers for Mother's Day. It is never too early to think about "mom." Buy her some shoes, dress her up real nice and take her to **HAMPTON'S**, 1342 N. Highland Ave. If your mom is like mine, she'll trust you to order her meat, and I highly recommend the wholesome, foodlike, yummilicious Slam Dunkburger ($5.00), not to be confused with the Slam Dunk*er*. There is no dunking dish but ma won't be sorry—there are no cooties, no nosehairs either (the hygiene is A-1). The topping? Concord grape jam and dijon mustard, of course, to remind her of her girlhood on the "farm." (5.)

Bringing us at last to Burgers in Bars. In the whole South Bay there is no finer beachcreep/pleasureseeker/newrepublican/ aerospacecocksucker taverna than **THE SHACK**, 185 Culver Blvd., Playa Del Rey. Bud: $1.25 (cheap). Shack Cheese Burger: $3.25— better you should spend it on The Poor. This Burger is nogood! Contents include—hold yer hoss—a wiener! Patty and a wienie b/tween two buns!! Worst mustard in L.A.! Worst lettuce, sixth worst Burger, (excellent weeny skin). (2.7.)

And now, like all good burgers, it is well we are done. All that remains is to clip, perchance to eat: today; tomorrow; all possible tomorrows; and tomorrows after that. Clip—and post—in the Home . . . Office . . . Car. Fortunately, we *The Reader* are L.A.'s very own "throwaway sheet," so three copies of *your* own is alright by us!

GONADS
AND
CHABLIS

The one thing L.A. had been for me on all my pre-'75 visits that I felt quite certain—beyond all doubt—it would *continue* to be was a safe sexual harbor, er, haven. And I'm not talking "safe sex"—I mean womanlegs for-ever, womanlegs spreading (in pairs), their moist, aromatic intersections quivering, dripping, shouting *come 'n' git it, Rob—er—Richard, git it while it is hot, quite hot, and unconditionally eager to ride the "snake."* You might say there was an interchangeable, less than uniquely personal aspect to it, but, heck, it was floridly abundant—more than I was "getting" back home in New York. Plus, my *distance* from home tended to reduce the infidelity/guilt quotient—I was still at the time living-with-someone—all of which helped make my once-twice a year in L.A. the ginch-grope equivalent of the kid loose in the candy store—with no bellyache, no calories, no diabetic shock.

Maybe it wasn't bliss but it sure was glee.

And the abundance, the glee, had a topical edge as well: three, or possibly four, of these candy-gals had been Jim's gals. Jim Morrison. The King of Rock-n-Roll, *my* king of rock-n-roll (though I'm hardly a monarchist), the "Lizard King." Dead since '71; they were former gals of his. Though ostensibly a live-with person like me, he'd had *many* gals, local as well as international gals, and by lying down, in sequence, with a few of these many I felt (a) on my way to a many of my own and (b) as if, through these but few, I *was* (somehow) the

Lizard King Incarnate. The closest I came to an actual western *girlfriend*, in fact—I saw her twice—was the Jim gal who had driven him, that final time, to the L.A. airport, whence he slipped off to Paris to die. I *reminded* her of him, she said—I didn't ask how—and our last moment together, after driving *me* to the airport, she asked, perhaps sincerely, if she might be my "L.A. woman." I told her— why not?—*sure*.

In autumn '75, howev, when I and my bags arrived to stay, she was unavailable, "engaged" to a realtor, and all others, of those I phoned, who'd locally known my sperm were equally disinclined towards ever reknowing it. After two weeks of *nothin'*, old or new, I began to worry. The gulf between my wanting-it and getting-it had never, at this latitude and longitude, been so immense, and the former I'm sure stuck out like a sore banana.

As my appetite grew from snack hunger to meal hunger to banquet *starvation*, it dawned on me that the town's famed organ gratification apparatus might in fact be equipped to service only needs bordering on whimsy or inconsequence, that its much-vaunted easy-access release valve recognized, probably, only the lowest of libidinal pressures. In any event, it seemed fair to rethink El Lay Heterosex Babylon in terms of strict, coded carnal repression/ release—you got-some (when you did) by the numbers, and I had no fucking *clue* what the numbers might be. Late one night in a burger joint I overheard this 400-lb. hippie chick tell a friend, "I really like to *massage* before I ball"—chomp, chew. "Lemme just say"—belch, burp—"it is *the* bitchenest turn-on." What a lucky whale, er, duck, I thought. But if this was the sort of "number" involved—flinch, wince—I'd be lucky to get my unit wet by St. Paddy's Day.

But just after Thanksgiving my luck changed. I fell down a few times with an ex-Hare Krishna whose uncle or father once played alto sax on the *George Gobel Show*, and then in mid-December I was at some shitty party for I can't remember which band where after two- three drinks I started talking to this medium-yummy secretary who it turned out had just written a piece for some mag called "At Home with the Manson Girls." Gwen, that was her name, had either roomed with Squeaky Fromme or at least known her—well enough, she claimed, to have taught her how to load, aim and fire a handgun. Not too ably as it turned out (joke! joke!) but okay, um—pour another drink. She then bragged, somewhat more crucially, of having once starred in PORN—as a runaway teen back in sixties San Francisco.

And thus began—I fuck a porn queen!!—my first L.A. *relationship*. (My tattoo, she would later confide, had led her to believe I was a *biker*.) Every night the Sexual Olympics.

And, because I was such a great *listener*, she eventually got real specific in her tales of porn queenhood past. Titles, plots, everything. There was this one she told me about (there'd been "about a dozen," she said) with her as a "horny nymphet hitchhiker," another featuring "homemade carrot salad" (the carrots taste-altered by vaginal entry 'n' exit), and a third wherein she'd "peed four times on a high-school principal." I so bought—and appreciated—this round of rap that I even went to my friend Liza Williams, then teaching Women In Film at Cal State–Long Beach, and suggested she have Gwen lecture some week on a non-dehumanized life in filmic smut. Which she did—great job, questions/answers, captive audience—and somebody took her pic and they wrote her up in the campus paper. And I was, yes, *very proud of her.*

So of course it turned out—you were prob'ly expecting this—'twas all bullshit. No porn, nor even any runaway. Totally made up. Which I found out, well, subsequent to her dumping me to "three" it with a husband/wife country-music duo somewhere in Texas. And which, the revelations (incl. additional goodstuff, like she wasn't *really* allergic to bee stings, nor had she ever, as claimed, been bit by a rabid squirrel—she'd just recited such stuff to *impress me*) (I was so impressionable), couldn't help but jolt me into recalling what a major-league sap, a fool for love and moisture, I had more or less always been.

Hey, I *began* as a sap in New York; I'd been one since puberty. But all my years of sapdom had ill-prepared me for Gwen or her successors. Yes, ahem, there were others—any *number* (and still counting) of penis-sanctioned, penis-governed over-the-falls relationships/flings/encounters . . . with my brains, meantime, on

121

vacation, on hold, cooling out in a Southern Cal ice chest. This is, was, always will be the major *leagues* of sap/heat/sizzle, a league I'd probably have been "too smart" to ever play in, to suit up for, in smartypants New York. Having played, though, having let my heart and pecker supply me with a richly diversified experiential base, I've occasionally managed—here's the socially redeeming part!—to turn critical sexthink corners that might've remained remote from me in Smart Town, regardless of my smarts.

'S the old theory/practice bit, and through many a spurt of L.A. practice I've held hidebound N.Y. theory and *run* with it—into deader, triter deadends of la vie hetero-hot-nuts than you'll find in Henry Miller. And by dead and trite I mean emotionally, culturally, politically, etc.—deadend bullshit for the *dumper*. By such means— repeat deadendings; consultations with deadended self—I've actually overcome certain long-held creepster orientations. I'm no longer especially youthocentric or meatocentric, for inst, preferring the company of womanpersons *my own age* and dealing with them ultimately as womanpersons *qua* person, i.e., as the persons *behind* the meat, bodily *occupying* warm and bouncy carnal *matter*, who in the final analysis are essentially warm, bouncy *persons*. Y'know not "objects." For an ol' piece of pigmeat I've come a long way.

The problem—even when you're part of the solution there's always a problem—is these persons as PERSONS. Dumb fucking stupid *L.A.* persons. But that's a whole 'nuther separate bag of shit.

VOYAGE
OF THE
DUMB

Just now, like five minutes ago, I stuck a bank-deposit envelope containing $160 down a (US Postal Service) mail slot, the kind of thing you used to see on *Abbott & Costello* or *My Little Margie* without batting an eye, reminding me what a fucking stupid jerk I am and have always been, reminding me too (great moments in solace, like now I gotta fucking call the post office and the bank and the fucking check people and fuck me I'm stupid) of times I was even stupider than six-seven minutes ago when I took a mailbox on Cloverdale and 3rd for the Day & Night Teller at Wilshire and Detroit. Like the TIME I SHAVED MY CHEST following the Far Rockaway High School boatride of '62, on the theory that hair *grows back faster* after you shave it; before you shave it it just grows. I had little and wanted more, so I shaved this one spot clean where to this day none has grown back, nor been replaced, nor nothin'. Leaving me with a "comical" bald spot in the heart of an otherwise furry *passable male chest*—what a dumbo.

17-yr-olds must've been dummmmmb back then—times're sometimes like that—altho 31-yr-olds (circa late '76) weren't such great shakes in the undumb sweepstakes either. F'r inst, I am thinking, THE TIME I TOOK ACID FOR NEW YEAR'S. Or as I referred to it myself at the time: "a date with LSD #2." Number one, the one I *wanted* a date with, Lona Susan Dennis, hot eternal love interest of my growed-up life to that point, was unavailable. Actually she was but she wasn't *willing*, so I got drunk (and drunker) and talked myself into stepping out with an alternate version, namely the one that's lysergic.

"Blotter" I think it was, or "windowpane"; I hadn't taken it in any form since India '72. I was there (Goa) living with hippies for *Oui* magazine, and every morning this sharpie from Michigan would have everybody open their mouth and he'd hit 'em a drop of (pure) liquid acid, made in Bombay. And it was y'know *good* as far as all that goes, but this was like fucking *India* by golly, this incredible mix of cowshit and divinity and I'm seeing the elephant god Ganesh in fucking *worms crawling*—which I'm thinking you're supposed to be able to access *without* LSD in so spiritual a locus; I mean isn't that like the *purpose* of India (or something)?

I thought so but this Michigan guy is meantime leading the local international set (Yanks! Frogs! New Zealanders! Belgians!) by the numbers through the pluralistic gaga, the mixed topical bliss, of it all: yoga *and* meditation *and* vegetables *and* dope *and* lingering sixties b.s. like everybody's sign *and* exploiting the non-imported locals into thinking the imports are *holy men* (anything for int'l kicks). And it's not as if the and-dope is even like an equal *fraction* of how you're obliged to spend your day, y'know or be considered a killjoy or a square or an Eastern purist or something. Dope *is* your day and even when you're on this goddam Bombay acid that *is not subtle* you're still kind of obliged to smoke many tons of over-opiated hash like everyone else just to maintain the ruse they are separate hippo sacraments, so on top of hallucinating gratuitous godhead galore I'm gagging my cosmic guts every time the chillum—pipe—comes my way (and I hear some Aussie talkin' chillums spread hepatitis and gee that's a groove to contend with too).

So for three reasons—generally unpleasant intake history (in general); trips-are-for-dips (wisdom at 27); most *superfluous* merrygo-round ride yet with god's preferred drug—I was pretty for sure never gonna take the shit again or any related substance: 20-25-30 times counting mescaline, psilocybin, DMT and all the other usuals was plenty for this returner from the land of Gandhi. For one, two, three lifetimes—plenty. But here it was four years later and I'm in love with this terminal alcoholic of 23 who won't see me New Year's Eve so I take this stuff somebody left at my house the year before which for some *stupid reason* I'd accepted, saved, continued to save, and finally—when the going gets going, the stupid get stupid—took.

Took on top of being drunk as a skunk (bourbon, beer) (wine?) on the night following the day she got out of Cedars-Sinai after busting up her face. Busted it crashing into a parked Volkswagen. On a bicycle; not wearing her glasses. No light on the bike. At night. A face unlike any other face: busted like a watermelon, this face which was like *some* other faces, pretty faces, very pretty. Before.

Afterwards she was still lookin' okay except for this scar on her chin and an eye that suggested the hit sensation of that very month and season, *Rocky*. Actually she looked like shit, but nothing that time and healing would not have cured (or reduced) and I was this goddam smitten romeo anyway so it wouldn't't've mattered—really. What mattered from the beginning was less the usual standard surface crap than the usual standard depth crap, y'know "substance," latter of which she was loaded with anyway as evidenced by this one time at my place, an early Saturday morning. She came over, totally from out of the blue—we hadn't been getting along on account she'd just wrecked (totaled) my '75 Rabbit (um, drunk) after I'll tell the rest later—she comes over on her bike, knocks on the door and says "I want to do something *kinky* with you" and she's also got bagels. We do things which would not've been out of place at the Pasadena Museum of Mysterious Arse and at one point this one particular part of her is doing something to or with this part of me, and she sez: "Wow, I just now realize I have for several minutes, without even thinking, been *tasting my own s--t*. What a liberating effect you have had upon my very *system* of inhibitions!" And I'm thinking 'I really *like* this person,' her and her depth of persona; I really love this terminal alcoholic (regardless of her wrecking my car) of 23.

And that night she goes and crashes into a parked VW, not a Rabbit. Some sort of belated "guilt thing" for having terminated my vehicle 9 days before? Dunno. Dunno either exactly what triggered the termination, actually I've got a very good idea. She did it 'cause I was in San Francisco with this Marsha woman (life is complicated) with her permission. Linda's permission, Lona, whatever name I'm calling her here.

In San Fran following a week of me and LSD #1 fasting on carrot juice. Literally just juice and you know I'm not the sort who *does such things*, not now and not then but—as mentioned—I was head over heels over whatsername (so what am I doing in Frisco with some-body else???) and juice fast was her idea. Strongly suggested by the Friday before when she smashed up both a party and the house it was at: fistfought with her employer's wife, broke lamps. (Drrr-*runk*.) So to cleanse her bodily plumbing—and get started on a "brand new life"—she fasts on carrot. And to register my moral support (before the party I'd saved her literal face from a sizzling fry pan of smelly fish by happening to be in the so-called right place when yumteen units of chardonnay made her lose her footing and tumble face first into hot greasy grub; caught her, mega-luckily, so maybe I like had an *investment* in her not drinking no mo') and meantime try on a new intake experience (for size), I fast myself and *lend her my car.*

'Cause I was sure she'd treat it okay, and maybe 'cause *I* was feeling guilty 'bout going north to see this old flame even though she (new flame) said it was jake. This was old travel plans from before me and new-person were busy being in love, and like a dumdum I take her at face value when she says it's okay—modern (California?) dating tolerance. So I'm up in SF and she has my car and drinks like a fifth of something and crashes into an embankment near the entrance to the Hollywood Freeway at Silver Lake Blvd. and it's such an extensive mess even the tires are destroyed and she's not even scratched (but they throw her in jail) and I tell her on the phone from Frisco *it's okay it's OKAY* (and I mean it) and except for the fundament frolics and bagels the relationship gets worse and worse to the point of being grave and dire and she won't see me New Year's Eve so I take the acid.

And I'm up all night talking to the walls and I can't sleep so I put on bebop records and try with no success to *write* the anguish and weirdness and every time I look in the bathroom mirror I see multicolored masks spinning radially at so many r.p.m. and I think this is the most self-destructive thing I have ever done and finally I get to sleep for a couple hours and wake up feeling like a lump of grey putty on the cold stone floor and (at the same time) some speedfreak hairdresser's nineteenth nervous breakdown and realizing I still have one hit left of the poison (blotter? windowpane?) given me by Fred B., husband and conservative father of two, I flush it down the toilet (sink?) and settle into a boundless, unrelenting horror-round of *what a happy fucking new year I have got in store* including:

Earthquakes, bone visions of earth a-quaking terminal, a 20.6 would do it Richterwise (I'm hopin'), where's that end-it-all tremor when you *need* one to match your own devastation? . . . was already scheduled for a *massive hangover* just from the drinking, so here I am massively *tripping* on hungover-baaaad . . . starving to death and all that's open is this falafel stand where the falafels aren't ready yet and I'm standing there, *standing* there (time distortions on acid) thinking, in spite of the "liberating" aspect of the wonder drug I swore in India I would never take again, that I can wait no longer, I must run home and watch the Cotton Bowl, or the Sugar Bowl, for some piddling low-paying bowl piece I suddenly recall I've been assigned . . . so I watch without sound, without reception adjustments, paying cursory but unbroken attention, chewing stale bread just to stay alive, feeling like (physical, emotional) death warmed over . . . having put all my eggs in the LSD #1 basket, I am now alone, aloner than Henry the Hermit in a children's book that never was writ, and there's no one on earth I can even *imagine* calling . . . back in New York, where I *knew better*, I could never, *never* have "done such a thing" (I tell myself), been such a flat-out romantic fool, surrendered to such an obvious dead-end James M. Cain "go for it" sham . . . frightened and bone-weary, I visualize *yet another layer of the onion* peeling away— where do they get all these layers????

L.A. Is the Capital of Kansas

YEAH, that was a pretty dumbstupid one with repercussions and all, I guess it takes the nod over TIME I STUCK THE CHLORINE TUBE UP MY NOSE IN CHEMISTRY CLASS when it looked like the thing was no longer generating, TIME I TOLD RENA RUBIN THAT LEGS FORBES WAS IN A COMA as an alibi for being at a Southhampton (Long Island) pop art show when she was expecting me at her Oceanside (Long Island) door for some boring date-night fun, and that TIME, AGED 10, WHEN I DRANK FULL GLASSES OF SIX DIFFERENT FLAVORS OF SODA at a party after some horrible school concert that I played clarinet in and not only didn't I have room left for ice cream, I had trouble walking home (two blocks) and thought they'd later find me dead with bubbles bubbling out. It also probably gets the nod over shaving my chest ('cause dickheat, brain cells, death of the soul and all that shit are involved).

THE GIRL WHO NEVER ATE PIZZA

Or burgers. A little tofu, but that's about it.

She had my tongue in her mouth but no meat *per se*.

After vegetables and rice I read her my poems and she read me hers. That was her gameplan. Mine was I'd've foregone the veggies for an eat of her clam. Rice, tho—brown rice—is good roughage. That I can always use re the dread constipation.

She ate her bowl faster than me, then a refill. But no—not a fatso. I lifted her up, she was light, very light, tho taller than me by a good couple inches.

I don't usually like blondes, but she was attractive. Small breasts, nice face. Like a blonde model—if you like blondes. Enough, for starters, to take my mind off the silence of the Void. I just generally like 'em darker.

And older. At 21 how much can anyone—heart, mind, organs— really know? Or even at 30. A lotta dumb, beautiful 21-year-olds, and she wasn't even beautiful, merely attractive.

So I picked her up, this cute, not exactly wise 21'er, and danced her and swung her and kissed her and put her down. She didn't mind the lifting, the jouncing, the mouth stuff, merely the carrying. The illusion of being carried *to*. As if—ha—I was aiming her at the couch or [some other room] the bed. Well sure, if that had been the ticket, what the hey. Cushions, fine—what have I got against bouncing in relative comfort? If she'd led me to her favorite mattress, swell, but I'd have just as gladly sexed her on the hardwood floor.

I drank wine. She drank "strong Brazilian coffee." Recently 'round the world, with a stop at the U. of Zurich (whose painting department displeased her), she'd brought back a tin. A crummy hostess, she offered me nary a sip. Nor would she touch my wine, *fine* wine, storebought special to warm, fuel and add that certain "glow" to our v. first encounter-in-flesh. It cost me $3.09 (plus tax) a bottle. I bought two.

'Cause I'd thought—ah! the dreams poets dream!—her roommate might join us and two would become *three*. But just two, heck, I could handle it. A youth-meets-experience cataclysm *in vivo*—in body—for me, her and the whispering floor. The floorboards were saying . . . well they weren't saying much.

But me, her, we were talking a stormsworth. Food, poetry— according to gameplan—many wds. on each.

"Did you notice the tofu?" No, I hadn't. Not thru all the sticky-sweet curry slop w/ raisins. And chutney. "It's about the only protein I eat."

"What, no chicken? No fish?"

"I've tasted them, but I just can't . . . eat them."

"Cheese?"

"No."

"Ever taste beef?"

"Yes. I took a bite once and spit it out."

"Hamburger?"

"No, it was prime rib."

"Rare?"

"I don't know. What's the difference?"

"Well, there's all this blood. It's a great foretaste of death."

"It *all* seems dead to me."

"And even just from a poison standpoint, right, these are like poisons that are not instantaneous killers. You're not gonna drink house paint or eat, y'know, roach poison, but you *can* eat beef enchiladas and pepperoni pizza."

"I'm hooked on vegetables. It's all my mother cooked."

"Yeah, but you owe it to yourself, just take some bites. A beef *taco*. Experience the dark side as a neophyte—you're lucky you've waited this long—and live to tell it. And write it."

Our cue for let's wheel out th' poems.

I'd received invites before, come on over & *you* know, but never like Rita's. That's her name—Rita. "I'd really like you," she said, "to appraise my poetry. As honestly as possible. Now that I'm no longer painting, I need to know if what I'm doing instead is... worthwhile. I'll even cook dinner." Geez. To hear it even now is to sigh. (Write 20 years and a *payoff*.)

So okay, here we are. Verse time. She reads me this *hey dad, father dear, put up or shut up; take it out, wave it, show what you can do with it* whatsit, excellent actually, then two more, longer than a night in Umptember, not quite so exc. but who's in the mood at this stage for appraising? Not this bozo, and I whip out a few of my own for to read them.

Mistake? Well, they're better than hers and she's, hey, for a second she's visibly pissed. But impressed—"Those are... very... good"—and we kiss and I suck on her nipple. Nice nipple, *very* nice, and the back of my hand's in her dress-to-kill trousers. Back? Actually the whole thing, but from the angle of entry only two-three backs o' fingers get to meet and greet her m-m-moisture. Oboy, and she gets up to go take a pee and there's no bathroom door and the stereo's off and oboy, I in fact hear her tinkle.

Oboy *oboy*, I've had a bottle-plus wine, I'm content, she returns, I resume groping. On my lap straight on, her legs circle me tight, my hands on her ass and the tops of her thighs and we kiss and we kiss— luv that youthtime-ish eagerness!—then *stop*. Whuh?

"Look. I didn't ask you here for... I wanted to read you my poems."

"I uh thought you *have* read. Read me some more."

"Well, that's all I've written"—3 goshdamn pomes?? "Besides, I barely know you."

"Oh *I* don't know. It's been two weeks, we've been in the same room three-four times. *This* is getting to know me." A *great* poet line, right?—then I realize (voilà!) she means *courtship*. Wants, craves, demands, deserves the fucker. (When you're my age, you grow out of touch with the "ways" of the young.) "Okay, how 'bout we—"

"And what did you *mean* when you told me Eunice was your 'girlfriend of record'?"

"Wait"—lemme get this straight; suitors have been phoning all night; more interruptions than from weewee and uncorkings—"you wanna be my *girlfriend*?!" If . . . then . . . so I go for her girlfriendly bra strap. No dice.

"Really, I have to study. You'd better leave."

"Study?"

"My journalism class . . . UCLA Extension . . ."

"Yeah? Well that's nice . . . didn't know . . . getting to know *you.*"

"I have to read about the Holocaust."

"Great. I'll read something too"—grasp at straws, Jim! Must be 12–13 books in the place.

We settle on her roommate's room. Black sheets, great for reading. *The Modern English Poets*—who they?—my first choice. Fat paperback. I open, check the contents, she says: "This isn't working."

"Huh?" I have not so much as stroked her puss thru pants.

"I can't *concentrate* with you here."

"Jesus, you're like a 15-year-old."

"Okay, that's it—go." Damn, forgot today's youngsters need to have their age-coding stroked . . . blew it! She hands me my boots.

1¾ bottles to the wind and sea, I squint, thinking suddenly of the v. good shit which (thanks to the rice) will likely make my hangover bearable, and see the gal who would not be mine, boo hoo, tonite or ever as a blonder Kelly McGillis in *Witness*. Lovely Rita! I could *like* a person like you . . .

Rotating on my left heel, then my right, I notice *no paintings anywhere.* Has she left them all in Zurich? (Some things you never get to know.)

"Mainly"—go ahead, shove me out the door—"I don't think I could *handle* showing up in somebody's poem." I forgot to tell her I also write prose.

TITS
IN
TITSVILLE

When I was eleven some kid brought a pic to school that really opened my eyes to b-b-b-breasts. Jayne Mansfield had 'em and the ones she had had *numbers*: thirty-six or possibly thirty-eight (thirty-nine?). Whatever, it was somewhere in the mid to upper thirties, and as I navigate those same advanced three-ohs in the age-digit dept. I feel compelled by reason of place to consider the subject like I ain't in a half-month of annums. Like here I am, here you are, here are we all in a town *lousy with tits*, where they flutter like a floating theme park eights days a week, fifty-three weeks a year, where suntanned cleavage is the official Unofficial Civic Coat of Arms, and I'm wondering what people (heteromales in particular, m'self included), *see in tits anymore anyway*, like how come after decades of BRANDISH-MENT by every Jayne, Dolly and Raquel they still "play"? In other wds. (this should be an essay in the L.A. public schools): What's so eternal about female mammaries? What *gives* with their persistence f'r crying aloud?

Thinking cap firmly in place . . . . . . GO.

For starters, okay, all us guys're just a buncha babes who miss our mom, that sly devil who (chances are) shoved cow's milk and a rubber nip in our mouth before we'd had sufficient taste of the *real stuff*—the whole superobvious "Freudian" biz. In our mixed-up, shook-up heads, milk = milk & cookies, which translates to *breasts as implicit dessert* or, as we get farther ever farther from the source, *as hors d'oeuvres*, namely an official round of snackin' that merely accompanies the standard sexist operating procedure of, uh, getting laid. (Even the most liberated among us are occasionally compelled by deep dark *psychology* to think of a lady's sacred knobs this way—'s the breaks so what can we do?)

Symbolic munchies aside, even diehard grownup heteros've gotta have something to actually *suck on* from time to time, something more substantial than a piña colada through a straw. In any shape or size, surrogate mom mamm is just loaded with oral substance, plus it's gotta be a heck of a better place to rest your grownup juvenile brow than anything this—or even the other—side of the (vastly overrated) womb. In extreme cases, this can lead to the sad male ballpark of *women as icons of security*, and as I for one am averse to pinning male neuroses on half the world's bazooms (ouch!) let us drop that one teat, er, toot sweet . . .

Okay. Let's forget function for a minute and pretend that tits were, say, asslike things on chests. Abstract roundish forms that frontally protrude from torsos, fighting against restrictive garments to be free. So on one hand we're talking the poetry of containment/release, and on the other the whole shebang of *objets d'art* per se.

Tight clothes were not designed to fit the female chest-thing; they'll fit (with effort) a gal's buttocks but not her teats. Long has the law conspired to prohibit their voluntary exposure to the cooling breeze of day, and bizarre contraptions have been contrapted to *keep 'em in their place*—while meanwhile they continue to unabatedly bounce bounce bounce like they got minds of their own screaming "We want out!" Won't somebody *please let them out*—somewhere besides dirty movies or the privacy of their own house? How 'bout Dodger Stadium for inst? (Breasts are the *voice of freedom* in us all.)

The artist in us all is just as keen on titties, once again for verrry good reason: They deliver. They deliver circles, cones, parabolas, hyperbolas, sine curves, ellipses, asymmetry and symmetry. There's more going on in the *world's meagerest tit* than in six dozen bushels of apples. Throw in the fact you usually got two at a time and we're already talkin' theme & variation in *a single pair o' paps*. An eyeball or two of cleavage and we're talking mighty landscapes in a nutshell; space is the place and craggy snowpeaked mtns. ain't telling fug-all better'n bazoongas—or with more *economy*.

Which brings us to the doorstep of *classic philosophy*: the jolly Plato; idealized forms. Even if it's horrible accidents like *sexist programing* that started you noticing knockers, 's highly possible you're noticing 'em more than toenails or nose hairs, and the inevitable issue of *formal comparison* impels you t' deal with esoteric baloney like *universals & particulars*. Ultimately, you're forced way the fuck up to a *higher aesthetic plane*, and therein lies the *continued fascination* with feminine protrusion (it had to lie *somewhere*). So as fate would have it, *even if you can't count higher than two*, you can't HELP being a motherhumping *intellectual* when you're ogling a pair—ain't life funny!

The World of Tactile Sensation: They're *good to squeeze*. Pecs may not have it all over glutes, but they're glands not muscles and that makes 'em softer than Charmin—yet still firmer than a falsie. Add a nipple for textural interest and all an ass can respond with 's an occasional pimple . . .

Tits Are People Too: If *hearts* could see, breasts would be their *eyes*. Some jugs have been known to flap like *ears*. As alluded to earlier, they're also *minds* (of their own), they're relocated *butts*, which is to say they're *cheeks*, come to think of it they're not too far afield from bent *kneecaps* and/or *elbows*. Aerodynamically sound models will stand (unassisted) on their own two *feet*. People sometimes beat off between them as they would in an *armpit*. Not to mention their aforementioned function as *glands* and *nerve* conduits to the complex of ms. whatsername's *sex organs*. They are a whole organism rolled into one, and *people who need people* are pleased to meet 'em at parties or down by the beach. Fondness for chest flesh = humanism on parade!

A TRUE
BOOKSTORE
STORY

. . . until you re-a-lize it's just a story!
—"Treason," The Teardrop Explodes

Magazines, comics and stuff I never had trouble with, but till quite recently books were a bitch. I never used to read 'em 'cept for school or reviews; was far easier to write-em than read-em. Black letters on white pages—no ads, illustrations or typeface change(s)— 've always been an eyesore; no less an eyescore now that I finally "know better." Ditto for the cagelike prison *geometry* of the printed page—hey that's tight—which always itself seems to bear some metaphoric relation to the goddam UNIVERSE.

Reading: *still* hurts the eye, *still* close-quarters the soul, and yet (in spite of) i.m. nowadays a reader and a half, and not just 'cause i.m. working a bookstore (on weekends). Is 'cause (1) I do not any longer WATCH TV, not even 30 seconds per week—month—year. I did not watch the Super Bowl. I do not watch nothing. So I got lotsa *time*. (2) Literacy is the FINAL CONSPIRACY, was prob'ly also the ELEV-ENTH or TWELFTH as well. Arcane biz: a secreter code than

L.A. Is the Capital of Kansas

Tarzan-speaks-to-apes or Jah Rastafari. Appeals to me that code/ decode I can. So I do. Making up for 30 yrs' lost time, and acting very *pompous* about it, in the last month I have actually read: Robert B. Parker, *Promised Land*; Ngaio Marsh, *Spinsters in Jeopardy*; John Giorno, *Cancer in My Left Ball*; Lawrence Ferlinghetti, *Her*; Louis-Ferdinand Céline, *Journey to the End of the Night* (in progress—400 pp. read so far); Wm. S. Burroughs, *The Soft Machine*; Wm. S. Burroughs, *The Last Words of Dutch Schultz*; Wm. S. Burroughs, *The Book of Breeething*; Wm. S. Burroughs, *Cities of the Red Night*.

Burroughs, I'm reading lots of Burroughs. He writes about hanging, he writes about colors, he writes about virus. Got (I have) next to no int'rest in such stuff as *content*, whole lot of int. in such as *voice*. Howling voices/written, howling voices/read. Reading (the activity) is somewhere between writing and crossword puzzles. Somewhere. In fever, in death, and in certain lights, all the somewheres intersect, are close to being *one*. Burroughs knows this, is the only writer (with so many books to his CREDIT) who *writes* like he knows it, is the only one who genuinely writes for the reading = writing PEER GROUP, writes *from* the writing = reading = dying = zzzzzzzzz (= *you* name it) flesh 'n' blood PLACE.

(Also, he writes like *me*, that's what they tell me, so why not, I'm thinking, read him & read him & try 'n' figger how he *gets away w/ same*, y'know with *income on the line* ...)

Stores that sell Burroughs: few. Mine isn't one. Stores that sell lots of Burroughs: fewer. Stores that sell lots of the Burroughs I haven't yet read: one. A Different Light, 4014 Santa Monica Blvd., Silver Lake. Featured: HOMOSEXUAL-authored lit.

I go, I find, I buy. *Port of Saints, Exterminator!, Roosevelt After Inauguration, Early Routines*. Expensive, I pay. *Getting the Most Out of Cruising*—not by Wm. S.—I notice.

I leave. Am followed.

Pimply Filipino, male, teenaged; traces of experimental razoring, facial and recent. Stands in the doorway to A Different Light, splits mere seconds after me, carrying—it is drizzling—an umbrella.

I do not take his tailing seriously, pay it no more heed than his raingear or the rain. Leisurely gait, purchase in bag in hand, I cover

138

one block, two blocks of Silver Lake, thinking (this is true) of SILVER LININGS.

He is there at the car fast as I am at the car.

Can I take him down Sunset? he wantsa know. Not *going* down Sunset. is the truth & I tell him. Where *am* I going? he cannot help asking. Down around Pico. and that is no lie. Okay, so how 'bout to Melrose? Okay, to Melrose we will go.

Open: doors. Close: umbrella. Take: seats. No time elapsed, south on Hoover, passenger axks: "Do you live alone?"

Me (v. fast w/ the impov): " . . . . . No."

Him: "Are you married?"

Me (faster): " . . . Yeah."

Brief gap; him: "How long married?"

Me: "Four. . . uh . . . *five* years."

Him: "Huh?"

Me: "Four and two-thirds."

Gap.

"Can I ask you a personal question?"—him again. "Are you gay?"

"As a matter of fact, no I'm not."

Long gap. Melrose. Whew.

"I think I'll go to Pico"—not so whew. "IS YOUR WIFE A HOUSWIFE OR DOES SHE WORK?" This guy is worse than me with the ladies.

"Works" I say and he says "What's she do?"

"Acts" I tell him, he wantsa know "Today?"

"Uh yeah . . . uh . . . no" and at last I know how females feel. I know how they feel when even verbal is more than too much to parry, when these persistent s.o.b.'s are just so . . . *annoying.* (I have learned my lesson—GALS TAKE NOTE—& will never persist with 'em, uninvited, again.)

Final last-ditch gambit: "Do you buy *all* your books at that bookstore?" He thinks he's got me but I do not slip: "No, I've never been there before just now. There's this one author. . . ." I do not finish the sent. (it is not nec.).

DUBIOUS, he's dubious, he is also plenty pissed. All the way down Pico—he hasn't copped penis or anus—raining hard now—'s a long hitch back. Back? Y'know somewhere. Pico/Vermont in a downpour (is no where to cop). *"Thanx"*—oof, slam—but he isn't thankful.

(There is no punchline to the story.)

ANY OLD
WAY YOU
LOSE IT

Well, simply, there've been three basic, distinct phases to my involvement in and with rock rock rock (& roll) in the eighth of a century I've hung my buns in L.A.: before punk, punk, and after punk.

BEFORE. In the late sixties, the only time its rockscene had meant much to me even from afar, Los Angeles had been the Doors, the Byrds and Love. If you want, you can throw in Buffalo Springfield and Frank Zappa, whom I never really liked much more than Henny Youngman, but I've still got a couple of his albums—throw him in. It had also been the mega-loathsome Monkees and hippiekids getting *ass* beat on by the LAPD—I'm glad I wasn't around.

By the time I *was* around there were no more Doors, Byrds, Love—not a trace—and what there was of Frank interested me less than, well, *less* than Henny Youngman. The last trace of Buffalo Springfield, Neil Young, had by then pretty much coalesced with a singer-songer zeitgeist (Joni Mitchell, Jackson Browne, Linda Ronstadt, et al) which at *best* might've been a musical correlative to Gary Hart *with* Donna Rice. Glitter-glam fops, unreconstituted hippies and reconstituted Monkees lurked about, as did aging Brit imports in the canyons and hills. And a million garage bands—in a million garages—with Beatles-hood (or bust) in their craw. (Talent scout designate-in-chief: Kim Fowley.)

Which tempted me about as much as having my legs cut off.

DURING. From mid-'77 through somewhere in '80 or possibly, on the outside, '81, L.A. (believe it 'cuz it's true!) was not only the hottest, hardest-core punk-rock venue in the U.S. but the second most vital such culture-seat in the world (behind the U.K.). With bands like the Germs, X, the Screamers, the Plugz, the Bags, the Weirdos, the Controllers, the Flesh Eaters, Black Flag, B-People, Black Randy & the Metrosquad, Fear, Nervous Gender, UXA, 45 Grave, Vox Pop, Monitor, Catholic Discipline and Gun Club, and a pair of swell mags, *Flip Side* and my all-time favorite rockmag, *Slash*, this shithole came as close to being a fertile musical oasis as any I've stumbled over.

Very little of which I bothered to write about. Aside from the fact that my rockwrite licks had already been worn to dysfunction, I was just too busy *experiencing* it all, gulping in the most atypical mass of fresh air I've encountered in this burg. I did, however, have an FM punk show, "Hepcats from Hell," on the local Pacifica station 'til they axed me for letting musicians use cusswords, and I even, for a total of eight horrible gigs, had a band of my own called Vom, for which—as "Mr. Vom"—I sang (and the less said about which the better).

In retrospect, what L.A. Punk *was* was a rock-roll stripped of nearly all glitz, pomp, bourgeois confectional gesture/intent. With hardly even passing obeisance to "professional standards" or conventions of rock-behavioral strut, it was raw, uneditedly human, unchoreographedly headstrong, yet neither macho nor wimp (which helped *me* for one—honest!—clean up my own lingering rock-sexist act). All told, it was arguably the most *specifically* anti-totalitarian U.S. rock-roll ever, and the one true Southern Cal "underground music" after Central Avenue bebop of the forties.

And the great shocker in all this, greater even than the mere fact of anything so substantial 'n' life-supporting actually *happening* in L.A., was its ultimate source. Basically this wasn't kids working factories, or on welfare, but the lawnstained, hot-tubbed progeny of "safe middle-class homes" in Endless Summerville. To which their basic measured response—bless 'em, may their tribe increase—was fuck!-this!-shit! in Beast Town, U.S.A. Way to go!

And it did go, it went. The whole thing lasted maybe three-four years, which I guess is a longish time in the general scheme of things, and then *poof*, it became the same old shit as everything else. As the rest of rock.

Rightwing assholes from Orange County, to whom punk amounted to little more than non-supervised contact football, started showing up at shows—to trash 'em. Soon this became the clubscene norm—gee what fun, bottles flying—rock as usual.

At the other end of the behavioral spectrum, punk became a non-ironic fashion, style, dress code for conformist simps, all but coalescing, once and for all, with Melrose yuppie ticky tack. You wanna see 14-year-olds (or 30-year-olds) looking like, dressing like the punks of *ten years ago*, go to Melrose.

And I.R.S. Records seduced-and-destroyed some bands, and other labels, other bands, followed suit, and eventually, well . . . which more or less brings us to:

AFTER. The biz goes on and on, corporately huff-puffing not only as if *punk* never happened, but as if nothing has really changed since 1972. What used to be a force of liberation (I'm talking *rock*—a longgg time ago) is now but an age/class consumer-demographic's musical dosage of *required entertainment*. Between New York and L.A.—which is slimier, greedier?—the whole country's pretty much sewn up. The Grammies, corporate breast-beating at its most mega-hideous, are here; so maybe it's here. (But MTV is there—so who knows?)

In any event, I no longer listen, I no longer go. Not to rock, just jazz, which corporations hardly give a hoot about, and which this town treats like . . . I'll tell you *later*. Some other book.

But rock clubs, sheee, I won't go inside 'em even to see people I like, and by like I mean *personally*. Every time I step inside it's *torture*.

And rockwriters, my erstwhile colleagues, my roots: I talk to L.A. rockwriters about as often as I talk to the Rosetta Stone.

EXCELLENT PANTIES IN NESMITH'S *THE PRISON*

If that's what you call 'em. Y'know 'cause they kinda stretched up past the butt and crotch to the belly and beyond—but for sure there was plenty-o-garment visible about the groin. In such provocative colors as black and grey (*real* good grey). Worn about the procreative area of Katherine Warner as Marie. Also about Carolyn Hauser as Janey's organ region as well, altho the first few times she got danced around by the skinnyboy she was paired with YOU DID NOT SEE MUCH. Guy didn't lift her high enough. Next time was okay tho, and the fine outline of her pudding was revealed.

Setting for all this clothed-privates excitement was opening night of ex-Monkee Michael Nesmith's *The Prison*. "Concert/Rock Ballet" read the program and indeed it was. A band of 6- and 4-stringers picked away at stage left amid potted flowers and ferns (nature in the raw) while Mikey narrated and dancers mimed the brazenly lysergic theme: liberation of the human whatsis from its self-imposed bonds. The mind reels to think that this same Mr. Nesmith once picked & sang for the most heinous anti-psychedelic out-of-sync-with-the-rest-of-'67 beat combo in all of phonus balonus L.A. As mentioned, the fleurs in pottery were real.

Excellent Panties in Nesmith's *The Prison*

Anyway, Nesmo's narrating this thing about how, well, you're in this prison, see, but it's of your own devise (theme borrowed from the late Jim Morrison) and all you gotta do's step thru this hole, um, into the void. The void'll bother you for one whole night (soft soil underfoot) but by morning there's clover and purple skies and a cabin with Janey and her stringbean dancer as your guides. They guide you back to the original hoosegaw and tell you all y'gotta do's remember the walls are false (memory's the key). So the guy goes back (name's Jason, he wants some womanlove, which as fate has it this particular jail's just *lousy* with) and, sez Michael, "The thought at first gave him courage to resist the sense input he was getting" (*damn* good way of puttin' it) till eventually he forgets and starts seein' walls and bars again, his subsequent panic necessitating act number two. . .

Is it still intermission? No, it is not. The belly dancer is part of the show. As are the oud (oud?) and tabla players, one of each. They're playing, she's dancing and sweating, this goes on and on when on walks—could it be??—Jason in street clothes. The guy who played Jason has returned! To hassle the belly, oud, tabla AND the audience! A taste of PIRANDELLO and act the 2nd is underway. . .

Capsule summary of this amazing, incredible, outasite act: lots more dancing, picking, plants and narration. Lots more slips-o-tongue than first half too (gettin' more comfy and casual by the minute), but Mike's tongue work on the tricky w-h's—all the whys, wheres, whats, whens, whiches and whencefors—remained *solid*. Also real good: a film strip, *Cycles*, featuring forest fires, atomic nuclei, sky, skydivers, red, blue, yellow and white. And orange. Ultimate message: no space, no time—they don't "exist"—love is all.

Only two misgivings about the whole two and one-half hour *thing*. (1) Why no horses on stage? (2) Old "fogey" in act one moves his feet too fast for a fogey with a cane. But blame that on the foot coach—not on fogeyplayer Dan Orsborn or his feet.

TWO is not a bad number at all. Six or seven mighta been but two is just jake.

LINDA'S WAVE: A WIPEOUT

First things first. You may not have this problem in NY but out in LA we got this farcical cross between Nixon and JFK of a governor named Jerry Brown who occasionally "dates" Linda Ronstadt so we've gotta like see her on the news all the time being/acting as guilelessly open-mouthed dumb as the sow (nonsexist "generic" term) she is. I've never liked Linda, maybe two cuts total, so it well may be a HATCHET JOB is in the works (call your friends!). Gonna listen to it (*Mad Love*) once and that's all . . .

Next things next. I know I've used the term "new wave" to refer to uncompromisingly visionary hardcore things like Public Image, the Germs and the Fall but that was then. Having come to my senses, I currently call that stuff PUNK, is what it is. Now that the new wave banner has been used to cover every tepid, retrograde anomaly from the Knack to the Fabulous Poodles y'gotta know it doesn't designate shit, generic or otherwise. If anything it's naught but the most insidious marketing ploy since the Bosstown Sound and a thousand times more EVIL, purporting to be "of the new" while effectively camouflaging the goddam industry's hell & gone TERROR of the Real Thing.

(There are record guys out here for inst, A&R people, promotion, publicity, who after work put on these silly narrow ties and tell their wives: "G'bye, I'm off to see some new wave." Or if they really feel like deluding themselves, or alarming the missus, they'll call it punk—if I can err in one direction they can err in the other. But try and get 'em to go see some *actual* headbang of a punk unit—I know, I've tried—and it's like asking them to stick their dick in a blender.)

Okay, the disc spins . . . dig that Farfisa! . . . Linda goes new wave! (Gotta be honest, the pink & black cover tipped me off or I wouldn't've done that second paragraph quite so soon, ain't tryin' to come off like some sort of *shaman* or anything.) In any event we see unfolding before our very eyes the ultimate "crossover" attempt by the queen of *that* wretched genre—pop, C&W and now, perhaps, NW. Hey, Little Anthony's "Hurt So Bad" is on here too, maybe she's also being processed for the R&B charts as well (or did she already make 'em with "Tracks of My Tears"?), let's move up a few grooves and *check it out.* Hmm, Frankie Valli cum '70s incarnation of Dionne Warwick, don't really think it'll chart—sorry.

Don't think it'll help John Rockwell's buildup of her as the new Maria Callas (classical charts!) either. "Don't stand in his . . . *way*" shows pretty glaringly that she still can't handle those, er, *tricky transitions*, and the "NO NO" screams at the end're *embarrassing* (no they don't embarrass *me*—I'm impervious—just one of those generic usages again). I mean when is everybody gonna 'fess up & admit the bimbo—oops—broad (Christ that *is* sexist)—gal (you know what I mean, when you're dealing with "sex icon" dinosaurs like Linda it's *catching*) CAN'T SING A LICK? Sure she's got a dandy swell "voice" like that other prisoner of pipes 'n' bombast I also can't stand, Joan Baez, but the only real expression, feeling or any of *that* generic shit that ever filters through the sloppily modulated (look out, here it comes again) *mush* is just an inadvertent trickle here, an accidental dribble there—like your Aunt Winny or sister Sue (or even YOU!) could probably hit the emotional nail on the head *at least as often.* (Hey, I believe this or I wouldn't be writin' it.)

L.A. Is the Capital of Kansas

Getting back on the NW track we see she's got THREE "hot ones" from the E. Costello songbook: E., whose tunes were no doubt *conceived* as hostile weapons aimed directly at the jugular or aorta of the shallow, self-satisfied, "pretty-faced" likes of someone not unlike Ms. Ronstadt herself (let's just say her *ilk*). She knows no more what she's singin' on these items than Tanya Tucker, age 14, did on "Would You Lay with Me in a Field of Stone?" (I know *she* didn't have a clue 'cause I once asked her.) Engelbert Humperdinck could do 'em with more "conviction," and if you wanna get tough on me and say he's male how about some droner like Mary MacGregor? Or maybe not Crystal Gayle, but how about—don't laugh—Anne Murray? Let's just say as far as cover versions go Mae West did a better reading of OTIS REDDING'S "Too Hot to Handle" in *Myra Breckenridge*. (But—hey—it should also be kind of obvious that E. himself, that veritable J. Cocker/B. Springsteen of new wave fluff in a nutshell, can't be too, um, "revolutionary" or any of *that* claptrap if she can even *hum* his mighty opuses without croaking. Or something.)

Then there's the matter of L-L-L-Linda's new brigade of backup hacks, the Cretones (fab-yoo-lous name you say?). Shit, if you wanna go Orthodox New Wave on me and claim there actually *is* such a thing lemme just say the Topanga Canyon incarnation (getting *merely* generic this time, I know it's tiresome, but perhaps they're actually from Malibu) is, if possible, even more corrupt, gawky and anachronistic than such regional stalwarts of '60s-revisionist NW as the Pop, the Naughty Sweeties and 20/20 (all recorded, all signed to labels, while Nervous Gender, Catholic Discipline, the Screamers et al—headbangers at the gates of DAWN—remain un-). Linda's biz consort Peter (w/out Gordon) Asher must jus' *love* all them Mersey chords!

Oh yeah, her "dirty songs": "How Do I Make You" and "Justine." The vile, loathsome Knack could do 'em better/smarmier (obviously), so could (for that matter) utter mainstream twaddle like Billy Joel, but even with all the pander machinery the industry can muster Linda can't *begin* to compete in the lasciviousness sweepstakes with Deborah Harry, those idiots in the B–52's or even (she useta be quite slutty) Diana Ross—let alone whatever her name is in the Pretenders. (Let double alone Lydia Lunch.) What's she good for "sexually" anyway?

I could go on and rant about her being one of our more immediately accessible examples of everything that's wrong with lowest-common-denominator culture, with LA, this country, the world, the very "human experiment" itself, but I'll just close by saying I hear she's got a hit and am glad (therefore) my car radio is on the blink.

(Hey—I hope I hope I hope—did I wound &/or maim? DID I DRAW BLOOD?)

SHIT,
NO CHASER

I love to shit at KPFK
seven minutes left on "Sister Ray" is how I've planned it
all week long I've been waiting for this
all week?
no a couple hours
knew I'd hafta "go"
so I brought the Velvets
hope their budget for paper
has not been diverted to
baklava for the
Balkan Festival

I love to shit at KPFK
I often use the girls' rm.
where paper is all but
guaranteed
tho I've got

Shit, No Chaser

other reasons
tampon/napkin disposal
is usually empty
do they take it home?

I love to shit at KPFK
marker in hand
"has anyone ever tasted Anita Frankel's cunt?" I write
and 6 months later someone answers
"who would want to?"
no response for that one
comes easy
I ponder
I ponder
I drop my dump with 30 seconds to spare
the Child Molesters from South Pasadena
are waiting
I must ask them
for all 37 listeners from here to Tarzana at 4:23 in the morning
"what is your mom's favorite brand
of disposable douche?"

I love to shit on KPFK
where are their commies
now that we need them?
K-fuck I call it
and wait for the flak
tired '50s leftists in matching socks & tie
afraid some snoopy badass will hear them say *please*
and quote them "out of context"
and Reagan will take away their toy
I stripmine the airwaves
and wait for the flak
I puke freedom in their sad, sad faces
they are as free as a schnauzer
in Beverly Hills

L.A. Is the Capital of Kansas

won't someone please *walk me now*?
isn't there one commie in the house?

I love to shit at KPFK
door to the hallway is open
as always
echoes of whatever
echo for no one
as no one
is listening
no one disturbs
the privacy of my exhibition
I am too fucking solemn for words

ANOTHER GRAMMY YEAR WITH THE MELTZER CLAN

> i have seen the gray flanneled suitors of my gen-
>   eration
> abandon their suits for rock rock rock (and roll)
> i have likewise witnessed rockboys and rockgirls
> smacked out on the jing-jang jegs of mainstream
>   pluralotropism
> furnishing their smelly kitchens and drugrooms
>   with flannel wallpaper, gray
> > —from "Les Fleurs du Pee" (in progress),
> > Eck Osiris Meltzer, age 15½

Sometimes kids say it all. Sometimes, well let's just leave it at sometimes. At all times, however, some things apply. Is there anything more important in this Life, for instance, than music—and TV—in that order? I think not and neither does that extended herd of Meltzers I am proud to call my family. We would not miss a Grammys for all the sin in Sweden, and '84 was no exception.

On odd numbered years we Meltzes—and related offshoots—plant ourselves firmly in front of the tube: awarding for to view from cushions and couches. As this was an "even," I, not one to shun my patriarchal duties, sprung for tickets: nothing beats live and in person for honoring MUSIC. While my respect for the National Academy of Recording Arts & Sciences may have waned a tad since "Louie Louie" failed to top the '63 voting (an event which caused me to burn my academy card in protest of my colleagues' unwilling-ness to change with the times and begin recognizing the Now Sound of the sixties), and a tad more since the fateful balloting of '71, when "I Watched You Rhumba" by Hackamore Brick got creamed by James Taylor's "You've Got a Friend," I still have my memories of the glory years—ah! fifty-three I remember you well!

And '55 for crying out loud, Haysoose *Christ* what a yr. for winners: five Grammys for Mantovani, four for the 101 Strings! And the incredible '54 by golly (year Eartha Kitt finally broke the "color line" by presenting the award for household how-to recording, since deleted), I'll trade you one '54 for '68, '73, '74, '78, '79 and '83 put together. . . oh but don't forget '52! I won't and I don't, I in fact do a rather serious "take" on the magical five-two as, brood to the left, right and rear, I enter the Shrine and (to quote my late—and close—personal friend Jimmy Morrison) "walk on down the hall." To the nearest usher, to get everyone seated and ensconced—and to be excused.

I 'scused myself to visit the press tent, my first trip back since g-d known when, to check out the "action" and show off selected family:

—grandson Eck, 15, sophomore (and honor student) at Spokane Jesuit High;

—granddaughter Jujubeena, 17, of "mixed" parentage, recently accepted by the collage department of Vassar University, tho she may just study art "on my own";

—grandson Bellamy, 12, totally cured of cerebral palsy, thanks in large measure to the Telethon (so don't knock TV—not to *me*, buddy!);

—daughter-in-law Woosni, 23, third wife of my youngest son Otto, a real q.t. who I wouldn't mind . . . only kidding! . . . whose interest in music is for very good reason (cousin of the late—and great—Les Baxter).

No sooner were we PRESSED W/ THE PRESS than there they were (sighted, spied): ole friends and lifers, "industry" hotchas I have known, terminal critics of the "Big Beat" from coast to coast as well as abroad. "Why there's that old sodbuster Ed Wallet"—currently with the Austin *Tex-Dispatch*—"your gramps and him used to *bust sod* together!" (Covered Bo Diddley's tonsillitis in nineteen forty and eight—for two papers, long since folded, in Cleveland.) And there goes Sylvia Sternhurst, metal critic for the French dogmag *Hounds*, with whom—hup hup—the author was once "unfaithful" to his late wife Cora. "Hi Syl"—the kids are watching, I can say no more—"how's tricks?" And great googa mooga if THAT THERE is not (holy cow!) my *extreme* pal-o-mine Ralph "Bub" Scuba, why Bub used to work for several *companies* (Hermes, N.M.A., Artista) and I wonder what he possibly is doing now. "I am working for *Record Music Magazine*" sez the smiling Bub; gosh—time sure flies—me and him used to watch *football* together...

Two former cohorts I am not 'zactly pleased to engage however: (1) "true bee-liever" (in ????) Biko Skidmore, whose anti-"factionalism" cooties I will die before I let rub off on ones I love, and (2) the great (she is *great*) Susan Brunette of Chris Columbus Records, who I am *embarrassed* to run into—hi Suze, love ya—on account last time our paths crossed I had officially "dropped out" (i.e., boycotted the Grammys for one year to protest—that's me, always a protest!—THE CONTINUED, ONGOING, UNINTERRUPTED MARKETING OF THE SICK AND FESTERING ROCK & ROLL CORPUS, MAKE THAT CORPSE). That was a yr. I would rather forget: treatment for ['tween my doctors and myself].

"Grandf-father"—Bellamy tugs at my sportjacket, only the slightest lingering trace of c.p. in his speech—"who is that large-b-b-bosomed young lady over there with the old person?" My lord! can it Be?

"Well, grandchild, that 'old person' as you call him is indeed ancient. Ever since the collapse of his recording career, and the subsequent demise of *Hollywood Squares*, he has been searching, rather futilely I might add, for gainful employment. Evidently the 'frail' with the—ahem—protruding *stack* out to here is the 'prop' he aims to utilize in manufacturing a new vocation. She is the one and only Elvira, Queen of Darkness; he, the sadly over-the-hill Alice Cooper." (O! doth weary sadness encircle me: how to 'splain to a youngster the pathos of cultural entropy, the patheticness of rube flesh, late of pig farm, returned to pig *pen* as stool? So I don't even *try* to explain . . .)

From the very old to the very new: Best New Artist. Nominees include: Men Without Hats. "Men Without Hats?" I hear myself asking, the kneejerk voice of incredulity—have they (migod what a cynic I must seem!) slipped us a "fast one"?

"Come on gramps, get with it," sighs Eck with ill-concealed condescension towards the "square" who stands before him, "Men Without Hats are *Australian.*"

"Whatchoo talkin', you dumb Eck-head"—there's my Jujubeena, I just *love* to see cousins in conflict!—"they be Belgian."

"I think they're from D-d-denmark."

"Quite possibly you're right, Bellamy, but I myself vote for, let me see . . . Uruguay? . . . no, . . ."

"Canada, R., they're Canadian." What?—who? (I *hate* folks who use my old name.) Why if it isn't none other than [bad with names] English fotogperson. "What brings you back, R.—your gig as a sportswriter never pan out?"

"The name is Richard, mr. shutterbug—Richard. As Ray Charles, and later the Kingston Trio, would say: *If you don't want you don't have to get in trouble*, so I'll trust you to remove your hand from the unprotected hip of my lovely daughter-in-law *toot sweet.*"

Which is merely my way of saying I can dig it: lifelong friends have a code of their own. Quickly we are conversing, specifically this yr's Grammys (versus earlier installments). Fotog has a *theory* and, trusting my judgment, tests me of its worth: "This is the year they finally decided to let Rock in on the awards."

"They uh what?" (Am I hearing correctly? Was Men Without Hats merely the setup for something far, far more insidious?)

"Okay let's look at the winners so far: Duran Duran, Culture Club . . ."

"Whoa—" (I am hearing!)

"Performing live: Big Country. . ."

"Nuh—" (Can my heart endure it?)

"Ozzie Osbourne is scheduled to present . . ."

"MY DEAR SIR I have had enough. Is it your intention to imply, nay suggest, that such combos as you mention are of a *different ilk* from, e.g., the Doobie Brothers, winners of quite a stack of cookies in, if memory serves, year of our lord 1979?!?@#$%¢! Culture Club indeed! Show me a more *antiseptically produced* third-hole version of shall we say the Classics IV—who never received *their* Grammy due if you'll remember correct—and I'll show you . . . something. Duran Duran? Big Country? Fuck 'em, pardon my French, *screw* 'em. No, don't screw 'em, put 'em together, teach [the former's rock-vid] elephants to play [the latter's rock-vid] bagpipes; then, and only then, will mumble mumble tut tut tut. Or like, the uh, these, hum, was for instance Fleetwood Mac a different *order* of b.m. than, y'know, the Eurythmics? Answer me that one—if you dare. It is my contention that, ilkwise, I can pick your face out from the front or behind, you may look pretty but I can't say the same for your mind. Meaning: it is only because . . . homogeneous . . . everything equals everything else . . . I mean Ozzie may have bit the bat's head, but did he swallow it? Billy Joel has bit more heinous things *and* swallowed, for *specific* heinous profit I'll grant you while Ozzie bluh bluh bluh, so what I'm saying, my man, is you are talking illusion, do you read me? The illusion that (a) 'new stuff' is as we speak being welcomed in the door, and (b) its isomorphs in the ilk dept. have not been *previously* rewarded, in spades, for their sick contributions to the final surrender of the human spirit. 'Rock' you say—Paul McCartney but no Minutemen—pshaw!"

The weight of the world thus off my (increasingly arthritic) shoulders, I crane my (equally arthritic) neck for a peek at the nearest monitor, and am (instantly) sorry I left my puke bag on the plane. For there in the seats—this was a seat shot—seated behind my beloved sister Persephone, inotherwords within proximity of the very seat in which my own writerly fundament would be planted should I choose to "use" my ticket, sat, together, not one but TWO faces

from the slick and smarmy covers of *People* mag, two REPRESEN-
TATIVES of the "new breed" of entertainer, together, oh my bowels
& innards: Michael Jackson & Brooke Shields!!! I know how costly
this evening has cost me—a year's supply of Stravinsky lps,
roughly—but at times such as etc. there are *higher priorities* than a
bleeping record set, I mean to say. "Eck, Juju, etcetera, I *forbid* you
to sit near those—yeesh—yuckos. While you may feel like calling
me . . ."

"Hey I think he's kinda cute. And I really enjoyed her in *Endless
Love*." To think, Woosni—I've loved her like my own flesh &
blood—a slut! [Harlot, begone! Exits.]

LIFETIME ACHIEVEMENT AWARDS. Chuck Berry. The
Man (!). The Myth (!). The Music (!). In 1984?????? (As opposed
to, say, 1961 or—to be charitable in the Fiefdom of Fools—some
arbitrary date like let's say seventy. . . *two*.) To think that Chas
Chaplin's geezertime invite to the Oscars once seemed a mite, hey,
anticlimactic! Chuck!! Hey!! Late (slightly)!! Need men, living, be
half *dead* before their times receive *ya* know. . . or, simply, must
Wayne Newton first "do" their tunes? (Or, likelier still, is yours truly
just another crotchety crotch?)

THE SHAME CONTINUES. Herbie Hancock, promising
young keyboardist/jass of 19-early-60s, who once had it in his power
to be the second coming of Bobby Timmons, or the third or fourth of
Junior Mance, up upon a stage not far from where certain Meltzers
now stand (the legs they buckle, the head it throbs), functioning
muse/ically like the thought (jass) never entered his mind. *Electronic*
instruments, yech tho hey we're liberal—8 miles high and when you
touch down, you'll find that it's stranger than known—but would ya
get a load of those GOD CAN YOU *BELIEVE* IT, BREAKDANC-
ING IS THE CENTERPIECE OF THE ACT!, finally I understand what the Shangri-las *meant* when they said "oh no oh no oh no
no no no no" . . . or something, equally chilling, to that effect. (I
contain the thought so as not to scare the children; they are entitled
to a—knock knock knock, on wood—trauma-free adolescence.)

"Hey gramps, isn't that whatsisname, *you* know. . ."

"Right you are, Eck, Bob Dylan. Why I've got anywhere from 16 to 18 of his discs in my current collection—none more recent, of course, than *Blood on the Tracks*. Pitiful—isn't it?—the tragedy of the Formerly In-Touch. The gentleman sure has come a long way from 10,000 miles in the mouth of a graveyard to, ulp, *this*."

"Y'might say 10,000 *inches* insida this one now!"

"Or at least millimeters, Juju, heh heh—hmm—WHAT TH-?!? Turn your heads quickly, offspring, avert yon monitor with your glance—Mike Love is *kissing*... the rhinestoned glove of Michael Jackson... and Dennis Wilson not yet cold beneath the ground!!!!! *Tell me that you've heard every sound there is and your bird is green* rant puff" and then it happened: my very first nonfatal stroke.

Past the Caddy limos, black, beige, cerise, they carry me, past the chauffeurs—was that *marijuana?*—of the very rich due to LP sales and/or airplay and publishing, crashing, flashing, my life in music flashcrashing before me: my last moment of recorded consciousness (could it be?): the Grammys of '49, which one scribe dubbed the Sammys (Davis Jr. had just copped three, a record at the time); my interview with Sam, the first of many; Cora? where are you Cora?; Sammy Cora core core your caw caw... crows??

donchoo worry Grampa, this Jujubeena, we write it for you. you jus recover, that your job, we write.

you know you racist what you say bout breakdance, maybe I jus so-call mulatto but my 'colored' part know you racist. that ok, I realize you talkin *sound*, Herbie Hancock music be lacking that dee*partment* you mean to say. and so what all this theatre-rical jivin in the spectator event? that what you mean so jus you lie still in you hospital bed.

one thing you *not* racist Grampa the way you hold back on that trash Michael Jackson. you too polite—he trash. People's Magazine, he bigger trash than a Magazine. I of sexual age—maybe you guess?—but I wouldn take a *shit* on Michael Jackson *face*. but i don know nothin bout Doorang Doorang or Big In The Country, that stuff inter*changeable* so who care, not me, what I care this Grammy revue say what special. bout this year Grammys. and that be Michael Jackson who trash. a embarrassment to the part of me colored.

I won show you this paper cause maybe it kill you. Examining Herald. Biko Skidmore, you know him? 'Michael Jackson Rewrite The Book'. it say. 8 awards, break the record Paul Simon, one them inchangeables, or do I got him confuse the Paul in Michael Jackson video? (tell me when you better). Skidmore say: 'irresistible appeal'. he say: 'half-shy mystique'. that very funny. he say: 'biracial audience'. well *I* biracial, count me out that! he *don* say: sissy boy who sing like a rat cause the whoremones—that a pun—and a operation the skin on his face. so he look like the panther lady Island Of Lost Soul, you know the movie, some say Diana Ross. either way that *sick*. I believe it sick. (don his daddy mommy love him)?

what it cause him is cancer—and cause you cancer jus listen. they give *award* to cancer?? that make no sense, not enough you sell it, gon give you reeward for sellin?? you right Grampa, this world so sad you cry a Pacific ocean. get well or I cry a wet planet Earth.

okay, now it stupid Eck turn, I don know howcum you like him. (guess it because he family).

Hey pops, Eck here. You spelled Ozzie wrong. Should be Ozzy. I'd be bummed if you kicked it, really I would, so take your medicine *lying down*.

I tol you he stupid, Jujubeena back again. in case you spec Bellamy revue Men With A Hat, he have c.p. relapse (cause by traumatic). so nex year maybe we gone the Telethon—it make sense we pass the Grammy.

$13.01 BEFORE TAXES

It's always a bad sign to find a penny. You find them because they're valueless, nobody wants 'em. Soon it'll be nickels, eventually dimes, quarters . . . so far pennies. Pennies *every*where. Who, dropping a penny, any longer stoops to scoop it up? And someone else's penny—the zip-valued mini-Lincoln of another—*sheee*. Do they even bend for 'em on Skid Row?

A penny found is a micro-death knell for *plenty*. And a penny pocketed—! I spied one—shiny, new—at the foot of the piano and foolishly made it my own after stepping on stage at the Lhasa Club.

The headlining poet, which is not to say headlin*er*, I began with the recently conceived "Gotta" ("—for the youth of America"), the one that starts

> let's see
> what I remember of our love
> first
> it was on the floor
> usually on the floor

and next was . . .
was there a next?

but hot as it was I got heckled. And before that ignored. Two or more gals—you could tell by their talk—were ignoring me. Which led— this was really quick—to Bob Forrest attempting to shush 'em with Budweiser.

What? No, they do not sell beer at the Lhasa Club. Neither sell nor serve it—nor condone it. Nor do they condemn it. You purchase a beverage, bring it in, slowly sip it w/ thirst-quench the goal, or you swallow the ocean, nearly drown, crawl through the sand a dripping, sodden *lout*—well that's *your* biz, Jack. Or Bob as the case may be.

And so *this* Bob, a famous Bob—he's that dickhead in Thelonious Monster—has by the time I get on "had enough to drink," thanks, enough that he hurls an unfinished surplus Bud at the talkers. Unfinished, in fact barely started, it carries pretty good, from a table at the base of stage left to this pillar 10-15 degrees off the base of stage right, rising as it goes, splattering (a lucky shot) at least one talker, thereby triggering the nearby Stev-o, another groovy "star"— the night was full of 'em—to get antsy and heckly.

He heckles *me*, Bob Forrest immediately heckles *him* (at double-triple the volume), I haven't got halfway through a poem of, oh, let's see, 23, 24 lines, *short* lines, before the pattern for the whole goddam reading's been set. Primary hecklers, secondary hecklers; ten-line poems, *three*-line poems—none're exempt. And after the first few I'm yelling back at them to just fucking shut the fuck UP—I could be home reading Proust f'chrissakes.

Look. To call myself the featured poet, ha, that's silly. A total misnomer. I'm hardly even the featured "reader." What I am is fifth—sixth if you count Iris Berry/Pleasant Gehman separate (Stev-o, in business suit & tie, was fourth)—"spoken word artist" on a bill topped by (that's correct!) MUSIC. Crimony a.k.a. Mike Watt/Paul Roessler. A swell band, coupla swell guys but C'MON now: I do not "speak words" left over in lyrics I never recorded, or which never managed to work as part of a, uh, TUNE (so whaddaya, duh, do-with-'em??). I WRITE—this is what I *do*, full frigging TIME—in a town that couldn't give two shits in hell for the printed word, and when (for whatever perverse reasons) it makes provisional sense to publicly, audibly READ a snippet . . . fine.

Maybe it's doomed to failure by definition; I dunno.

But let me get back to the chronology. They're yelling at me, I'm yelling at them, I can't get through half a poem without interruption. And what's really piss-shitty is it don't matter WHAT the poem is. It ain't CONTENT that's burning their ass—this poem versus that poem—it's the mere fact of poemhood. I.e., non-music. Five-six non-musics in succession: far too many for their overtaxed rock-roll hormones. If I'd gone on second I'd be fine . . .

Then another beer whizzes by. Bob again.

I'm in the middle of this one about a "fuck motel" in Zanesville, Ohio, I look over at Doug Knott who runs these shows, I shake my head and say: "I hope I'm getting paid for this. 'Cause if not, g'bye. I could be home reading Proust."

"Of *course* you're being paid. Go on, continue."

I do but so does Thelonious. I say: "Shut UP, asshole." He claims: "I'm on *your* side"—remember, a *secondary* heckler. I say: "Okay, annihilate yourself." He doesn't.

So now *I* throw a beer. My nearly empty Tecate. It misses. He continues his rap—at me, at Stev-o, whomever. Doug comes over, plays bouncer, tells him *Outa here.* He stays, gets louder, I jump off the stage, knock his table over. He lunges at me, Doug and two other guys grab him, hold him, he busts loose.

Back on stage, I'm at the mike, he jumps up, comes at me with this lunging shot—can't recall if it was a left or right—that catches me below the hairline at the end of its arc. I'd been backing away; impact but no pain. I touch my forehead: blood.

My poems all over the floor . . . footprints on 'em. While I gather what I can find, Doug returns, having somehow dragged the dickhead away. "Hey, man"—*proud* of having dragged—"now you can finish your set!"

My set? My set? "No thanks, I've already bled for this audience."

L.A. Is the Capital of Kansas

(And, really, I am *not* precious about my wds., my "art." But if I'm gonna read this shit, if I've gotta *headline* reading this shit, they better find a way to goddam listen. If they don't wanna listen, let *them* stay home and read Proust. Or fuck themselves.)

Oh, and I made thirteen bucks.

THE
EMPEROR'S
NEW
SPORTCOAT

In my dozen-plus years in L.A. I've gone from being *very much* a sports fan, i.e., your basic rabid can't-get-enough-of-it type lout, to, well, hardly a sports fan at all. One of my first brainstorms after getting over the intial shock of the place was *O.K., I'll be a sportswriter*, a zealot (if some paper or wire service would have me*) occupation- ally *welded* to an uninterrupted 365-big-ones-per-annum sporting gestalt. Today I don't think I catch ten events a year, and that's including TV.

Whether my residence has been the necessary, sufficient *cause* of my fall or its mere geo-occasion is not an issue over which I lose much sleep. Sure, it could certainly have happened in Green Bay (or Portland)—anything's possible. A new town, new perspectives, bridges burnt, interests forsaken—or some such hooey—right?

Dunno. All I know is it was in THIS illusion-rich, artifice-heavy burg that I came to "see through" bigtime sport as illusion, as artifice, as modern-age maya like any other and, ugh, ofttimes *worse*. 'S where I learned to recite, with terminal import and feeling, *Oh give me a break* to jock-media dogma; to peruse the daily sports section for *no more than* the scores; to watch televised contests, when I watch 'em

---

*Closest I came was a brief, unsatisfying stint as L.A. stringer for the Japanese edition of *Sports Illustrated*, which insisted on easy-translatable copy ("He hit the ball. Jackson caught it."), none of it, fortunately, extant.

at all, with a book on my lap and *without* the sound; to grasp, without flinching, the fundamental fact of sport as slime-grimy market-shuck, and of *all* offerings thereof as Miller Lite commercials writ large. Or small. In any event, *writ*.

All of which swept over me—universally, particularly—in the LAND of Lite Beer adverts *per se*: of movies, groovies, shimmer as substance, mass delusion as High Culture, the latest/greatest Big Lie as bottom line. In sport as in any of its more renowned entertainment-biz snakepits, though gen'rally with additional binary malice, x is, as a matter of course, equated not only *with* not-x but more or less *exclusively* with it. On a "micro-management" level, for example, you've got the charming phenomenon of fans not only *swallowing* increased ticket prices but duly regarding them as an ultimate *reward* for their loyalty. Going macro, binary as bulk *content*, as structure and shape of sporting *significance*, the ongoing theme—natch—is all or nothing, victory or self-erasure, mega-profit or bankruptcy, a Guinness record or the garbage dump.

Follow this to its logical generic conclusion and either Southern California is "the sports capital of the galaxy," as shills in its press corps have been whistling as gospel since, oh, the '81 World Series (Dodgers beat Yankees in 6), or it's not. Well, hey, let *me* be the bozo to tell you, it's not even close.

Heck, as long as you're listenin', all it's really *got* is the wrongside-o-tracks *miracle* of clubfight boxing (a 40-year bust without a boom-time prayer in Hell) and the Oakland, er, the L.A. Raiders, interlopers still, whose carny-style "antics" have only minimally (thus far) coalesced with H'wood horseshit. The high-flying Lakers, you ask? Fast-break-till-you-upchuck can get bor-r-ring; anything dubbed "Showtime" is just a *show*.

But what the hell do *I* know?

[NOTE: All refs in this section to racism were written *before* Al Campanis spilled the beans!]

DAMON
RUNYON
SLEPT
HERE

NO SE PERMITE TRAER A LA ARENA BOTELLAS BO-
TES O OTROS OBJETOS reads the sign over the general admission entrance and below it BOTTLES & CANS NOT ALLOWED
IN AUDITORIUM, suggesting that if you're Anglo extraneous
objects're cool. I have none on me but the sloppy once over I get from
the T-shirted security person is so unthorough I could probably've
snuck in a half-pint of scotch in my sportjack pocket. It ain't the
intoxicant itself they're concerned about—hey the cerveza flows here
like agua fria!—it's only that empty bottles and cans can do a lot
more *damage* when hurled ringward following an unpopular decision
than a cup o' beer, empty, full or in between. A Thursday night like
any other at the Olympic Auditorium, 18th & Grand, the only fight
club in America with boxing every week of the goddam year. This
must be my 35th trip inside.

A paraplegic with a loud, booming voice sells me a program for a
quarter that is so crudely mass-produced you can see the ink from
the other side, announcing this time a "double main event" of Rocky
Garcia vs. Roberto Torres followed by Roberto Elizondo vs. Norman

171

Goins. No, I've made this mistake before, program person is only birth-defected and cannot walk right (deformed arm & hand and a shave that looks it). Not everyone is buyin' however, an apparent response to the jump in price to ten bucks for ringside (not long ago it was five, the current rate for general ad., and once in while they even had these giveaways of ringside for *one dollar* if you bought it a week in advance), people're saving their coins now for brew. At the beer stand a trucker from the Valley, presumably just seeking contact with an available Caucasian face in the midst of so much Aztlan overkill, borrows my program and finds he's never heard of any of tonight's attractions although he comes here "almost every week—to get away from the old lady." 'S okay though 'cause midway through the conversation it turns out he's never heard of Marvin Hagler, merely the uncrowned middleweight champ and a network TV performer a good five times in the past year. Among Olympic regulars rampant unconcern for the particulars of a given weekly card is par for the course though usually it doesn't take such an, uh, epistemological twist. Beer this week (buck seventy-five for a large) is Coors, in the last couple years it's been Hamm's, Busch, Olympia, Tecate, monopoly seems to rotate on let's say a monthy basis like Pepsi/Coke at the Greek burger place on *Saturday Night Live*.

One thing that never changes is the fabulous decor. Palatial height to the walls and ceilings, not exactly art deco but art *something* you can bet your boots. Framed yellowed blowups of leatherpushers of yore Tony Canzoneri, Ace Hudkins, Mickey Walker, Bud Taylor, the less antediluvian Jose Becerra and whoever "The Popular Sporty Harvey" might happen to be; at Madison Square Garden you gotta pay extra (the M.S.G. "Museum") for a photo of anybody. Lots of dust and grime in every corner and alcove. Peeling coats o' paint, new and old, with non compos mentis color themes (paint is paint). What used to be a classy marble floor, so cracked & cruddy it could currently pass for weathered linoleum, your feet sticking to it from beer than ain't been mopped since 1938. A place that really lets the customers in on its crust and crustiness. In spotless, germ-free L.A. this joint is an existential godsend, been around since '25 but more relevant now than ever.

Program has no amateurs listed, perhaps one of the *welcome* changes wrought by Rogelio Robles, Aileen Eaton's recently acquired partner in promotion. For two-three years the first three fights of the night featured starry-eyed youngsters from local gyms whose main proclivity was holding—holding an opponent's glove with *both* of theirs, for instance, thus freeing the guy's remaining fist to bash their babyface in—fine fun & games for sure (and fewer bucks off Mrs. Eaton's ass) but even the meagerest of pros have a firmer grasp of those parameters of fistic firepower the fans would *prefer* to see. As the first pair of fighters climb through the ropes and dapper ring announcer Jimmy Lennon flips his oversize "coin" to determine who goes to which corner, names on the robes are the tipoff that pros-only is indeed the policy: Jaime Garza (17-0) vs. Lorenzo Ramirez (12-4-2), super bantamweights (122 lbs.), six rounds. Lennon, uncle (or something) of the Lennon Sisters, reaches for the overhead mike being *manually* lowered by a guy all the way up in the belfryish rafters, does the introductions, apologizes for his "bout with laryngitis" and the fight is underway.

Nothing much in the first as each combatant neither finds an opening nor initiates anything approaching an attack, but in round two the crowd comes alive as underdog Ramirez staggers Garza with a combination to the head, burst of life owing to both the former's underdog status and the fact that it's the first anything by either man that so far hasn't missed. Hometown fans're watching and Garza is pissed, recklessly lunging at Ramirez only to be met with a series of shots that puts him on his trunks. Up real quick and *really* pissed, he again abandons all thought of defense (let's end it now!) and is jolted with sufficient low-calibre artillery to upend him for the second time in 30 seconds. It's ruled a slip (crowd boos 'cause it certainly wasn't) but in any case Ramirez is neither powerful nor resourceful enough to parlay his advantage; by rounds-end Garza, having apparently decided to stop fucking up, is back even with his foe. Your typical Olympic prelim, in which the main eventers of tomorrow—or at most a month or two from tonight—are tested by lessers who can at least "make things look interesting," emphasis on *look*.

No real threat but illusion counts for plenty, and after measuring his man to no avail through all of the third and half of the fourth Garza finally capitalizes on an opportunity to end things, connecting with a short something or other (ref was in my way), its impact enhanced by the collision course a sudden burst of mutual wildness has put the pair on. 'S all over at 1:57 of the round and Ramirez takes a l-o-n-g time getting up, prompting one general-admission regular to yell, "Fake! Fake!" (Tank jobs are *not* uncommon). "Still undefeated," announces Lennon to a roar, less than deafening, which echoes through the half-empty building.

More than half actually, can't be more than maybe 3,000 on hand (full it holds 10,000), of which a greater percentage than I can remember ('s been many months) seems Cauc and Asian. Could be the actual body count on these two groups is same as always but the proportion has definitely changed a tad, aforementioned price rise being the likeliest explanation (i.e., white/yellow make more bread). Usual mere sprinkling of blacks and otherwise it's like 97% Mex/Chicano, used to be around 99. In the five years I've been coming here the predominant Hispanic hairstyle has gone from greaser to razorcut/mod but there's still a decent helping of plaster-downs and hardcore DA's, even some oldtimey mustachioed types. Everybody (all races) sports this well-practiced "I get laid a lot" look, a very specific brand of macho you don't get at, say, basketball games at the Forum. Thirteen or fourteen females in the house plus ten or eleven noisy, free-roaming kids (babysitter out of the question). On further perusal I change my estimate to 3,500 (pretty standard without a title fight or at least a title contender) and, avoiding the nearest usher, I move my act down to row G of ringside, five bucks'll still get you far in this palace of punch. The photog guy from *Lou Grant*, Daryl Anderson, is seated a few rows further down (AFTRA strike has apparently not affected his budgetary priorities).

Seat is on the aisle the fighters march down. One of Ramirez's cornermen knocks his bucket into my knee and apologizes—the second overt politeness of the night (Jimmy's laryngitis was #1). String ends abruptly as a handler for Rocky Garcia bangs the same knee with *his* bucket and just keeps walkin'. I pull in my knee for the Roberto Torres entourage and get a whiff of sixteen tons of liniment on Señor T, a sign of who the heck knows what. Stats on this pair of featherweights (126) have Rocky, from Placentia, at 19-0 and fragrant Roberto at 36-4, which you can take with a grain of NaCl as this veteran is, we're told, from Michoacan. Suspension of disbelief is the order of bizness when you're dealing with out-of-towners, let alone out-of-countryers, a suspension borrowed from boxing's companion sport wrestling (handled Wednesdays and Fridays at this arena by Mrs. Eaton's son—and convicted murder conspirator— "Judo" Gene Lebell). Wrestling metaphor is highly apt if you check the back of your program and notice the variety of hype employed: "Boxers from Japan are known for their fierce brawling style. Katsu Okubo is no different and he says he will prove it next week when he fights Cubanito Perez. 'Perez will fall just like his stablemate Frankie Baltazar'"—who you kinda doubt he's ever heard of—"'did recently.'"

In any event Torres doesn't *look* like he's 36-4, unless perhaps the 4 represents his last four outings, and if that's the case he sure don't look like he ever was 36-0. Guy seems beaten and bitter, bitter (1) about *something*, who knows what, down Michoacan way, bitter (2) about having to travel so far just to be done in by some local upcoming cheese. Bobbing and wriggling during the intros like a chicken awaiting slaughter, or a reprieve that as ordeals go can't be too much better, 's no way he seems even faintly preoccupied with notions of victory. Perfect setup (compliments of matchmaker Don "War a Week" Chargin) for a clumsy, untried newcomer with a less than impressive KO ratio (only 10 out of the 19) and a nose that looks like it's been whacked (repeatedly) with a baseball bat.

As expected, Torres is too terminally punchy to be aggressive in any functional sense of the word, but in the first couple rounds he occasionally flashes what might once have passed for skill, going through the motions of meekly one-two'ing at enough key junctures to throw off Garcia's timing and upset his opening gameplan of lunge-and-bull. Settling next into a tactic of waiting to be jabbed so he can counter with awkward roundhouse swats, Garcia is flustered as Torres either doesn't jab at all or he follows his jab with a right (rare as they are, there's a definite habitual purposiveness to the bitter one's surges of interest). In the third Torres momentarily switches to a southpaw stance, either to make it even less likely that the inept Garcia will be able to reach him or (possibly) to show off his sardonic taste for doomsday irony, but when nothing of any import comes of it he simply reverts to "orthodox." No diff that way either— nada worth writing home about. Ditto for the fourth, in which Garcia offers glove-fakes galore that're timidly retracted the instant he needs the glove to guard his puffy face (puffy before the fight even started) and Torres finds himself in the unlikely position of pursuer (somebody's gotta do it) but doesn't at this point seem able to recall the procedure for landing an actual meaningful blow (and appears downright *perplexed* when, almost inadvertently, he *does*).

As so often happens at the Olympic, what loomed as a surefire theater-of-cruelty performance piece has turned out (through its participants' inability to deliver even *that* idealized form) to be something wholly other, perhaps Pirandello by way of Bukowski, maybe pre-aesthetic ghetto street theater, possibly *Fat City* as bumbling improv (or maybe something else). But no matter how you look at it, this is the thee-ate-er bargain of this or any year, Mark Taper and all the Equity waiver pits can go take a flying dump. First round to last, something excruciatingly *cogent* is delivered re the frailties of human endeavor, a real authentic gusher that, locally, only this dungeon of sweat & poverty can semi-automatically deliver, week in/ week out. Oceans of concrete mystery too—like who knows if maybe Torres's reluctance to directly engage in combat is the result of his having once *killed somebody* with his lethal straight right to the adam's ap? It's unlikely, sure, but who the hell *knows*? So I'm tellin' you now (unsolicited testimonial): if you don't come and catch at least a week of this before they tear the place down for a shopping mall, a parking garage, you ain't got no culture that adds up to diddle.

Getting back to the fight at hand, one thing it surely isn't is street*fight* theater. Maybe in a free-for-all (biting and kicking allowed) they could each wallop the daylights out of your little sis, but here & now you'd be hard put to spot anything that might pass for street smarts or even good wholesome street fury. They're just circling in a semi-animated dance whose name is avoidance of danger. Torres, the minimally more adept of the two, is able to consistently avoid heavy leather simply by tilting back out of harm's way, so slow is Garcia to learn from exact repeats of this move (and/ or calculate a workable trajectory against a moving target). At times Torres leans so far back the merest of knuckle sandwiches would prob'ly tumble him like the proverbial sack of taters, but Rocky hasn't the wherewithal to manage even mere.

In the seventh El Michoacano's left eyelid is sliced by a butt (unintentional) and the sadsack registers his dismay in the coyist of post-life manners, as if to say nothing more than *well um y'know*. Time plods on and on 'til midway through the tenth there's suddenly this frozen moment following a particularly laughable do-si-do where they end up in a frontsy-backsy clinch with Torres's left cocked and ready to rip scant inches from Garcia's right kidney. It's cocked through no fault of his own, an involuntary boxing response of ancient derivation getting the better of him, and he's gotta decide whether to retaliate for the butt (ref cannot see so it's really up to him). Shakes his head apologetically—#3 for the night—and lightly (*lightly*) taps the organ. Crowd on my side chuckles and half a minute later the fiasco is over.

"Close but unanimous" decision for Garcia, the second lamest undefeated fighter of recent vintage (Garza is first); some halfassed boos but no one's really complaining. Nor are they throwing money into the ring as sometimes happens following a thriller, this was basic stinksville and the warriors better be satisfied with their purse. Pissing seems indicated so I make tracks for the nearest men's rm. (only two on the whole ground floor—architect was a sadist), foregoing the chance to see if the loser's liniment is still in evidence. Piss line is already immense, folks evidently didn't wait for the stinker to end. Sometimes these things're so long people're doin' it on the floor, in sinks, in garbage cans, whatever's around. Urinary freedom on parade. But naw, it can wait (I convince myself), hobbling down to an even better seat that hopefully don't belong to a pisser away on leave (ushers by now don't give a hoot in heck).

Bell rings for the mainer of the two main events without anyone claiming my "comfort contoured" hard green plastic chair in row C, and whudda ya know if I am not joined two seats away by Olympic Aud. super lightweight (junior welter) mainstay Victor Abraham, on hand it seems to root for his ethnic kin Norman Goins. Both are black. Goins's career has been spotty at best, a goodly number of "KO by"s contributing to his 13 losses in 51 bouts, but back in July he was the fallguy imported for the local debut of Guadalajara hotshot Juan Graciano and it was Graciano who fell (KO 4). Making him an even more attractive fallguy this time around for handsome Westminster hotshot Roberto Elizondo, at 14-1 (12 kayos) the Olympic's resident lightweight heartthrob. Goins in burnt sienna velour trunks with gold satin trim, Elizondo in purple velvet with gold block letters, classiest ring attire of the evening. At the weigh-in this afternoon both weighed 134½.

Not ten seconds elapse before a Latin-tinged voice diagonally behind us yells at the top of his lungs, "Send him back to *Dee*-troit!" Without turning around Victor matter-of-factly corrects him that Norman's from Indianapolis, and the yeller promptly changes it to "Back to Africa!"—which Victor ain't about to take sitting down. His professional fists're raised and a pair of sympathetic Britishers hafta restrain him lest all heck break loose in their laps. The yeller, beaming proudly with friends to either side, is a light-skinned Chicano in pink polyester (gold chains). Hispanics in our section get an enormous kick out of the disturbance and first time Elizondo connects a round of told-you-so "AAAh ha ha!"'s break out with Victor as ostensible target. As the round continues he seethes and I rush to empty my bladder.

Emptying in an adjacent urinal is a swarthy, stocky Hispanic who thinks the fight will go the distance. "You'll see, niggers' heads are too hard, they're very tough to knock out." As I shake off the last drop it dawns on me: what we've got here is a Hearns-Cuevas backlash! Last Saturday in Detroit, Thomas Hearns beat the living shit out of WBA welterweight champ Pipino Cuevas, the reigning glory of Mexican fisticuffs (and my own second or third favorite fighter). After the closed-circuit showing let out in Inglewood some people got stabbed—two fatally—by disgruntled Cuevas partisans equally disgruntled (more than likely) by the 25 bucks they hadda pay to witness their hero's demise. Sociologists would probably wanna add something about competition on the low rungs of the workingclass ladder but anyway this is the first L.A. fight show since that night and—hey hey hey—things could get interesting . . .

By the end of the second round Elizondo's face is lookin' reddish in spots, a sign that either Goins has been landing more effectively than has been apparent or maybe he just reddens easy. At the bell for the third an asshole gets up to encourage Elizondo to "Put the nigger down this round!" followed by the night's first chorus of "Meh-hee-co! Meh-hee-co!" (Which would've been ambiguous or redundant for the previous bouts.) As obliging as he's capable of being, Mejico's man of the hour still has a pretty face to protect, so he just crouches forward with both gloves flat against his forehead—what in Floyd Patterson parlance used to be known as the "peekaboo" defense. Like a chess opening that compels imitation, this posture is instantly mirrored by the trialhorse from Indy, who meets him head to head in center ring, literal tops touching, no way to get flesh on your mitt without going underneath. For the next three rounds uppercuts become the shared m.o., some three-quarter underhands, couple-three sidearms: dislodge that right from your face and pump it somewhere quick.

Human chess is indeed all we're seein', so much for all that Norman Mailer claptrap about primitive masculine rituals under arc lights, this is pawns moving out one or two squares, knight to king's bishop three—the tension may be high but so's the tedium. At least once per round there's a "Get the nigger!" to remind you where the real action is, ringstuff's just a blank slate for the customers to embellish with their own plot of Gippering it for Pipino. In the fifth, as was probably inevitable, an uppercut finally meets a groin, Goins performing the honors, sparking a deluge of "Killll himmm!"'s as knees knock the backs of our Anglo-darkie seats. Revenge for the blow comes in the sixth when Elizondo hooks Goins to the jaw on a break, late, but Goins knows where it's comin' from and doesn't scowl or shrug. Mejicanos meantime read it as stereotypical docility and *eat it up*.

Noise is pretty intense by now and the fighters finally seem willing to partake of the house's recommended level of hostility. Their rhythms suddenly in gear, they swing at one another with the night's first instance of two-way abandon. The younger and quicker Elizondo scores in flurries, Goins in singles but without a miss. Ultimately Norman tries to up the ante and leaves himself wide open for five or six unreturned beauts that put him to sleep with less than ten seconds left on the clock. The bell can't save him ('s the rules these days) and he's counted out. Hell that's been on tap for the past, um, 23 minutes finally breaks loose.

The polyester jerkoff taunts Victor. Victor throws down his wallet, makes moves to remove his $39.95 beige vest-or-something but once again the peacemaking Brits restrain him. An entire row of the jerkoff's buddies are up outa their seats, duking up and hurling bilingual epithets. The UK'er holding Victor's right arm tells the two-three of 'em most likely to tee off exactly who their livid tauntee is—in case they don't recognize—"He's a fighter, are you sure you wanna mess with him?" and really they're not. With only slight ado they drop their fists, their pose and fortuitously opt for non-engagement, sidling as a unit to the nearest exit epitheting louder and nastier than ever. Victor, released by the limeys only after the coast is clear, angrily exits himself. The limeys stay—there's still a four-rounder to go—and so do I (gluttons for boxing).

Gary Vinet of New Orleans, racial ancestry uncertain, vs. Rodrigo Aguirre, less uncertain and he's from Chihuahua. Lightweights again, no records supplied as it'd only embarrass them and you alike (politeness #4). Hold, poke, miss, outa position, no leverage, no footwork; hordes leave with each passing round. Reason even most diehards're staying is to (1) get that last red cent of moneysworth and/or (2) too lazy to deal with the parking lot just yet (or too drunk). Fight ends and even though hardly anyone's actually been watching everyone boisterously applauds—conceivably themselves for their own endurance. Decision to Aguirre (I'm telling you in case your cousin works for his uncle), the whole thing's over by 10:16 P.M.

A relatively harmless evening (no blades brandished or bottles thrown) and now that it's over 's testimonial time again, this time for *sports fans* (theater folks, I'm sure, have already ordered their tix). To wit: you may watch the occasional worthwhile TV fight and you may watch the dregs, but there's a whole genre of fistic thrills and/or swill which you'll find only at the Olympic. No other major U.S. population center has anything remotely like it, I mean there might be some dive in Fort Minor with similar permutations of pathos, passion and macho-gone-cuckoo but not so for New York, Detroit or St. Lou. Sophisticos there wouldn't put up with the stunts they pull here, least not every week of the goddam year.

Look at it this way. It's like getting an invite to open house at the fistic *factory*—you watch bums, non-bums and in between in the process of crudely coming to be (or coming to not)—if it ain't crude, it ain't primal. You'll see washed up nobodies of 22 drag their two left feet from a premature grave to "give it another try"—the human drama of athletic decomposition. Brains, eyes, looks: all laid on the line for *almost no marbles*. How reckless! How poignant! How mercenary on the part of so-called creeps! How what the fucking ever you wanna call it!

Time's a-wasting though, you hear wrecking-ball rumors all the time, this ain't the sort of place they save and stuff and ship to Long Beach—even though it's *the greatest living testament to body madness in all of L.A.* If today's a Thursday go tonight, otherwise wait six days or less as the case may be. Or if you're really fussy you can wait until *postponed to a later date* for Alberto Sandoval vs. Alfonso Zamora, that should be an actual hot one with more customers, more noise, etc. Any longer than that, you ain't got no culture and will die miserable, alone and without benefit of clergy.

THE BOONIES

Hey, I'm just the messenger so don't blame *me*. Message: This is one amazing bush town (sportswise) and I'm not talking bush babies, Bush Tetras or somebody's cunthair. I'm talking bush as in bush *league*; the literal boonies. In most or let's say *many* ways; at least a countable *some*. And those parts of the pie which aren't totally, *thoroughly* bush are often this odd mixture of bush and post-life b.s. (Podunk Meets 1984). And those rare spots where it ain't a variation on bush at all it's just plain generally fucked up, y'know anyway. All in all, a really jive corner of the sportsworld toilet.

Okay. In terms of media glut, number of teams, and resident sports-consumer population, L.A. has to in principle qualify as a major outpost de sport; so far so good. One of only six North American cities (the others being Boston, New York, Philadelphia, Detroit, Chicago) with one or more current pro franchises in each of the big-four team sports (baseball, football, basketball, hockey), L.A. would seem to be covered vis-à-vis criterion no. 2. But take away the Kings whom you might've heard of (they play hockey), take 'em away 'cause they don't by any stretch of the imagination *belong here* (only National Hockey League town without natural ice) and basically *are* here only because the NHL thinks they *should be*, and you're left with three; no big deal but three is less than four. No big deal *at all* you might say, considering the quasi-major status of certain teams representing that local fab *collegiate* duo, USC and UCLA, but (taking nothing away from the Pac-10 in the qual department) therein lies a half or at least a goodly third of the *problem*.

To wit: The time-honored preeminence of college shit in these here parts has made it exceedingly tough for homebred fans 'n' media to grasp the full import of teamsport without all the rah-rah-sissboom-bah. How many years, for inst, did this town have a Lakers before the profeshnal brand of bouncy-ball artistry-in-rhythm finally worked its way out from under the long quaint shadow of the John Wooden Bruins' lesser-version-of-same. Ans.: as many years as it took 'em to acquire Magic Johnson, who in most ways is still shackled with his original media persona as an NCAA primitive/innocent. Or take the Rams, who've only been here like 37 years but who in the eight I've been around have pulled such stunts as the protracted starring role given 'SC shorty Pat Haden and the Chuck Knox offense: three yards and a cloud of "student body right" cliché. (Whereas even the Cowboys—Podunk on *so* many levels, right?—could give two shits in hell about topically tapping SMU for either personnel or style of play.) And for a taste of *bush per se*, lemme just say this is the first NFL town I've seen—heck, I'll throw in the CFL—where paying pro-grid customers appear to *enjoy* halftime shows.

The point being: A town's college dimension (once again, bracket the qual) is not necessarily an additive factor in the overall sporting gestalt. In every other big-four sportsburg, local college hoops and pigskin, if and when they aspire to majorhood at all, do so only sporadically, and only sort of like sprinkles on a cake, never really altering the ongoing flavor of *basic sports perception* or—more to the point—making functional waves re the marketing of *teamsport-as-product*. Bush (at this nexus) meaning: the superimposition of a bill of sports consciousness/consumption particulars that is—for want of a better phrase—*less sophisticated*, in any event less up to contempo sports-evolutionary snuff, than the given sports qua form/fulfillment mind-manifestingly *merit*, leaving this town an easy 20-30 years behind even a scumhole like Detroit in terms of, y'know, eschatological sportish etc.

And woe to the sport, and the team, *without* a college equivalent—so it's gotta cover all that ground itself. Case in point: the so-called Dodgers. Like that's what they're called, y'know officially, but why they even kept the *name* after splitting Brooklyn is beyond me. Nowhere in the annals of franchise shifts has a move been more fraught with intentional discontinuity, more by-design translatable to instant something-else. Well, no, actually there's the St. Louis Browns/Baltimore Orioles, but there you had so-called *shame* to live down. Anyway, before becoming Frank Merriwell U. they were the *Brooklyn Dodgers*: a team that drank more whiskey than milk and never washed its socks; even after the '55 Series they were still "Da Bums." Emmett Kelly (as the *ur*-bum) was semi-official mascot and their yearbook always had Willard Mullin cartoons of some poor disheveled slob.

Not that there was anything specifically "bigtown" about such a trip, or that the *calling card* of grunginess was anything but a matter of familiarity and convenience, but there was something about the whole thing that did smack of casual/urgent workaday-populist whatever-the-hey. Image-*as*-image was not yet something superimposed from above, certainly not as "Dodger Blue" frathouse parochialism (or Steve Garvey/Don Sutton/Rick Monday whitebread-uber-alles), and all stripes of urban rats-in-a-cage could (and did) huddle mass-ively for nine innings of three-strikes-you're-out without feeling put upon to coalesce with any sort of team-mythic I.D. You were all just part of . . . whatever.

The move out here took the whatsoform Dodger soul up the Yellowbrick Rd. to a place where everyone bathed twice daily and was funnel-fed unspiked cowjuice and affable relations with bankers (in seersucker) (on the golf course). Raw, unvarnished rural hick is one thing—the melting-pot Dodgers of Bkln. surely had their quota of same in the stew—but antiseptic afraid-of-its-own-excrement *suburban* hick, the ruination of all life as whatever hypothetical gods could conceivably have intended, is something *wholly other.* (Tom Lasorda's "Dodger in the Sky": a terminally constipated Calvinist with Herbert Hoover posters over the crapper.)

The first time I ever caught a game at Dodger Stadium, built on land where actual human beings fairly recently (in the scheme of things) actually lived their call-it-a-life, some polyester insurance exec told me not to *lean so far forward* in my seat, as I was obstructing his theater-seatish *"pure* view of the game." Now they're not even selling beer in the bleachers, all the easier to keep the prole scum from getting off and getting a little, uh, rowdy. Not that it's a snap even in the upwardly mobile sections to simultaneously cop a brew and a cereal-dog (for balast); in many locations separate lines segregate kiddies (and wholesome-adult eaters-only) from hardline belching beertrash. (Not to mention the fact that the Stadium is the last place on earth where I'm still asked for I.D. Hey, I'm only 38 and can no longer—on my *best* days—even pass for 30!) During the '74 NL playoffs at Shea Stadium an entire section, a good ten thousand outraged Met fans, stood as one to yell "Rose eats shit!" after Pete had spiked Bud Harrelson. If *one person* used the vernacular for doody at a Dodger game, y'know slightly louder than conversationally, there'd be a demi-section of outraged "family persons" telling him/her to *watch yer language*, such being the nature of—and likeliest trigger for—outrage at the So-Cal ol' ball game. (Screenplay by George Orwell; technical adviser, Horatio Alger).

Dodger TV. No home games; selected handful of away. Dunno what it's still like in New York—or ever *was like* in Seattle, Milwaukee or K.C.—but in N.Y. they actually used to televise ninety-plus percent of *everything*, both home and away. As late as the mid-'70s, you'd get every away game but two or three and every home game except maybe five-six of both Yankees and Mets. Having 300 baseball-viewing options per season felt like an approximate birthright, and even more crucial than the obvious *treat* of all those hours of home-screen green (pull up an icy-cold something and *enjoy*) was the direct access you thus had to the ebb & flow of the true unit of baseball cognizance, the season. Without such access—radio plus newssheet writeups the next morning is the frigging 1930s—you don't catch *dick* in terms of a team's actual continuity, reducing baseball consciousness to a level that's fundamentally *digital*. Which is ridiculous for a sport that barely *has* digits per nine-inning monad, forcing you to cherish those moments that fall in your lap, to glue your focus on 'em like they were boxing or something. (Which is no mean feat with Vin Scully, blander than George Peppard, at the mike—and I wouldn't watch the Angels if you paid me.)

But anyway, TV, cable, even the fact that certain Dodger home games're now available on cable hardly changes the *economics* of the game as locally dealt: You want curveballs and sliders, *you* pay for curveballs and sliders. As opposed to, say, advertisers shouldering the home-access burden, like ain't it enough to be a crass consumer in general (of tires, carpets, Farmer John shit-dogs) without having to be a consumer qua consumer of baseball? I mean how many extra billions does that sissy zillionaire O'Malley *need* to get his zillionaire rocks off annually? 3,000,000 live fans ain't enough, he's gotta go for 4,000,000? I may be a dunce, but it seems to me he could get a channel 11 package for the whole season that'd keep him in ties from here to 2012; what's he need, a new cravat for *every remaining minute of his life*? Sure, baseball *is* money—on the field as well as in offices/front—but there's *lotsa ways* to finesse such shit without being a mid-/mod-American scrooge incarnate. In sick/gone capitalist megasuck L.A., Dodger greed is the megasuckiest.

FOOTBALL DIGRESSION—Not that local consumers especially even *want* things free. Or cheap. The Rams, for inst, rarely got televised at home when they still played the Coliseum mainly 'cause they could never manage to unload this one section of seats in time for the blackout to be lifted. The seats, in the *further* of the two endzones, true, but no worse than something for let's say $7.50-$8 at Candlestick Park or RFK Stadium, would go unsold week in week out in spite of their low-low price of two bucks a pop. So what happens, this is like '78 or '79, they eliminate some seats outright (you don't want 'em, you can't have 'em), raise the rest to $10 and *voilà*: sellout city! 400% increase made them *more* desirable. (With thrift as the tune they were tainted merchandise.)

Back to the Dodgers: fuck 'em. For acquiring Rick Monday (for

The Boonies

Bill Buckner, who's been *missed* ever since) just 'cause he stopped
some hellion from setting his Bic to Ol' Glory at a Dodger-Cub
game, summer '76. The hellion chose the outfield for his deed, only
to find outfieldin' Rick's opportunist ire in overdrive. Go ahead,
beat his ass!—and get rewarded w/ the golden op of growing old 'n'
useless in the land of Eddie Albert and Raquel Welch.

Fuck 'em also for two-seasons-plus of not-nice-to-Fernando.
Y'know Valenzuela. First year ('81) his instant appeal all across the
league was in too high a contrast to any trip they could improvise
themselves for exploiting his image to *their* whitebread ends. Guy was
a *natural*, and that sort of thing can be dangerous under any
circumstances, plus his spirit and genes were too goddam *alien*—not
to mention his belly in fitness-sick L.A.—so who knew what sort of
customer such biz might ultimately *attract*? Like it's fine & dandy to
finally have the means of tapping this ethnic consumer pool that's
always been out there in the local ether, one which has gotta mean
instant trillions and all you hafta do is let the floodgates *rip*, but when
you're the *L.A.* Dodgers, not the J. Robinson Brooklyners, even
trillions take a backseat to something, the something being physical
(and cultural) anthropology. Like what if Fernandomania gets so out
of hand you've gotta deal with Mex nationals streaming in from Baja
with their horrible taco-breath and pints of mescal concealed in the
instep of their huaraches, running loose amid (and upon) Stadium
throngs to wink lewdly at receptionists from Covina, to splash acrid
Mex-piss on the sneakers of boyscouts from Woodland Hills?

Don't want *that*, heh, so until they could manufacture *controls* for
the setup they played it phenomenally cool—if not cruelly cold. Shill
number one Mr. Scully, never mr. emotional breadth to begin with,
did these play-by-plays of the rookie's heroics that were even *less*
warm/fervent than is his norm. Every chance he got—to keep the
novelty firmly *in context*—he'd throw in wince-inducing geo-
racialisms like "strikeout *siete*" and "He's really got the *bull* by the
horns." Instead of condemning such shit, the local working press
tripped over itself to ensure that you knew, on ev'ry occasion of the
guy momentarily almost *stumbling*, that "the bubble has finally
burst." Next year ('82) O'Malley, Campanis and company hailed the

bounty he'd dropped in their lap by demeaning him and his agent for not speaka da English, giving him a laughable token raise, waiting 'til arbitration at seasons-end to have *someone else* certify his value (so the taint of fairness would not be on *their* hands) before they would ink it official.

HOCKEY DIGRESSION—And why do people go to hockey in L.A.? They go to hockey, which used to be my favorite sport, because (a) it's white, (b) the fights, (c) it reminds them of the Ice Capades: guys skating around in silly, gaudy outfits. Few people here actually know what hockey *is*, the sport not having been on network (U.S.) TV since '75, and there's even folks who've had season tickets longer than that who still don't know (or care) what *icing* is. A minute remaining, Kings trail by 3—anywhere else the stands would be empty. Here they stay, cheer; perhaps Dave Taylor will hit a grand slam. One of the most inept stickhandlers I've ever seen, Gene Carr couldn't pass or receive the puck (literally) to save his life; his shooting wasn't even *that* good. When Carr played for the New York Rangers, TV colorman Bill Chadwick once commented that he "couldn't hit the water from the pier." Traded to the Kings, howev, he had to 've been one of the two or three most popular players in all the years I've been seeing 'em live. Reason: fast skates, no helmet, blond hair (long) billowing behind.

It hardly bothers the fans that the Kings *stink*, that they're in fact one of the mediocrest franchises in the history of franchisery. Gosh— just imagine!—to be able to not only skate but to skate *on ice* and handle sticks, pucks 'n' opponents *simultaneously* . . .'s tougher than jogging, for inst. Or dry-land racquetball. Not that it's easy for all these Canadians who even *can* do it—not once they've docked in the land of sunny sunshine. You take a youngster from Saskatchewan where the temperature (F) never goes higher than minus-12, he's made a name for himself with some junior team in Moose Jaw and you move him down from the tundra to a condo in Manhattan Beach with surfboardy surf lapping at his frozen feet—you think he's gonna remember, for more than five minutes, that hockey's what got him here? Same deal for veterans, only worse; they'd just as soon *retire* here, the sooner the better. Pandora's box for everyone has gotta be double-triple for folks from Up There. Which means Kings teams have very rarely even *intended* to play hockey...

BASKETBALL DIGRESSION—I'm too lazy to look this up, get the actual dates and stats, but I remember these years even after they got Kareem when the Lakers were consistently outdrawn by the arch-lacklustre Kings. It was probably only marginal, a thousand, maybe 750 average extra customers per game, maybe in fact it was only one season—no, it had to be at least two—but for the Kings to *ever* outdraw the Lakers, even a piss-shitty Lakers-in-transition, is a joke of the sickest whitebread order. All things being equal, a predominantly black team at the Forum has gotta be winning *up its ass* to be turnstile-competitive with sub-.500 whiteys. And without *some* white, even NBA titles won't wash. So now that Mitch Kupchak's knee is a thing of the past, look for Jerry Buss to twist his act into a pretzel trading for white should something happen to Kurt Rambis.

What was I digressing from? I forget.

HOW I
SURVIVED
THE F---ING
OLYMPICS

Thurs., July 19—It won't be easy. Not with all these goddam flags, banners, WHATEVER THEY BE on them poles in the street. Not that they're exactly ugly, or even in fact unattractive; possibly in fact attractive (from certain angles, in certain lights) and *that* is the prob. 'Cause of what they SAY—to locals not tourists—in no uncertain terms: That this scumtown of artifice uber alles, of facade as a Way but not of life, of systematic sensory ruse like there's never *been* a tomorrow, a ruse itself subject, even as it grips without quit or mercy the sensitive flesh of our eyelids, rectums, and unguarded tissues down along the Achilles tendon, to phases of no known (all known) moon(s), to winds which blow any which way but windward (yet can & will blow-is-not-the-word our ass to Kingdom Fuggo); that this place wherein we live or at least reside, which has never for five seconds been kind to our senses (or sensibilities), which has never, even with condo megabucks on the line, had the wherewithal or inclination to give us even *half a block* of non-eyesore/continuous, is serving up linear *miles* of not-half-bad Happy Face, all of which in its lavishly simple not-half-bad-ness is so outlandishly foreign to this town's true ongoing essence as to constitute not only one of the bigger cultural lies of this trashiest of all possible decades but surely *the* most conspicuous gift (of anything) by the least generous of all possible towns, and it surely ain't for *us* (nor, what the hey, is it a gift); serving up same so that rich sissies from Belgium will notice something besides smog, and Beverly Hills clip joints can thus raise the price of gold chains for two weeks, two and a half; all because of a Games that few among us can even pretend to want, that both the *Times* and the *Herald* are finding it exceedingly hard to shill for even *sports*wise, and whose Arts adjunct is looking more & more, in its unfolding cantaloupe-boxed entirety, like an average no-big-deal weekend in New York, Zurich, or Nairobi/Mombasa; a fester which thunders toward us blander than 10,000 Rose Bowls, more joyless (at best) than the last million innings of Angels vs. Seattle *writ large*, something the full travesty of which no sports metaphor can quite cover so what say we try so-called politics, and here we go rolling over & playing dead, quite dead, f'r the fucker: Hey rube! hold that banner high!!

Mon., July 23—"When the U.S. wins, YOU win." I *do*? Really? Well ain't that sweet—it would be a first. Or at least a first for the post-lamebrain-adolescent Me. Last time this wretched counry *did* any-thing—overtly, in the name of officially Doing—that didn't sicken or embarrass me I was like 16 and it must've been like Alan Shepard getting launched for his big fat 3-5 minutes; he had a flattop and so did I. I & I makes for viable I.D.—but U.S. and U??? Mc-DONALD'S SEZ YASSUH, and I get myself a last fuggin' quarter pounder w/ cheese, last ingestion of shit/material for weeks, maybe months, first doc I've seen in 15-16 years says high BLOOD pressure, Jack, time to start thinking (eating) 2 salads a day, every day, for life—thanks, I'll start tomorrow!—and whuddo I get with my farewell to shit but this: a McDonald's 90kg weightlifting card. Which who knows what that is in pounds, but I won't be watching so never fear, I fought in the TRENCHES to evade the draft and *this* is what I get—gold wins a Big Mac, silver a regular fries, bronze gets a reg. Coke-a-Cola (w/ or w/out ice)????

L.A. Is the Capital of Kansas

Fri., July 27—Ten P.M. and all I want is a head of lettuce. Ralphs has got; I will go to Ralphs. Oh no, what is this? The GODDAM TORCH, which has for the last several daysdaysdays been circling around at $3,000 per carry from Oxnard to San Diego, is scheduled for carry RIGHT now between my apt. and Ralphs; let's forget the lettuce. Oh no, sez my truelove gal Maureen, why don't we go see & enjoy the wonderful flaming motherfugger as the (no joke) A.T.&T. rep in blue satin shorts takes the handoff from some equally monstrous corporate goon/geek, a thrill we will only witness once in a lifetime so witnesseth with me, o.k.? *No* o.k., you watch yourself, babe, while I shield my eyes and trot over quick for my vejtable. Wonderful person that I am, I also grab her an imported British chocolate w/ hazelnuts and seek her out amid throngs of redneck yoyos, which is not to say I have got thing one against cultural descendants of the dust bowl, I have got MERLE HAGGARD ALBUMS up the old gazoo, fuck me with a crane but these folks are red-white-&-blue-ing on the fightin' side of *me*. Geez I can't *hack* this shit (Ole Glorys a-waved—"U!S!A! U!S!A!"—by gugs from the Valley or Norwalk or where? . . . and for WHAT? and for WHY? and for WHOm? . . . the Goodyear Blimp circles, A.T.&T. scratches his nuts, the Blimp, the blimp, the BLIMP joining copters more in force per night than used to be the case per—truth! truth!—*per year* and I ain't kidding) so I'll be off, Maureen, observe ye torch yeself and think on this: Were this New York the city, or certain areas of New Jersey, Massachusetts, Connecticut, etc. the states, someone in all this circletime would surely have *doused* said symbol of olympic greed & buttfuck by *now*, doncha think? Plus, Maureen, seeing as how you're an unemployed, underappreciated artist cum actperson drooling assward at the doorway to H'wood, why is it that NOT ONE SO-CALLED LEFTWING H'WOOD BIGCHEESE, f'rinstance J. Fonda, E. Asner, M. Sheen, has forked up the three thou, taken possession of a righteous piece of torch, and hurled the fucker (willy nilly) in the great Pacific sea? I mean fuckaduck, there'd hafta still be *some* party *some*where in town or environs where they'd *welcome* the bustard, give him or her a healthy "toot" up the old schnozzoo, blah blah blah blah gimme a break, I'm dyin'.

I go, she stays; she returns with a story. Old family of Mexicans in beat-up car; leathery faces, selling flags of a nation whose Congress has legislated their status down to that of the cucumber beetle. Their English so crummy the verbal side of commerce is impossible; hard times as well a-calculating change, they hold up traffic, are busted (while flagwaving fascists, loathsomer, noisier as a group than your average Halloween coke party, go free to noise up the night, loathsomely). "That would probably 've upset you, but the torch was *fascinating*."

Unfascinated, I go berserk/bazoony care of upsets older/ primordial. If this was *Night of the Iguana* they'd've tied me up/down, let the rage pass thru me, outa me, *out*. Untied, I spew bile/vile at the walls and windows of every room and closet, louder, more noisome than your average U!S!A!, Maureen's "Why do you hate America?" spurring me to heights of au-contraire-but-the-America-*I*-love-is-barely-even-the-compost-heap-of-etcetera absurdity.

BUD POWELL!...LENNY BRUCE!...HERBIE NICHOLS WHO YOU NEVER HEARD OF!...CAN'T EVEN WAVE MY DICK ON WILSHIRE BLVD!...THERE'LL NEVER BE A STAMP FOR COLEMAN HAWKINS!—till I'm hoarse. (And the damn thing ain't even started yet.)

Sun., July 29—Second full day and I still haven't watched. Caught sonic suggestions of opening-day garbage off neighborhood TVs through windows but did not see (vowing I won't). Saw the *Herald* headline ("WOW"), they must've had W on hold since the last War. A once decent sportsheet, shills for far less than the *Times*, if suddenly they're leading cheers they can go and get fucked. While I drive to Long Beach, perchance to avoid, ignore, evade, y'know be less a *part* of it.

Which is easier said.

There's these *kids* in the street, streets named whuddo I know from Long Beach, underage kids in Olympic t-shirts hawking Olympic programs, main streets of a town, a town not L.A., a Sunday drive: unavoidably Olympic. "What they got down here?"—curiosity never killed no one—my pal Casey asks a hawk tot. "I think," says the hawk tot, indicating *possibility*, "I think it's races." Well it's NOT RACES, KID, well maybe yachting's a race, but not so (as we find out *not* from dumb kids, *not* from liquor store persons or streetfolk on the street—nobody knows!), not so for: archery, volleyball, fencing. Which it's a whole hour before we 'scover by deciphering the cute little "designer" hieroglyphs on various scattered signs & shit: nobody knew. And nobody cares—poor dumb kids have still not sold their 'grams. Tired old Long Beach will thus not be saved, reborn, by minor-event Olympic traffic & trade. So maybe the whole THING is a bust. (Pant, pant; suppressed premature yippee yay hey.)

Wed., Aug. 1—Frenchies, two, buy me beers at Kelbo's and mine my mine, Olympic, mine my mine, ABC. One of 'em's *assignment* is ABC—their coverage of the Games—and the other's, I dunno, he's just a stringer or freelance essayist; both from this French daily, *Libération*, hanging out in a mansion off Hancock Park, rented back when 24 writers were coming, then came the Soviet boycott, number got trimmed to 7 or 8. Prompting me further with offers of passes— they got *so many* left over; something LUDICROUS like field hockey might be bearable—they get me talkin' Jim McKay (who never seemed like a sure bet to get through sentence one, not in 1960, not in '64, not in years divisible by 2, 3, 5, 7, 59, 61, etc.), talking ABC as a sports network (before *Monday Night Football*, when the only football they did was college not pro, ABC was *the* hick network, the Voice of the Farmer—am I *really* this anti-agrarian?—as they remain unchallenged to this day). As swimming or cycling or something flashes the screen above the bar, well I don't know about *as*, I'm continuing my boycott of their JINGOIST POISON so I'm faced the other way—while Monsieur ABC Assignment, facing towards, takes notes on me and it . . . two pitchers gone.

Fri., Aug. 3—Boxing is hard to turn down: freebies. Not from the French but my pal Teenage Rick, who got 'em from his mother, who got 'em from someone she works for or with, who none of 'em (save for me and Rick) wantsa see boxing 'cause they think it's *boxing*. The amateur version is more like fencing with gloves on, but still it's BOXING (my first cultural LOVE) so hey, I'm going. Even tho I've been watching less and less of the *real* version lately, tho maybe that's just 'cause I been working weekends so I ain't had time for it, or maybe because it actually stinks, or maybe who knows; anyway it's free and I'm going.

On a lousy day for driving, so-called Black Friday, max projected traffic for max events—track starts today at the Coliseum, boxing next door at the Sports Arena—but I can't beef about everything, even with the smog so thick the all-new FUJI BLIMP looks simultaneously cubist and misterioso Von Hindenburglike, no contradiction there and I only bring up the latter to intro, gratuitously, Bill Reed's comment on these Games versus '36's: 1936, Hitler's Games, the Triumph of the Will Games; 1984, Reagan's Games, TRIUMPH OF THE SPORTS CONNECTION. But, really, no problem with parking, just ignore the ground-level capitalist pathos of these guys trying to sell you their driveways—"All Day!," 25 bucks, it's enough to make you cry—and park free (all day) directly in front of their house, only 5-6 blocks from the event, a snarly march thru mobs of poster sellers, flag sellers—"Only *three dollars*! Cloth, not plastic! It's *four* inside"—one-dollar soda sellers, dollar-fifty orange juice sellers ($1.50 for a half-size small-size *cup*; I snarl, they snarl back: communion), flags-of-all-nations *pin* sellers; a seller's market and nobody's buyin' . . . boo hoo.

I'd've bought a program tho, a boxing program—if they'd've *had* a boxing program. Instead all they've got is something called *The Olympics Today*, newsprint, three dollars, not much more'n you'd get for a quarter from any of the regular dailies. Which is plenty cheesy, not having a separate program, it don't even have to be glossy or a new one every day—just photos of the participants, vital stats, maybe throw in flags and maps in full color, charge *five* bucks— which I'd gladly 've paid. I *love* programs, have got hundreds of them—Precious Object City—and as far back as I can remember this is only the second time (anywhere) that I've gone live and there hasn't been one. Other occasion was the ultra-laughable Joe Bugner "comeback" fight at the Forum, one of MAPS's dying-ember cards before going belly-up (behind bars)—even those dinky shows at the Pico Rivera Arena where they'd get 100 people outdoors (in summer) they at least printed up one-pagers, hey you *got* to—so, anyway, I've got nothing to remember this fucker by besides:

—3 thousand max (place holds like 17), tourists from Oshkosh and such, first time to boxing, many fatsos, few flags, fewer foreigners;

—an actual bat flying out from down near the ring, up towards the rafters, back down to humans, then *disappearing*;

—a Chicken Man type idiot with chicken suit and gloves, a red, white & blue parody of the boxing kangaroo in that Robert Mitchum/Elliott Gould stiff *Matilda* (1978), prancing and prancing and finally prompting the normally sports-tolerant Teenage Rick (who—this is true—can even stand halftime shows at *basketball*) to proclaim, "Now that is *gross*";

—no acoustic correlation *at any time* between happenings in the ring (too much jabbing; frequent awkwardness; three or four premature stoppages) and fan mutter/mumble, nightclubbish in character even following knockdowns and kayos, "full response" seemingly withheld pending replay (on a magic screen—somewhere—neither activated nor revealed);

—a half-assed "U!S!A!" for a CANADIAN (super heavyweight Lennox Lewis); two hardly rousing but full-assed choruses of same for American super heavy Tyrell Biggs, each discontinued when the big fella, hardly impressive (tho dominant), fails to respond with combinations unsubtle or effective enough to play the Oshkosh Civic;

—a fat German and a fat Austrian (super heavies) who can hardly stand up halfway thru their match, which happens even to fat pros— but this is just *three rounds*;

—compulsory helmets which, lookwise, make it all look like ice hockey;

—Howard Cosell, in Olympic banana-orange, looking like death warmed over at his ringside ABC mike;

—(afterwards) three-dollar flag guy, on same street corner, now yelling: "*Four* dollars! Inside it's eight!"

I dunno, I just don't have FOND MEMORIES of it.

Sun., Aug. 5—Still no TV for me; I don't care about Carl Lewis and I don't care about Mary Decker and I certainly don't care about Bobby Knight and I don't care about dunno, I just don't care. In 1960 I cared, an oh-boy nascent interest in sports—*any* sports—and I watched the entire goddam thing; missed most of '64 (college); watched all of '68 on dope; by '72 I was writing while watching, doing both all day, using TV for trans-content, post-content writerly triggers, shuffling the Olympics in with everything else that was on (but remembering none of it). Since then I've basically just skipped it, having gotten too arch selective about g/Games I'm gonna monitor; '76 I caught 15 minutes, in '80 there wasn't, '84 I don't even wanna *know*. Actually that's not true, that's bullshit, I'm still ridiculously—neurotically—attached to data for data sake; I glance the papers, not quite as thoroughly as a casting director might check out current films but just as obsessively, just to keep my hand in that universe. Just in case . . . what?

So anyway I do read the *Herald*—never the *Times* (an old grudge?)—I buy it every day, throw out the news part, cop a peek at selected sports results. But these 'Lympic headlines have been getting to me, it's getting tougher picking the thing up just to glance it, I mean "Gross Busters"—German swimmer of same name gets beat by U!S!A!—c'mon. Getting to me, but still not enough to make my buy the *Times*; not, that is, till today's headline: "THE NEW MISS AMERICA." I will never buy the *Herald* again. First piece of salable whitebread comes along—Mary Lou Retton—and they write off that cunt-eating Negress (th' old Miss Am) while her photo ain't yet jizz-dry in the grave. Death of a sportsheet—reverting to Hearst "type"—get fucked.

Fri., Aug. 10—Boycotting the papers too, what a nifty guy I am, media-ignoring the what-was-it? (starts with an "O") and now it's almost gone. But the Frenchmen call me and, well, an *experience* is offered & I don't refuse. Event of my choice for tomorrow, Saturday, we'll use a fake I.D. No choice necessary, field hockey is still on: field hockey.

Sat., Aug. 11—But they blow it 'cause some other Frenchman's I.D. got confiscated when the photo didn't match; so they need all the I.D.'s they've still got; so I don't gotta go!

Sun., Aug. 12—'S over and it wasn't so bad and now all these foreigners will go home hating America like it was probably in the cards for anyway and we'll all live happily ever after and the fucking helicopters will finally leave us be.

Tues., Aug. 14—And with this fake bomb-squad rescue thing even the LAPD gets to look like shit so yippee yay hey!!

THE
EVERYMAN
BLUES

A couple years ago I was driving an old pal around L.A., a writer friend in from New York en route to Hong Kong, when he remarked—it was his first night in town, and the day had been hot—how *cold* it was. Well, I told him as it had once been told to me, this is all actually just a desert wetted-down, and deserts, once you turn the sun off, get colder than most elsewheres, once ditto.

It would be colder still, I went on, not to mention hotter by day, if not for the moderating influence of an ocean currently serving little other purpose, having become as unswimmable, as unfishable, as your average full-service sewer. "A desert with a sewer," piped my pal, "what a place!" It was *nice* having a friend, a colleague, around, however briefly, who didn't take offense at my cheery read on things, my delight at the Lie whose throat has been silenced, and insulation *stripped*.

We drove through cold silent this neighborhood, cold silent that; through cold silent theater districts and cold customerless all-night drive-throughs; past cold silent sleepytime sleepyheads in cold cardboard boxes on cold cold skid row cement. We drove on, mostly in silence, until, feeling at last the *emotional* desert chill which is L.A.'s and L.A.'s alone, my companion had had enough. "God, who'd have thought the place could be so . . . forlorn?" He's lucky we didn't take the *daytime* tour of same!

L.A. Is the Capital of Kansas

Day—when sun animates and *illuminates* the desolation, *non-metaphoric* desolation, for wet or dry spectating eyes to BEHOLD.

To wit: For all its swimming pools, "lifestyle" and jacarandas, L.A. can surely be a town without pity, a hot-cold bottomless misery pit for the poor, the past-it, the unattractive and the merely unfashionable . . . and for absolutely anyone on any given day. In due time, in real time, the passing parade will pass HERE.

SILENT
NITE(S)

Three of 'em . . .

South side of Olympic, just in from Hauser, a driver pulls into the first available spot and shuts off his engine facing east. TOW-AWAY, NO STOPPING 7–10 A.M. EXCEPT SAT. & SUN. (in red); 1 HR. PARKING 10 A.M.–3 P.M. (in green). The spot is legit, Sunday before Xmas, 8:35 p.m.; no one in uniform will bother the bloke as he sits and stares at the 7-Up machine (fully lit) across the street.

A red dot separates the 7 from the Up, both in green; a yellow-and-red sunburst pattern completes the design, a jolly and *familiar* design that smacks of the sixties, maybe even the early sixties altho more like mid or late, in any event the *summertime* sixties (it's like 50 degrees—or less—but he isn't shivering). Above and behind the machine looms the Garden of Something—a dwelling of some sort, northeast corner of Hauser and Olympic—the something obscured by a willow type tree but not a willow, y'know whatever you call it. At machine left sits a weathered aluminum/plastic lawn chair and a potted plant that, judging from its placement, would receive nary a ray unless the sun started rising (or setting) in the south. In all directions, not a soul (or sole) is awalk as far as the eye can see; tires hiss by, followed (and preceded) by the standard doppler of cars headed west or east, and the idle of engines momentarily paused (facing west) at the Hauser stoplight.

From beneath the Malinow-Silver Mortuary bench at 7-Up curbside right a white cat emerges with brazen intent to cross Olympic. A third of its death-surge complete, it hesitates, eyes straight ahead, is beeped by a white Toyota (that does not brake) and beats a hasty retreat, disappearing beneath the bench to, presumably, wherever whence it came. To Malinow-Silver right sits (stands) another bench—a big corner, apparently, for buses stopping—this one hyping Murray's Soul Food King, Open 7 Days, Chitterlings (featured). Headlights continue their optical *thing* on the dewy rear window of he who watches.

After 15-20 minutes of hisses, dopplers, 7-Up and no more cat, he (meaning I) steps forth from his bucket seat, crossing (at the green) to more closely peruse the northeast corner. Garden of Eden is what it is, and the coin-op soda dispenser, for all its accessibility, is out of order. Also available (once upon a time) were Coke, Diet Pepsi, Dr Pepper; hand-writ out of order is old and faded, or old and rained on. A good use of electricity (is keeping this thirst landmark lit). Some sort of lobby, Holiday Inn style carpeting, is lit and attended.

He (still meaning I) braces himself against the cool nite air—for which he has ill-provided himself—and wanders eastward, toward the bright marquee one block hence which appears (possibly) scriptlike in its calligraphy. Trodding upon rubber studs imbedded in the pavement, wondering as to their purpose (surveyor's points?), he/I/we pass what seems like a secondary Garden of Eden, one less moderne than the G of E proper but subtly identified as Garden of Eden Rest Home for Seniors (thoroughly deserted). A black-on-white painting of seniors at play squints from the beige facade; it's too dark to tell but what they're playing might be cards. Further on, terminating at the corner of Olympic and Ridgely and marked by an aged and damaged Garden of Eden 'lectric sign (oval, unlit), a faded umbrella poked thru a metal tabletop, and equal desertedness, is yet another once-operative edifice in the Eden family of fine homes for folks, the geometric pattern of its pink cinderblock fence whispering "no" to would-be intruders.

At eyeball distance—other side of Ridgely—the script is clear: The Intermezzo. Fussy looking trees and shrubs out front, one of 'em (tree) totally dead and groomed like in *Flash Gordon on Mars* (the serial with the Clay People), its meticulously truncated branches fatter than most trunks and at least half the diameter of this one's; maybe that's why it had to die. Traffic keeps hissing, but nary a muh-fuh out walking so much as a dog, nor are dogs (anyfuckingwhere) walking (or barking) themselves. Backtracking to Hauser, I and my clinging loneness notice no more than before, only the modrin bench area fronting Garden of E #1 (which was noticed but not noted—one long elongated red strip of *bench*) and the illuminated bus stop enclosure at southwest Olympic/Hauser, hyping tonite (and for the foreseeable future) *The Dark Crystal*.

So as not to *miss* anything, a right at Hauser is walkingly hung: Miracle Mile sign (gateway to excitement; white on blue); Garden of Eden parking garage, containing 1 (one) white sixties Cadillac and 1 (one) beat blue Datsun. Oh yes, the lobby light has by now been switched to off—it's 9:05 and seniors (as we all) are in need of rest...

"Show me the sound of one hand clapping & I will personally show you a man outside a Burger King, finished with his meager though wholesome repast, continuing to sit among the leavings of his take-out order that he might (in solitude) glimpse the hand-painted Xmas design on the windows and, weather permitting, snow on the ground" (Robert Penn Warren).

Monday before Xmas, 10:02 p.m., Burger King on Wilshire, couple blocks east of La Brea. Whopper with cheese, small fries, no drink. Inside: Xmas tree with lights (on-off string of white; separate, yet hardly equal, string of red...green...red), low-sheen paper streamers, red, fat guy in a yellow T-shirt, cheerleader type girl in light blue, prancing, pacing and kicking up her visible thighs, chubby. Outside: windo-rama of Santa and his merry deer, upper section of the Four Star marquee, Lena Horne/*Stormy Weather* (now playing), white Robbery Prevention vehicle, tall male in tan hunting jacket (entering).

L.A. Is the Capital of Kansas

As the dimensions of his Whopper inevitably diminish, catsup spilling on his jeans and tomato on his shirt, our eater finds (quite to his liking) that his elbows have finally gained room (to maneuver). The driver-side window, which during daylight use would be open, thus allowing his left wrist and forearm to more casually swing and sway, is tightly closed; it's c-c-cold out there, and only slightly less so within the space he has unfortuitously chosen to gobble his meal, a space a few timely tugs at the dashboard panel would surely have warmed (but such is life). In midprance the cheerleader cuts short her number, her jello-y gams still quivering, to lasciviously—or merely curiously—peer out at he (handsome) who has taken-out but not gone home. Roy Orbison's "Only the Lonely" plays neither loudly nor softly from a California radio or juke; he who chooses to dine alone is often *alone*; tan huntsman is at least alone *inside*.

Burger ingested, mr. outside reaches for his final fry, only to find (fate is cruel) that the last of the fries has gone the way of the next-to-last and the last-but-two. Large fries (and even a drink, as he is thirsty) would have been a smarter move; next time (if only he remembers) he will purchase *wisely*. He continues to sit—go home to *what?*—and is rewarded by the sight of fatgut in yellow splitting the King, walking to the nearest receptacle, depositing a rolled up wad of mostly paper, returning inside. Is Roy Orbison singing (anywhere) for fatgut in yellow?

Cheerleader takes another look, her last; handsome person, altho finished, remains in the lot. In the lot, nose towards the King, he hadda back *into* the spot (which no one ever *does*) she is thinking. She is also (perhaps) thinking *if Dad doesn't get me that moped for Xmas I will throw a shit-fit* or (less likely) *I wish this attractive whiteboy would take me to Sacramento where Aunt Edith has a condo and I hear the TV is really neat.* It is 10 something—and she's still staring—as goodlookin' possibly-me turns the key and heads out for whaaaaaa . . .

In an undreary apartment off Third Street, not far from La Brea, there's this guy sitting on his hands (figuratively; actually, he's lying on his back) a-waiting, waiting, *waiting*. He is tired, weary, almost dizzy, and could use at least a nap tho it is only 7:43; he has had a busy day, and the several beers he's downed (in the course of writing; he's a writer) have not helped matters vis-à-vis remaining awake for the *nite ahead*. It is the birthday of a loved one, and something (tho he is hardly sure what) is in the offing. Several options have been discussed, including the 8 o'clock showing of *Time Bandits* and *Monsignor* at the Pan-Pacific, altho right now that seems far from likely, unless (that is) she shows up in the next five minutes. She (no one you know, so don't ask) is the raper of time, the disregarder of time (public) like nobody's uncle; she sets her own (physical, mechanical) clock an hour and twelve minutes *ahead* while her emotional clock straddles the ether. He no more, no less *expects* her to show in five, he hastens a guess, than to appear at his door in time to make *That Championship Season* (option #2), 10:25 in Westwood. She is *out somewhere*, unreachable by phone, sequencing two-three interactions (of which he represents the fourth) as if they were co-temporal trifles, spanning (in toto) no more *real time* than who the fuck knows what— in any event, *small time* (she thinks), while meantime the world's public clock, and this guy's biological ticker, keep right on ticking. Tho he has come to no longer take these things *personally*—numbers 1 thru 3 are as likely to be *fucked with*—still he cannot help feeling shortchanged.

At 9:17, the Tuesday before Xmas, he (meaning him; this could *never* be me) arises to shave. It is more than an hour since he showered (clipped his nails, both finger and toe; applied Old Spice Musk for Men to his pits; replaced the day's shirt with a fresh one she is fond of) and the razor scrapes his face, twice drawing blood, the beard-softening effects of his shower having long since subsided. He aftershaves (the scent of which she's also avowedly fond), styptics his wounds, prepares a pot of tea, perchance to caffeinate his tiredness and give his pathetic waiting some renewed vigor. For the first time since he bought a tin (along with a teapot, his first) at the People's Republic gift shop in Chinatown, the jasmine doesn't taste like soap. Water-to-tea ratio is finally all right, if (however) not in the wake-up range, and he returns, mournfully, to a bedwise supine mode, contemplating the twin bedlamps' reflected glow in the turned-off TV, the curvature of the doorjamb as refracted by his specs (which perhaps should be replaced by his contacts, tho his eyes are *shot*, as such a transition is often half-enough to jolt him from semi-slumber), the fact that the heels of his socks are grayer than the toes . . .

Is this any way for a thirty-seven-year-old, one who has known *many* women and no longer particularly regards them (as such) as a *threat*, to prepare for a date???

As the hypothetical *Championship Season* deadline nerve-rattlingly approaches, he recognizes his earlier reluctance to visit the Day & Nite Teller of his local bank—his wallet is empty—as clearly a mistake; tho he might have missed her in the process (and missing, after so much waiting, would have totally defused the *nobility* of the wait), he will now have to rush like a motherfucker to withdraw cash and still make it to Westwood for the opening credits (she, an unemployed yet reputedly talented actress, considers credits de rigueur professional *reconnaissance*).

On his back, a preferred grouping of pillows supporting his throbbing head, he listens to his breath, *counts* his breaths when merely listening begins to prove boring, stops counting when counting becomes boringer still. He farts a couple times, wondering (in abject terror) whether the tenant a wall away can hear. Tho jazz and reggae often fill his digs with joyful sonic mystery, no music of any sort now issues forth from his speakers (what to *select*?—one wrong choice and he's *doomed*), the disco-funk bass line from the apartment below rattling the floorboards like a digital telltale heart (what to cover it *with*?). A paperback Céline, only 20 pages read, beckons from the nitestand, but black type on white page would prob'bly kiss his waking ass goodnite, and—hey—it's only 10:36, still plenty time for a late-nite birthday snack at (Canter's or) the Figaro.

Jesus Christ (whose own fucking birthday is itself but four days away), *why don't they just kill me*, he is thinking, *why don't they wrap barbed wire around my face and yank from both ends; why don't they strap me tight with bonds of (flexible) steel that snap my bones, dislocate my shoulders, crush me like a goddam twig and get it over with.* In the last year of their relationship he has been stood up (like this) once, twice, fifty times, but it is not being stood up (per se) that makes him feel lower than pus on a slug; it is the realization that, as spoken by the one he *loves*, yes has come to mean no more than maybe, which has all too often come to mean nuh-nuh-nuh-no. Never, until rather recently, could he have entertained the dire thought that *this one*, the love of his goddam *life* (no less), would stand a chance of surpassing the infamous Lynn Deegan for mind-thudding, soul-thudding *unreliability* (a no longer implying b, c, q or anything in the fucksucking alphabet); tonite (at 11:53, officially) she has finally, indeed, surpassed.

At 12 oh something (a.m., Wednesday before Xmas—lights-out plus several minutes) r-r-ring goes the doorbell, as his fucking truelove arrives with warm (and edible) snackshit from Pink's.

...AND CRAZY FOR LOVING YOU

There's this woman I used to see a lot, no what am I saying, I've seen her four times total, on Wilshire. Twice I'm walking and she's walking towards me, well I don't know it's towards me till she actually gets there, shopping bags and ripped stockings and I don't really pay her no notice, not till she plants her feet two strides in front of me and there she is. Sez: "When are you gonna marry me?"— neither insincere nor sincere, diction tiptop, w/ bitterness or irony or both; an old crone (= female geezer), not particularly shabby or unshabby, not exactly a bag lady in spite of her bags, late 60s or thereabouts.

Without missing a beat—sometimes I'm fast in my shoes—I tell her "Not today" and I don't regret it. Could've regretted, like if I was a real cad or something I'd've been p.o.'ed not having said something *nasty* like f'rinstance "Haw haw hey, I would rather marry, um . . . um, like y'know this, uh—that's right—this here *clump of cement*, granny." Said nothing of the sort, just a simple, witty 2-word reply that smacked of neither condescension nor rejection. One of the things I really *like* about myself, y'know these days when I kind of hate myself left & right, is I'm still capable of being supremely kind—as well as laugh-a-minute spontaneous/creative.

So I guess I just filed it away, somewhere in the circuits, 'cause months later when I see her again, same exact spot, she asks the same Q and I give her the same exact A—*instantaneous*. Like this time there's no question of option, nasty or whateverwise; 's automatic. Third time tho it's summer, I'm wearing cutoffs, and she's got a new one for me, delivered unambiguously rude in *her* own right, one I have adequate response for neither on the spot nor thru the marvel of months t' think about it: "Your pants are too long." Rather a good'un—doncha think?—and what's a gent t' say? Anyway so it looks like she's actually got a repertoire, subject to seasonal etc., until fourth time a week or two later—same pants, same spot—she's back in a re-peat mode and (dadgummit) so am I: " . . . pants . . . "; " . . . "

So you might wanna say she's a 2-track person, just leave it at that, meanwhile ya got' admit we're a real neat matched computer combo—oughta take it to Vegas or the Convention Center. Prob'ly tho you wan' me tell ya the lady's nuts, bananas, a genuwine *crazy person*; is that what you want? There's no limit to the hoops I'll run thru for you, so okay yes she's crazy, she's crackers, fucking nutso in my unprofessional opinion; I'm writing her up *because* she is nuts—satisfied?

And I'd follow her for you too, take a look she's maybe (already) got a wedding ring, possible additional poetic reads on the marry-me bit and etc., only I ain't seen her sour face since Aug. or so. Better bet for tailing would be:

THE MAN IN THE MELTZER-GREEN HOUSE

This guy, maybe you've seen him, he's around a lot, Beverly, Wilshire, 3rd St.—'tween Fairfax and La Brea. I've never seen him west of Fairfax or east of La Brea. White shirt, paper(s) in hand, nearly always a big fugging smile on his quasi-unshaved mug; wild eyes, he's got 'em. Mid 30s? Waves his arms sometimes—like he's trying to cast off his hands at the wrist. Does interesting public stuff like grab a handful of tickets, rip 'em up *real good* (County Museum), sit around 'n' talk to himself while lines of uptight customers gawk in fear 'n' amazement (Crocker Bank). Nobody ever tells him to stop or not do it here; nobody ever talks to him nohow.

Ain't talked to him (yet) myself—there's time for that eventually. Have made eye contact howev, he don't spook *me*, only reason I haven't attempted to exchange utt'rances is you know me, I'm basically the shyest bloke you've ever met. Me talk to strangers? C'mon—ain't it enough I write you these won'erful *entertainments* semi-regularly, formerly regularly? Can't do it all but I'm trying. Soon as I overcome my cat-got-my-tongue around strange'uns you'll be the first to know. Meantime lemme just tail this guy for ya, starting at his home.

Corner of Xth and Pgwuyi, that's *code*—decode it, you're sitting pretty for a tail job of yer own. Lawn: elevated up off of sidewalk, brick front, stone stairs lead to elevated walk. House: post-deco, well preserved, light green of a tint employed in the pre-acrylic paintings of the author (1962–64). A *class* joint, piss elegant and then some; happens in "the best of homes"—inotherwords. Crazypeople: fine homes have 'em. This one has one on the lawn.

Driving, wheeling, automotive up Pgwuyi—I spot the holy sacred sumbitch on his back. No screeching tires, I continue up the block and circle, pass the class address one mo-time, pull a "U" and park where nearest available, clear view of krazy muthafucka—inclined on butt, heels, elbows, *grassy*. He is not smiling; has the World got to him? Arrow shirt (or one of *those* brands), pink f'r a change, blue-grey slacks, face somewhat *dirtier*, or perhaps less *shaven*, than usual. Has the world gone to shit in a bucket? Envelope, possibly a letter or (author guesses) a junkmail, held not waved in (suspect's) left hand.

Gets up, peruses traffic left . . . right, sees me, spots me, eyeballs aligned but . . . nothing, smiles forced: none. I dunno, if I'd been feeling smily (that aft.) maybe grins or sparks 'd've triggered some sort of *shared experience*—guy'd've smiled too, love and/or friendship & universal mammal *something* would've opened them floodgates, many minutes of mutual wutsa followed by I finally break that interpersonal strangeperson ice, converse w/ (or speak at) him and

he speaks at me. And I tell you what he said and—more important—
I *hear* what he says, i.e., get t' know the nature of krazystuff, verbal.

Instead he disappears behind a tree—a man must pace . . . or is he
avoiding? *Please* don't be avoidin' me, mister krazy, I'm more
harmless than your muther and dad; look what I'm here in the car
for, *reading a map* for crying out loud (author takes out his Thomas
Bros. and pretends to investigate South Gate; boy is he lost, no
danger in *this* rube!). Reemerging from arboreal shadows, mr. k, no
life-stinkser after all, smiles, he's smiling, he's . . . well he smiled for a
second, went neutral. Eye contact: minimal, momentary, feeding
back in neither direction. Two glum guys, c'est la (call it a) vie.

Sits down and leans again, y'know *him*, gets up, examines the
ground beneath where he sat. Pieces of something, what's he got
there? I take my binocs, only kidding, they were stole when my
house was burglarized in '81, binocs not needed, pieces of . . .
ballpoint. Musta fell out, he rescrews. Gets up. Goes inside, door
isn't locked, they don't lock him out, he don't need a key. Welcome
in his own home—that's nice. If y'knew *where* you could go in
yourself: Xth and Pgwuyi (yours for the taking!). What a disappoint-
ment tho, performance was *nowhere*, lamest show of public oompah
by a formerly reliable kr-razy fuckin' guy (take my word); didn't
lead me on a tour of banks, museums—what shit.

And fuck, what am I gonna do now for a column, my first since
being demoted to once a month, now that it's me against *three* of
'em—not just vs. the everpopular Steve Erickson, did I spell him
right? (And damn, why am I always thinking in this *adversary* frame?
Why am I such a *hostile* putzeroo? Can't I learn to live in *harmony*
with my so-called peers f'r a change?) I am one mis'able wretch but
still I need a column, this one's too short even if I flesh it out with
"insights" and they run it 12-pt. type; no way either will they take
another "old girlfriend" piece—not for another 2-3 months or something.

So I'm at the bank, the automated teller, withdrawing for to
shop—food—perchance to fat out like a hog, when who should
happen by but

NAMED FOR ALICE KRAMDEN?

and her mom; a miracle. Usually it's her alone, sometimes both. But when you *need* 'em like me it's a miracle—thanx a heap. If this isn't tail meat—and I'm not talking "asses," not using meat "sexually," more like heart o' the matter: ain't it *nice* to see language twisted subtle 'n' metaphoric by a writeguy who knows how?—then my name is Edgar Flug. It isn't, nor is whatsername's actually Alice K, read on and you'll get the connection, maybe I'm spilling the drama but I am not Tolstoy, what can ya do?

Blonde daughterperson w/ mom! She: bleached or dyed, not quite platinum, aged 22–35—but I've been saying that for the last 8 years. So let's just say she's *eternally* 22–35, you couldn't call her 30–43, well maybe 28–38, okay: 27–40. 'Cause she *is* lookin' older, her 'brows—not dyed recent—are starting to grey. First time I saw her was buying a soda, trying to make the 35 cents or whatever at some taco stand on Beverly Boulevard. This was maybe late '75, one of the first neighborhood females I noticed after moving into this dump on Genesee. She was having trouble coming up with the change—all pennies—counting 'em again & again—and I'm thinking I could maybe contribute pennies, nickels, dimes of my own. A way to meet gals, then I notice she's nuts or neurotic, something in the way she's eyeing the pennies, *very* neurotic or just plain nuts.

Or maybe non-generically drastically poor, unemployable on account of ???, and so unsomething on account of the poor that in turn she's ??? to the point of she's *nuts*. But not terminal, nothing that $19,000 and a couple hundred visits to a reputable shrink couldn't reverse in terms of confidence w/ pennies & cetera. So I figure—call me mr. ulterior—this is not a 22–35-year-old I wanna meet *just yet*. I keep my coins, see her around now and then, then finally after seeing her mainly with her mom it dawns on me how come she was short to begin with: skimpy allowance! Mom: wicked witch of the (Beverly-Fairfax) north; mean looking, mean talking, taller than blondie—and mothers're usually shorter. *Emotionally* stunted growth—the worst kind. Poor blondie!

Anyway I'd see them together shopping and more & more they

seemed like a matched pair of not exactly goony-birds but *something*. Old nervous wreck barking out irrational commands, young nervous wreck hesitating—machine clicks on—complying to the best of her ab. Lots of universal parent-chile trauma, the kind that always drives me up the wall and here it was stretched to asymptotic infinity; plus something *non*-universal, specific to the screaming need of their particular bond, sort of like blondie's this poodle or something—a *pretty* dog, but mostly the result of excessive ritual *grooming*—and mommy's got the leash. The traumatized chile in me would always wince; rest of me, *part* of the rest of me, would stare fascinated. *Dig this trip*, I've always dug it, and here they *come now*, just when my write need is screaming loud as whatever else: blondie w/ shopping cart! mom at her side! northward on Fairfax as I'm out there withdrawing $$$.

Wow yes they are shoppin', cart/wagon/whatsis (2 wheels) is even empty, shopping has not yet begun so wow wow wowee—lemme jus' get my withdrawal and proceed to follow! Stick like glue!!—ring my bells!—but the goddam machine takes its time and they're crossing Bev'ly, they've crossed, light goes red, I lose sight just as the bucks come. I run like a demon to catch the next green, still don't see 'em, whoops they're at a bus stop, bus arrives, it was short & sweet (apparently). But they don't get on, just flounder around, and I huff & I puff, look 'em straight in the eye, too huffed & puffed for strategic concealment, diversion.

They've seen me lookin', what the hey. Then I follow them across Fairfax to *their* bank—great day f'r banks after all—and take a breather while mom withdraws (or deposits) (or transfers funds). Blondie meantime sits patiently, well maybe not but more or less *still* on a couch by the door, hands on her cart while I scribble in a pad on a bench by a flagpole. Philip Marlowe I'm not, 'cause just as I'm finished scribbling and look up they're exiting side by side, eyes straight ahead ('cause why not?)—straight as an arrow at *me*. Should've sat at an angle (I'm a writer not a dick).

Eye for detail tho, I notice mom's bright lipstick, color they used to call fire-engine red, black slacks, shoes and jacket, hepster shades (of a sort), sandals on the daughter, bandaid on one heel, prefaded

215

matching jeans & jacket; coffee-carton cardboard at the bottom of the cart.

Back across Fairfax, keepin' my distance but making the light. M. and d. enter Bargain Fair where I once bought a bowl (that cracked in a week—heat due to soup). Would be nice t' see what *they* are buying but I jus' know I'd totally blow any attempt at a close-quarters in-store tail. No better at peeping from outside—lotsa glass, no cover—I'm forced to scamper when they round an aisle headed directly my way. This is maddening, embarrassing, I'm a *very* crummy Marlowe. 'S my old neighborhood tho—and I still bank here—so I ain't too peeved having to play it safe & cool peeking in other familiar windows on the block, waiting out their purchase before following 'em home (or wherever).

I look in Merlo's, second seediest supermart in Greater Hollywood, in Honest Max's (which used to be a drugstore) and Emil's Shoe Repair, I step inside Merlo's and out to the unfinished furniture joint, I avoid a guy I know from punk shows by ducking in an alley, I stay in the alley and check my watch. Ten minutes killed and I still don't see them. Mebbe missed them, y'know inside Merlo's, it'd be just my luck, then I hoof it to Bargainville—there they are at the checkout. Blondie holds up some sort of red plaid thing (fake wool or woolen), ma shakes her head. Back in the alley, five minutes pass, what goddam indecisive shoppers. Couple mins. more and I opt to throw caution, step inside blindly—right into them stepping out.

Body contact, unavoidable, I brush between 'em, eyeball to eyeball, four of theirs to two of mine, too spooked (me) to gauge their response. Mainly it means I've gotta fake like I'm in the store for something, brief but not too brief, I'll pretend it's ballpoints—sorry, *not today*—and spin for the street. But they're floundering again, didn't really need to rush; as they're almost about to cross they reconsider, well maybe not *this* light, uh . . . make up your minds already. Suddenly they're stopped, frozen in mid-nothing by this store person sticking her head out & yelling them back for their purchase. Small bag, real small; easy, no doubt, to forget. Too tiny for wagon, blondie pockets it, but this time for sure they have SEEN

ME: coming, going, sideways and frontal—and also I've seen stuff in them.

Fear, suspicion, either or both, insect fear, rabbit fear, reptiles and little kiddies and fawns. Awareness of danger—or somethin'—something palpable, smellable, tastable, uh oh: something. Primitive, primordial—nervous system sez *go*, flee, fuck outa here *nòw*. So they take their flounder east instead of south, I stand and watch as they snail it east over Fairfax *then* south across Beverly, this time I'll give 'em some distance (feelin' *bad* about scaring them), kinda know where they're headed so why spook them—needlessly—to smithereens?

'S gotta be Ralphs they're aimed for, the route is right and I've seen them there anyhoo, Ralphs at Fairfax and 3rd. So I hop in my auto, windows still open, doors unlocked, in the bank parking lot, forgot about that in my 'riginal haste but nothing 'cept maps worth stealing. Snickering how easy this is, I pull into the Ralphs lot pointed north, clear view of the only possible approach I can 'magine them taking. 20 minutes later I'm thinking I've been had—they're smarter than me, or more scared than I reckoned, maybe they just beat it home. But that shopping cart, these people are function over show, shopping instincts are strong ones—they must already be inside Ralphs. Like they took a scenic route, sneaked around me, they're in there and I need some stuff anyhow.

Mustard and things. I'll get Gulden's, some yogurt. But I'll navigate carefully, taking each aisle slow, so I take half an hour and *nothing*. Faked me out, those sly ones. Well, heck, at least I got to know 'em a little better; nice people, I *like* them.

So out in the lot I'm signing some "Jobs for Peace" petition when the guy asks the next passerby "Would you care to sign . . . ?" and the passerby—passing behind me—IS: blondie! & mom! Hey y'know it *pays* to like someone—they will always come to *you*. So I run my yogurt to the car, they didn't see me this time (just my back), and I *know* it is K-Mart they're shopping, same lot, bigleague version of Bargain Fair, shoulda guessed it was bargains not non-discount staples they were after.

But what took them so long? Snack at the Farmer's Market? Too gratuitously expensive. Cart still empty, hmm, and three quarters of an hour gone by. Perhaps some *hardcore* rerouting, evasion, I'd better play it *real* safe. Like whatever that could mean anymore—I've been blundering all day. And what am I looking for anyway, intending to *do* f'r chrissakes? Whuddo I fucking *want* from these people? They haven't even exactly *behaved* like the mother and daughter I've known, not today—no wicked witch, no leashed poodle. But then again I've never been so conscious of me-and-them before, so *self-conscious* around 'em, so skittish in their presence that I'm not seeing jackshit, not acting altogether. . . sane. Or is it just more of that shy shit of mine pulling its number, keeping me from, I dunno, walking up and asking them 'bout red plaid things and the price of dust? Just dunno.

Into K-Mart, I scoot around snaggily, scooting, darting 'cause they're hard to linearly follow—this is their element, shopping, not crossing the street. Run into 'em on the price-reduced matzo aisle, the instant iced tea aisle; they don't seem to notice me nohow. I was dead wrong, miscalculated my effect on them—which makes me feel a little sad, alien—or can they simply turn it off and on? On-off but outside their control? Specific (but not currently present) triggers? Variable sensitivity? In any event: neurotic ballparks that smack of home, my home, me—alien feelings vanish but still I've gotta *do something*.

Finally they're on their own last roundup, mine anyway 'cause I can't take much more of this, they're shopping the K-Mart outdoor superduper "street sale" and I brush against mom, *intentional.* "Excuse me" I say, "Excuse me" she says too. Sees me right on— nothing. All that insect/reptile b.s.—my own (florid) imagination. Goes right on with her bizness, "How much are the paper towels?" A *benign* voice, almost sweet. "Audrey" she calls—so that's her name; did ma watch *The Honeymooners?*—and that most assuredly *is* sweet. Audrey I seek out and almost face—with ulterior sexual not-much; mammal innocence or some approximation—but just cannot do it. I settle for the back of her hair. A whiff: Johnson's Baby Shampoo.

Sun is setting, I'm lonely, curiously "uplifted" but sad, oh so sad, unto tears. Yogurt well on the way to rotting, I speed home; where is the love—any love—in this here world? Are Audrey and mom the closest approx. of the closest it (familially) gets? And boo hoo for the author, readers don't like him, they send him hate mail, call his phone, say "Kill your ass" and he thinks it's *universal*, sez something somehow about Life. Once a month column—hate mail cut in half. "Love" from readers—"respect," "appreciation"—is this what the poor boy wants & craves? No—just (if you can swing it) leave me alone. Jus' lemme write this shit; who knows why I write it.

All I know—or can imagine knowing—[HE SAID] is these are my peers. Audrey Jr. and Sr. If only I could (ahem) someday talk to them, if only, if only. . . then what? Fuck if *I* know, I'm just trying to end this lousy piece.

'TAIN'T KILLED ME YET

Anyway, it's home. Obviously I hate the place, but I seem to recall hating that other place—what was it called? (starts with an *N*)—as well. Livingwise, home is an overrated concept. Anyone expecting redemption *at home* is fucked from the start to, uh, finish.

So let's just say it's my office. Best office I've ever had. With so few distractions, so damn little I might actually wanna *do* out there—outside my walled, windowed apartment cum personal *office*—I stay inside most days/nights and get things done. Writing things, inner monologue/dialogue things, the "works." In Paris (or somewhere) I'd be too strongly tempted to go out and cop a croissant.

So I stay. Where's to go anyway? Cleveland? Unless you know something I don't, it does not appear to be much of a planet, a world, for living places. Certainly not for alternate offices.

And outside my office window, right out my *typewriter* window as I finish up this wonderful book, three residential whatsems are right now being demolished, three nice, okay two-story brick buildings that would otherwise, barring etc., have stood for (rough estimate) the next 200 years; reduced to brickdust so that flimsy condos may stand in their stead for rich out-of-town fuckos who caught last year's Rose Bowl on NBC, oohing and aahing at the color-enhanced images of skies-over-Pasadena and thinking, gee, a home in Califawnia would be *so neat*.

Well, fuckos, if you're coming I can't stop you. I hate your kind but I tell you what. I'm feeling magnanimous; lemme tell ya what you're in for that I ain't told already. First, the Italian food *stinks*. Really a joke. 'S what happens when you have no Italian neighborhoods. Italians, yes, but no street on which three consecutive dwellings have Italian-American habitation. Unless Dom DeLuise lives between Annette Funicello and Don Ameche. (And I don't think he does.)

And then, well, maybe you've read some Chandler. You've read Raymond Chandler and figure wouldn't it be a *kick* to "see Chandler's L.A." They've even got maps of that stuff, y'know like which building on Franklin Ave. might've been Dolores Gonzalez's address in *The Little Sister*, or the parking lot in Beverly Hills where Philip Marlowe picked Terry Lennox off the ground in *The Long Goodbye*. Those are good books, I don't exactly consider them Great American Fiction anymore but I did once regard them, 7-8-9-10 years ago, as more or less infallible *ciphers* for this place.

But not anymore. Too much of Chandler's "eternal L.A." has been digitalized beyond recognition, or buried under the relentless weight of non-related digital bulk. I mean sure, the police state shenanigans go on and on (LAPD chief Gates' final solution to the homelessness question: lock the bastards up!), and if you've got a downstairs apartment the sound of an *L.A. Times* delivery at the crack of dawn will wake you as it did Marlowe in '43. But the mystery & hunger of Place, of every last palpable nuance of Locale, so central a theme to Chandler both literarily and metaphysically, no longer really *plays* in these parts except as nostalgia.

And by nostalgia I don't mean "nostalgia," some easy-access pop-surface ripple or wrinkle; I mean . . . archaeology. This shit has gone *deep*. A couple years ago, half a mile from my house, er, apt., a bargain clothing store exploded, blew the fuck up (with customers within) on a Sunday afternoon. Apparent cause: escaping gas from *improperly capped oil wells*, abandoned as unprofitable during the thirties, over which *many portions* (but which?) of the current "city" presumably sit. And Chandler even *worked* for oil companies, right? But this stuff's rare, and show-and-tell *presentations* of it're rarer still, so don't hold your breath waiting for the ghost of a gambling ship, for inst, to run aground in Marina Del Rey.

And let's see, what else? Well, if you get here in May, don't park your shiny new Cadillac or Mercedes under one of those omnipresent and extremely pretty purple blooming tree type things—what are they, jacarandas? (after all this time I guess I still dunno know what a jacaranda *is*)—that always seem to be in full lovely total goddam bloom in the month of May. Park under 'em and you'll need two trips to the carwash (minimum) to remove the purple gunk-drip from your finish.

And if you're moving here from that N-place, please bear in mind that the director of perhaps the ultimate N movie, *My Dinner with Andre*, and possibly even the ultimate N-J movie, *Atlantic City*, had no more sense upon planting his tootsies in H*o*l*l*y*w*o*o*d than to MARRY CANDICE BERGEN. Hopefully you'll have more sense than that.

L.A. BENIGN: 36 ATTRACTIONS WHICH MIGHT NOT MAKE YOU SICK

From the outside at least. Some I have never been in. Some don't even *have* an inside. But all exist. No fake ones—in case you're thinking how can this known cynic, this mocker of precious, horrible, disgusting L.A. icons that normal folk (be they of Melrose or the Valley, the "art scene" or the surf, single or *en famille*) dig, cherish, prize & revere . . . how can such a hater of the holy even *come up with* three dozen whatsems that have not made him cringe, upchuck or reach for a handy prescription valium?

Well, 36 is not really *that* big a number. You could probably find *37* items which will not cause you grief in your own home, apartment, room, dwelling or memory bank. So it's not *size* of space that counts—or even, for that matter, quality. The human spirit finds ways to "endure," y'know? Places. Objects. Objects of place and inconsequence. Little here-there pockets of dusty or dustless whatever.

Which is purt near exactly the point: whatever.

'S no matter of life and death but, heck, you might wanna check a few, suss a few, out.

1. **Line of grass down middle of street**, 5th Ave. from 8th St. to 9th St. Widest towards 9th, just a great big ol' line of grass. (Between Wilton and Crenshaw.)

2. **Hollywood Reservoir.** You've seen the Silver Lake Reservoir, the placid waters of Echo and MacArthur Parks, seen them probably without a hitch from actual navigable sts. and rds. Well this one, sort of a Great Moments in Caged Mock-Rustic, has got them all beat but is kind of hid. One visit should be plenty; take Cahuenga or Cahuenga Blvd. West north to Barham, turn right on Lake Holly-wood Dr. and stick with it, it curves a lot and might even be called something else a couple times. If you get lost just keep circling, the maze is finite.

3. **Wah Wing Sang Gutierrez & Weber Mortuary.** Is there *anyone* who doesn't love a trans-ethnic corpse operation? 611 Sunset Blvd.

4. **Superet Light Church.** 2515 W. 3rd St. That old time religion: thirties L.A. hocus pocus, or is it/was it mumbo jumbo? (Hairem scarem??) Raymond Chandler had to 've known this place—either that or the town was so lousy with 'em then he didn't need to. But unique, generic, what's the diff? Where else you gonna get J.C.'s heart, valves and aorta in living lavender neon?

5. **Asthma Vapineze.** Whatever *that* is, but so says the neon at something-or-other [number obscured by foliage] N. Fairfax Ave.—between 1030 N. and 1022. Though probably newer than Superet, ditto on Chandler. Dark, spooky facade if you're snooping close, but basically it just blends with all the nothing on a nowhere street. Really, though, what the hell's a vapineze???

6. **Beautiful Nails by Kathy.** 7967 Melrose Ave. Non-New Age sign w/ long-nailed fingers holding a rose. I used to work across the street, so I'd see it all the time. Koreans run it, this guy would hand-paint signs like "Liquid Juliette $6" in purple, "Manicure $5" in green, then step outside to admire his work. It never made me sick.

7. **View of Glendale from Elysian Park.** Includes trains, tracks, the whole damn thing; good elevation; sound of pistols from the nearby cop academy. Great—y'know bearable—when it's cool, clear or rainy; awful—I mean *awful*—when hot, dusty, smoggy. Take Acad-emy Rd. to Park Rd. to Park Row to Elysian Park Dr.—or you

might have to park, walk and improvise 'cause sometimes they block things off. Anyway watch for broken glass, aim for the northeastern crest and try and spot either a stone wall or one of those big cylindrical water tanks or whatever they are (green with lots of graffiti). Between the two landmarks there's lots of trails with unobstructed views of the Big G, even some privacy and an occasional stump or fallen tree to sit your butt on.

8. **Republica Dominicana Consulada.** 12103 Jefferson Blvd. Swell little consular module, a storefront across from Hughes Airport with parking slots adjacent to those reserved for Hagar Tile and L.A. County West Mosquito Control. Nice coat of arms & wrought-iron filigree. I wonder if Pedro Guerrero ever stops by.

9. **"Gargoyle House."** Also known as Chateau LeMoine, so you'd hafta guess the LeMoines, who figure to be *silly*silly people, are the culprits. In neurotic geo-limbo 'tween Miracle Mile and Hancock Park, they've opted to "live out" a recollected fairy tale or twelve, or maybe *Camelot* and *Ivanhoe*, custom gargoylizing their turrets and prodding their fake brook to babble—or is it a moat? Sillysilly*silly* people! 846 S. Longwood Ave., a block east of Highland.

10. **Boxing at the Olympic Auditorium.** Wrestling and roller games, no. Rock concerts, no. Only boxing. (Now more than ever.) It doesn't matter if the fights are for shit, or whether the house is packed—10,000 strong—or there's only 900; when fists are featured this building *delivers*. The smell, the acoustics, the shadows—not to mention the sleaze, although middleclass as I am I've gotta say I have never felt anything but *serenely comfortable* inside the Olympic. An essential date with someone you really care about—honest! 1801 S. Grand Ave.

11. And for your pre-fight dining pleasure, may I recommend **El Comedor**, 408 S. Main St., in the heartiest heart of Downtown—home away from home of Jose Napoles' champeenship belt. Oil paintings—no acrylics here—of Ruben Olivares, Raul "Raton" Macias, Efren "Alacran" Torres. This is all up on the wall, and on the menu: Pipino Cuevas. And oh yeah, right, *foodwise*: second or third finest Mexican eat joint in town. True.

12. **Samson Auto Salvage.** 8103 S. Alameda St. During business

hours they used to display the giant whoozis of Jack Dempsey that 'til about five years ago was tacked on the front of the Olympic, but last time I drove by I didn't see it. It's only like a block or something north of Manchester, so you might wanna check it next time you're headed to or from LAX or the Forum.

13. **Pik-a-Book.** 8422 W. 3rd St. Well yeah, I have found good stuff on the shelves like De Sade's *Justine*, Jack Paar's *I Kid You Not*, and Barry Malzberg's *Oracle of the Thousand Hands*—all hardbacks for a buck apiece. And sometimes the guy is in such a hurry to break for lunch he'll give you everything in your hands for two bucks total. Or maybe he won't. Mainly what's so attractive about this shop is it straddles the line between thriftstore/junkstore and bookstore/used very well. It's the latter of course, but with minimal claustrophobia, no pretense and the right amount of dust.

14. **Old beat-to-shit residence.** Well actually it was painted recently. But still, compared to all the New Age chintz and fuckpus at this end of Playa Del Rey (6206 Pacific Ave.) it's as welcomely alien as that old beat-to-shit residence on Hollywood Blvd.

15. **UCLA boathouse**, Marina Del Rey. Okay, still in *Playa* Del Rey, continue on Pacific to its terminus at the little footbridge over Ballona Creek, cross it and follow footpath inland to marina proper, half a mile, maybe slightly more. First structure you'll see is this ramp and a building with *zillions* of dollars in 8-oared shells and smaller, the materiel necessary for this tax-supported institution to remain competitive in what must be its 145th hottest sport, rowing. Or the aggregate gift of richer richfolk—unless you're one yourself— than you'd prob'ly wanna know about. (For that extra little dose— you might need one sometime—of So-Cal contempt.)

16. **Marina Breakwater.** No, you can't get *on* it, not via land, but you can see it pretty good with all its birdshit from the far end of the jetty that juts perpendicular to Ocean Front Walk where Venice Beach terminates at the Marina Channel. Quickest shot is Via Marina to where it curves into those parking meters that didn't used to be there, park and be quick (they're good for just an hour), walk or run up the paved part of the jetty 'til you hit the fake decorative fence, crawl through, step across rocks (slippery when wet) and sit

'til your meter runs low. Especially good (in meter-size doses) during storms.

17. **Least Tern Natural Preserve.** Side trip, before or after breakwater. Down on the beach, right in the sand just beyond the volleyball nets, maybe a hundred yards in from the channel, there's this square of fences maybe three feet high that fence in you cannot tell what. So you move in to see and these *birds* swoop down; their turf, apparently, and they don't want you even *near*. Then you crawl *below* their flight path, crawl crawl as they buzz your back, and right at the fence is a tiny sign which reads: "Least terns use this part of the beach as a nesting area from May through August each year. These small birds are an endangered species because many of their nesting and feeding spots have been destroyed or disturbed. To avoid startling the nesting colony please stay at least 15 feet away"—at which distance you couldn't read dickshit. And I've been buzzed in winter and fall. I think it's neat though that *between the fences* is where they are based, that it's *right in the sand*, y'know next to volleyball. And inside their space there is NO GARBAGE. Interesting.

18. From fauna/live to fauna/dead: **The "Antler House."** 1218 14th St., Santa Monica. Stucco, shingles, plastic & aluminum lounge chair, 3 garages, 17 sets of antlers, 4 of them possibly caribou. Or elk. Or moose. Plus: horse-sculpture weather vane, whale-sculpture weather vane—if you need to know which way the wind blows.

19. **King's Head British Pub** (weekdays, mid-afternoon only). When even halfway hopping it's as horrible and sweaty as any yuppie wine pit in, f'rinstance, Westwood Village on, f'rinstance, Friday night. But at not-so-rare empty moments you can sit quiet as a ghost over pints of Watney's, Bass, John Courage, Guinness, Theakston's—all on tap, each loaded with more B-vitamins than a loaf of two-dollar bread. Nice coasters to steal (but the fish & chips're no great shakes). 116 Santa Monica Blvd., Santa Monica.

20. Symmetry's a groove, for then there's that dandy oasis for non-drinkers, the **New Way Beverage Company**, a real trip and I don't mean geographic. "Alcohol-removed" beer, wine, brandy, cordials & shit—as opposed to simply "non-alcoholic"—all of which you can con this cheery bartender type joe into pouring you a hit of

as he spills you his story of a life before and after. Only part I remember is how he went to some fussy Italian joint with a group of *former* drinkers, maybe it was even New Year's Eve, and in front of this pompous wine steward he whips out a magnum of alcohol-removed chianti—" 'Cuz we former drinkers appreciate a fine wine with our fine meal as much as the next et cetera" . . . yeah. (20127 Saticoy St., Canoga Park.)

21. **Drive-in w/ palm trees.** Right alongside the screen, tall muthas, one to each side—the ultimate California frame. I don't remember which drive-in, though, it's been like three-four years, could be the Centinela (Centinela east of Sepulveda) or the Studio (Sepulveda north of Jefferson). My guess is the Centinela.

22. **Town of Athens.** What—you didn't know we had a town of Athens? Did have and do have. To the west of Vermont, just above Gardena, about half a mile south of Imperial Hwy.

23. When in Athens, be sure 'n' picnic at **Helen Keller Park**, Vermont between El Segundo Blvd. and 125th St.

24. "Yes, we're OPEN!" reads the window card at **11609 Santa Monica Blvd.**, West L.A., but no, the oh so pathetic Golf Repair is not. Golf Repair, its full entire name, once inhabited 11609. It was a sad, sad, sad habitation. Even in our Land of 1000 Golf Courses, rarely did business look good. Window ads were in marker on newspaper—not newsprint, but pages of printed-on *Times* and/or *Herald*. People with clubs (they're such *snobs*, I hear) do not respond to such pathos. But *you* can I'm sure, so stop in today at 11609—currently a Super Sandwich—for a good, good cry over your jack cheese & mayo.

25. **Phil's Diner.** The matchbook says, and it does not lie, "The last diner of its kind!" I won't tell you what kind, just go see for yourself some lunchtime. 11138 Chandler Blvd., North Hollywood.

26. **Sixth & Serrano Building—Dentistry.** Plain facade, no dental kitsch of any sort; you just step in and they yank 'em. The epitome of benign—but not, alas, of ouchless. 3851 W. 6th St.

27. **M. Forman Pottery & Gift Shop.** Once I was walking in Venice and this woman in her late sixties, possibly M. Forman's mom, came up all bubbly and handed me their biz card. "We carry a complete

line of cement pots, glazed pots, stone ware pots, terra cotta pots, sand jars and many other kinds of planters," reads the v. classy print job, and in ballpoint, possibly the handiwork of M. Forman *mère*: "Terrific place!" I have no reason to doubt her. (8868 W. Pico Blvd.)

28. **Novelty misspelling**, 2037 Sawtelle Blvd. Every list is allowed one, and since they finally painted over "Pestrommie Samwich" on the wall of that burger stand at Fairfax and Santa Monica, ACUPRSSURE is my pick. Especially since it's right across from . . .

29. **Safe & Save Market**, 2030 Sawtelle. The only food mart in town that is *both* nonthreatening and economical!

30. **Clearman's North Woods Inn of Belmont Shore.** Maybe there's others, maybe you've seen one, but I really do think you should see at least *one*. Outside it's done up like a fake ski lodge with painted-on, sprayed-on or possibly molded-on snow. Inside it's Gay Nineties, guys with garters on their arm playing lame oldtimey dogshit on the 88s. The floor is all peanut shells; behind you at the bar is a dangling sign (backwards) which in the mirror reads dump 'em there. Bartop itself is unshelled goober city. A my-t-good place to try out your untested reprehensible behavior routines. 4911 E. 2nd St., Long Beach.

31. **The Devil's Punchbowl.** A state park or something, you walk through this immense, barely modified wilderness with rattlesnakes sunning themselves at your feet, these large, enormous furry red wasps called cowkillers—actual name—crawling around (they're wingless), lots of exotic crawlthings and the sound of falls roaring just out of view, you've had your nature fill & thrill and, exiting, you notice a sign you *did not read* upon entering: "Area contains rodents whose fleas may carry bubonic plague—enter at your own risk." (Gosh!) Take Antelope Valley Fwy. to Sierra Fwy. to Pearblossom Fwy. to . . . stop somewhere and ask, how many other attractions have they got in Pearblossom?

32. **Tony's Steak & Seafood**, 2009 E. Thompson Blvd., Ventura. If you can drive on Pearblossom, you can drive to Ventura. Fine little quaint little basic y'know *restaurant*, with the heppest name from here to Lompoc and beyond. Seven seas decor up the *gitgo* (from before

they had steaks?). On Friday and Saturday nights Tony himself comes over and blows tenor sax ("Theme from *The Godfather*," etc.) at your table. Reservations: 805-643-3322.

33. On the scenic route to Tony's: **Museum and main drag, Fillmore.** Dunno the names or approaches, but it's better you find 'em yourself. Fillmore (a short hop inside Ventura County, up 23 from Thousand Oaks and Moorpark, after that you're on your own) is the Town That Time Forgot. Parts of it anyway. If things look too new, keep looking. The museum's in an old railroad car; every eyeglass, scissors and pencil a townsperson ever owned is behind glass, labeled. And stuff like this old calendar from a Nisei-owned cleaning store with the inscription: "Mr. Yonekura, respected member of the Fillmore Chamber of Commerce, was relocated to an internment camp following the outbreak of WWII and never returned." Date on the calendar, no joke, is December '41. And the whole town, i.e., selected parts, is eye-deep in that same kind of capsule.

34. Speaking of capsules: **Carthay Circle.** Also known as Carthay Center. Where once, based on scattered evidence, things were possibly hopping. Before I ever lucked into it (my dentist—a kitschy nonpainless yanker—is officed nearby) I remember noticing references to film openings at Carthay this or that in news clippings under the varithane on a tabletop at a McDonald's somewhere; items that made it seem, once upon whenever, The Place. Mid to late twenties I think. Pre-H'wood-&Vine, pre-I-dunno-what, it might've been a coordinate to reckon with. Now what you got is a mini-park, trendy New Age offices, and mini-monuments w/ plaques. Like this one for the v. heroic Snowshoe Thompson (1827-1876) "who for twenty winters carried mail over the mountains to isolated camps"—which is more than they do today—"rescuing the lost and giving succor"—*certainly* more—"to those in need along the way." Dedicated 1926 by "The Native Sons of the Golden West"—who I'd hate to run into on a dark, deserted golf course or firing range. Also, well it's not there, not anymore but I did find it, crumpled at the foot of Snowshoe's shrine, one big *wowser* of a personal orgaz poem (or note):

L.A. Is the Capital of Kansas

Oh uh a OH
    Oh
Oh uh a Oh ooh
    OH ooah
Oh uh a Oh ooh OH uhnnh aaaah
uh-h-h-h jesus oh baby mm-n-h-h O-O-O
ooh fuckme fuckkkk mee OHHHH
        OHHHH
           etc.

—suggesting that "things Carthay" are still v. hopping today! (Between San Vicente Blvd. and Commodore Sloat Dr. at that part of Crescent Heights called McCarthy Vista/Carrillo Dr.)

35. But the *real* time trip: **Beverly Hills!!** Rodeo Drive equals Fifth Avenue (New York, N.Y.) '58. Where else anymore you even gonna find fifty-*nine*? Not in Boise, not in Great Bend, not even Murfreesboro. Certainly not as *per se* as in Beverly—an *amazingly* out-of-it place. It's still so, what's the word, *tasteful*. Melrose has not yet invaded. Its alien streak is from dead horse central: a necktie here with *speedboats*; a blouse there with *show dogs*; beer mugs w/ *Winston Churchill*; shoes made of...elephant hide? If L.A. is just one big doggone hick town (which it is), Beverly Hills must be its...its Beverly Hills!!!

36. **Southeast corner, Lorraine Blvd. and 4th St.** During the Olympics I saw a coyote there—three miles, at least, from any possible hills. Maybe he'll be back. Or she. You could wait around.

RICHARD MELTZER VISITS AMERICA

Searching for nothing, I found it royally.

Kansas: nothing. New Mexico: nothing. America: nothing.

(But ah! the varieties of nothing in our Land!)

I got this car, see, and drove it from Providence to L.A. Which is not quite the same as getting one at the top of Maine, say, the Canadian border, and tooling all the way to San Diego, Tijuana. And which, as an accomplishment, may not seem like *dick* but I did it, or came close enough. For the first time in my life, and I'm no youngster, I've "driven the country"—did it solo in fact. By design.

You're born alone, you die alone, you write alone, and on each hump of the journey I tried my darndest to *be* alone, massively alone, to be one isolated schmuck aswim, adrift, adrive in the heartlands, hinterlands of a huge neutral mess of GEOGRAPHY, a far cry (I hoped) from the endlessly stacked deck of my own neurotic terrain. I wanted, and got, a hefty, heady dose of highway as isolation tank; a hard drive as welcome respite, rest. And since, as a bonus, most stations of the mess turned out to be anything *but* neutral, I got to be alone, without distraction, with and within IT. This big halfwit country spoke and occasionally was audible. I wouldn't have heard half as much with company on board.

But no, it wasn't my object, certainly not at first, to "see the U.S.A." Nor was I aiming to "do a Kerouac," pull some functional update of *On the Road*, or a '60s-revisited "goof on America." Basically, these wheels just fell in my lap. My womanperson's father died up in Rhode Island, leaving behind a '79 Malibu with—due to his Parkinson's—under 18,000 miles. Which she wanted, right, but had no time to get—employment is like that. Fearing her brother would claim it if she didn't—property is theft—she dispatched me with gas bucks to fetch it. Since I had *nothing better to do* (I'm a writer, right?), and since it was her car, not mine, and I could thus do what I wanted with the damn thing, I geared myself up for the challenge.

Challenge? Well, I'd never driven more than 400 miles, in one swoop, before.

A quarter of my life ago, when I threw in the towel on New York, urban blight wouldn't have made my top five reasons for splitting, had someone pointed a gun (or knife) at me and said, *Okay, list 'em.* My motives were essentially "personal" (boy-girl, friend-friend, writer-editor), but framing it all was the fact that I'd just plain used the place up. When finally the day came that I found myself on a Circle Line cruise around Manhattan (literally: the last straw), I got me a one-way ticket to Somewhere Else—which I proceeded to use up in 30 seconds.

Thirty seconds and a quarter-life onward, having still lived in only TWO PLACES, really, neither proving ultimately satisfactory, in all my days, I motored south from Providence with mild trepidation, returning as I was to the place of my birth, germination and oowee with transit goals and stratagems I had never before employed. Since splitting for the palm fronds I'd of course been *back*—I'd visited, revisited those few remaining Gotham pals 'n' buds; I'd hugged, kissed, sat around, had drinks, laughs, departed. I would fly *to* New York, *return* to L.A. This time, howev, New York was neither principal target nor launchpoint for immediate return. It was but a stop, an ad hoc coordinate, a Mars en route to Jupiter (or a toilet en route to the bar). Having stripmined, from both ends, the whole frigging New York-L.A. *axis*—Essence versus Illusion as a great American "theme"—I craved nothing more essential than a free place to park.

In Manhattan, ha, the Village.

Which I knew would not be easy.

Which could easily break my spirit.

Which I dreaded more than all possible else on the trip.

But fug me, I did it, found something in just over an hour, a mere 12-13 blocks from where I needed to be. I even scraped a city tow-truck in the process, its driver too involved with an illegally parked sucker to even notice. A good omen: getting the compulsory 1st accident summarily over with. The remaining 3000 miles would by contrast be pretty much nothin'.

But the town. Between check-ins with cronies I still had to endure a town.

Since last I'd looked, the Apple's rich had plainly gotten richer, and its poor poorer. Where the chronically homeless—what we used to call "bums"—once confined themselves to certain neighborhoods, stairwells and alleyways, they were now *everywhere*. Every 25 feet. And the despair, shee, the kill-you-motherfucker on everyone's face . . . I'd never seen so many syringes, for inst, in the gutter.

Years without major break in a fake, scattered city like L.A. can throw you out of sync with the rhythms and sins of the Pavement. My capacity for blight as foreground thus diminished, I sat with my goodfriend Nick on a pair of folding chairs, taking it in as backdrop, as universal context, as surgeon general's warning in an eyeful of *anything*. Maid walks prize-winning schnauzer past staggering wino . . . yuppie mom wheels babe in yuppie stroller *sharply* around sleeping (dying?) junkie . . .

The LIES New York tells itself have clearly reached the stage, the scale, of the kind L.A. has always told *itself*.

"How'd you get through all that Statue of Lib *centennial* shit?" I asked my companion. "That must've been as tough as our goddam Olympics."

237

"Nah, it was quicker. Yours was like two weeks, ours was only two-three days. I just stayed inside, didn't buy the paper or watch the news, and stuck with stations less likely to hit that button. As long as there's a *Honeymooners* or two and *The Giant Gila Monster*—I think it was on that weekend—you don't have to pay attention to that other crap."

The rest of the trip, five or six days, I just drove, stopping only for gas, food, urine or sleep. Shits I took in the morning on waking.

Smog of New Jersey: I remember YOU. The sight, the smell, the life-is-poison *presence*; last familiar face 'til Oklahoma City.

Pennsylvania in autumn is a beaut. Yellows, oranges, reds, with splotches of green (or brown) that work like a congruous off-yellow. "The Fall!" hawk the billboards, "You've got a friend in Pennsylvania": nature as Product (& don't you forget it).

After West Virginia, which for the minute or so it lasted seemed ostensibly mountainous, terrain as the road served it up got flat (Ohio), flatter (Indiana). The degree of full-spectrum fallhood dropped radically, as did the height and distribution of shrubs. By Indianapolis, the few roadside trees were totally brown or totally green; at the Illinois border, everything faded to grey. Dry, grim and relatively unpeopled, the Land o' Lincoln at I-70 latitude seemed right out of *North by Northwest*—the cropdusting scene—minus (f'r contrast) the hills. Eventually the Land of TRUMAN—lush, rolling, citied Missouri—came along to cut the routine.

Dead animals helped. For decor you can't beat all the weasels, woodchucks, squirrels, rabbits, dogs, possums, skunks, snakes, hawks, deer and miscellaneous splattered on the blacktop and shoulders. Plus you had yer *higher*-mammal fortuities, those local bits, slices of what some think-tanker of yore awoke from a fever dream to dub "Americana":

—beat-to-shit 100-year-old barn w/ satellite dish (Cloverdale, Indiana);

—billboard, south of Pittsburgh: "The door to alcoholism" (football player, red jersey, beercan in hand);

—Howard Hughes Motel, Greenfield, Illinois (*He stopped here, see, on the way to Vandalia . . .*).

Mainly, tho, adverts & exit signs. No need to actually leave the highway and see, inspect, *eyeball* St. Mary-of-the-Woods College (W. Terre Haute), 24-Hr. Adult Books—Truckers Welcome (Yukon, PA), or the fair town of Teutopolis (Germany-opolis?), Illinois. It's NICE (or something) just to know they're there.

And mainliest of all: radio. With both AM and FM, I had it all. I'd be driving through some typical Smallville, East Jesus, what have you, and signals would come in off these little rinky-dink transmitters, joyful earfuls of smalltown crime b.s. ("14-year-old held in theft of waffle iron"), farm commodities shit ("Listeners often ask, 'What *is* a pork belly?'"), high school football *weather forecasts*, and local do-good baloney (an all-you-can-eat breakfast of *sausage, ham, bacon* and eggs—proceeds to go to "the mentally retarded of Korea").

What really tickled me was the precious, ludicrous, seemingly ineradicable AUTONOMY of these isolated, insulated fairytale locales. Wouldn't wanna live there, would hardly wanna visit, but receiving their alien transmissions—in coherent English no less—was more of a kick than Carl Sagan is likely to ever get from *his* storybook aliens. And it always felt TRAGIC—on the hour, the half hour—when master-program central, radio qua television, piped in current Big Lies (the "national news") to eradicate everything.

And along with national news: national music. Playlists that only varied by genre (rock . . . country . . . religious . . . a smidgen of black pop), not broadcast locale.

And national food. Wherever I stopped to eat—wherever I *looked* to eat—within finite minutes of the national roadway, the slop was exclusively chain, corporate, fast: Wendy's, Denny's, McDonald's. (Truckstops had Hardee's, Burger King.)

News, music, food; but how 'bout a national *nation?*—one "existing" unassisted by TV. To see if there WAS one—heck, I'd come this far—I opted to stay on the interstate. Only by continuing at double nickels-plus could I get an adequate sense of overlap, continuity, discontinuity, whatever. Only by hitting a decent ratio of states per day could I take the whole thing in as a single anything. (A single multiplicity; a single horizontal blur.) By mid-Missouri, even the *idea* of New Jersey was receding fast. Only by zooming THROUGH it could I possibly get TO it. Zoom on!

I should've guessed something was UP when Jimmy Webb's "MacArthur Park" began in Kansas City, MO, and ended in Kansas City, Kansas. "Someone left the cake out in the rain"—it was too sunny for words—but would I be up for *it*?

Kansas is flat as a cake. Flatter. Even with ripples in the wheat, alfalfa, whatever the hell it is, it's as flat as a '61 Gus Grissom flattop. I think the word is horizontal. It's also the first state I hit where they *groom* the grass adjacent to the roadway, inotherwords *flatten* it. Flat must be synonymous with neat, jake, as-suggested-by-God, cute-as-a-cuddlebunny.

Vladimir Nabokov, bug collector, would've loved Kansas and, worldly s.o.b. that he was, probably did. Butterflies attack you as you drive—at least they did me. Monarchs, sulphurs, fritillaries, swallowtails: a reg'lar Lepidoptricon. You see them flutter a ways off, the only real color in the landscape, and 'fore you know it they're the color and glop on your windshield. It's no great leap of mindset to imagine *The Wizard of Oz* as having been conceived, gestated and bouncing-babe written here . . . L. Frank Baum meets the author of *Lolita* (15 rounds—who will win???).

Maximum flat after harvesting—some acres had been reaped—is no more, no less, than Basic Flat minus the ripple, minus some inches and feet. You can't out-max max. You can't see to a FUR-THER forever in all directions. Simulated "infinity" is the upper, but also the lower, limit; the norm. I didn't hafta be a math creep to put two and two and shout eureka, hmm, L.A. was *not* geo-drastically diff.

Which exceeded my, well, they hadn't exactly been *expectations*. I'd for years been running this line by and at people re some culture sync between L.A. and a Kansas I'd never set EYES upon. Something to the effect that Kansas, some *possible* Kansas, was in fact THAT WHICH Los Angeles, CA, was the sole and logical culture capital *of.* Its principal industry made film after film "about" Kansas, based "in" Kansas, to be consumed by "Kansas" (or some such mid-American shuck).

But here I was in KANSAS, *literal* Kansas, and godamighty there were too many, too many points of literal concurrence: the flat, the groomed, the fake forever, the ontologically shitfaced-boring (masked as Divine). Outside Emporia, a billboard screams: "You must be born again." Please! by all means! *yuh yuh.* But don't, on the life of your ma, let H'wood buy it, film it, cast it, script it, precurse it, prefigure it, or. The temptations are immense I know (mythic congruence is Mythic Congruence; Ameri-Jesus bucks are ameri-jesus Bucks), buh buh but.

Then I pulled into Wichita, a compulsory petrol/pee/minimum daily requirement stop, and it's like I was ACTUALLY THERE: the cultural-cum-physical Los Angeles. Malls, sprawl, burgercruise, vacant faces/posed, ill-fitting clothing as statement of UNIVERSE, let's-pretend-we're-a-city-while-a-large-box-of-macaroni-would-probably-fool-us-as-well, nothing to block or filter the killer sun (which blindsmaimscausescancer).

And which came first? (a dipshit might ask)—film? concept? chickie chicken? egg? california? kansas? But the answer is too, too (boo hoo) obvious. 'Tis generic, 'tis Ameri-generic, and THAT which is generic is no grander, no hepper, no more life-nurturing than THIS.

This Kansas in Oct., as I drive and see lines, I see telephone lines but I don't see no linemen. "I hear you singing through the wire, I can hear you through the whine"—I'd give yrs. off my life to hear Jimmy Webb's "Wichita Lineman." And I'd give more than that for the code by which nothing yields something.

I've always like Texas. And/or loathed it in a Wrestling sort of way. Its bluster either plays or it doesn't. Been there time & again—to Dallas, Houston, Austin—the bluster of bluster-as-Culture. But never, 'til now, to *West* Texas, where bluster wears not denim nor waves its wienie: the bluster of nekkid land.

After all these states where residential mythos did not exactly jibe with the *lay* of the land, it was refreshing to see a hand dealt where A equaled A. Since Pennsylvania, excluding Missouri and a couple of urban accidents adjacent to rivers, it had been a tough ponder weighing the pivotal question WHY *HERE*? Why a bunch of Euros would come here for *this* land and, having come, why they'd *settle* for this—property-as-theft notwithstanding—or even tell their children's children they did.

Britain predates Rome—Stonehenge and all such truck. You wanna talk Brit mytho-history, you're talking archetype, paradigm, psychic protoplast; the "existence" of a Richard the Lionhearted no more cries for "verification" than does that of a Zeus or a Thor. But Indiana, Ohio, Kansas: none of these designated regions of habitation seem more than theoretically livable NOW, and you wonder what subspecies of migratory Humankind could have deemed them so THEN—a scant (non-prehistoric) 200-300 annums past. BOOKS tell us 'bout wagons and families, oxen and men, ladies w/ heirlooms in their burlap stockings singing (in French, Rumanian, Dutch) *Indiana, here we come.* I mean pshaw, I ain't debating the *veracity* of such tales—no sir, no ma'am, not me. But the Land, the Land in Question, does not meet the Legend halfway or even a third.

Hey: pre-Interstate travel must've been a fucker; the source of *many* odd quirks of spatiotemporal duh-duh. (Mere jetlag has caused teams to lose NBA championships.) American geo-history: last of the Eleusinian Mysteries???

Dunno, but here's a firm, sweaty handshake for West Texas qua PLACE. The no-pretense, no-alibi turf of not necessarily "tough guys," um, let us say "outlaws," no-home-on-earth "misfits," "desperadoes." Maverick: a motherless calf. "Mavericks" too. Such folk are eminently credible now/credible then. And the land: NO comfort from the land (only whiskey, orgaz, beer, the Cowboys or Oilers on Sundays).

No sissy, macho, jaycee, godswilling "immigrants" need apply.

And then: the Void.
Hours 'n' hours ('n' hours) of New Mexico.

Richard Meltzer Visits America

The major Nowhere that minor nowheres far and wide unwittingly aspire *to*, that *select* 1000-miles-from-nowhere watering holes and buzzard farms are by good fortune a thousand miles *from*. Before this jaunt I'd been to rural Quebec in Jack London winter, to cobra-bite tropical India, out on the Pacific with naught on the horizon but horizon. But aside from an occasional *psychic* mass disjuncture, I'd never felt this far afield from human-content Earth.

Hundredmile after hundredmile went by with few, if any, signs of Life. Fewer exits, fewer billboards, nary a trailer camp, no visible crops, maybe three-four cows, calves, colts the entire run. But rocks a-plenty, and dry creeks and red clay and sky. You drive along and the basic detail, the *only* detail, is lifeless plethora, inanimate muchness: a planet complete—and completely *full*—before dinosaurs, certainly before mastodons, at least before Stonehenge's grandpa breathed its first stone-hewn breath. Everywhere you look it's the Grand Canyon, sure, but hardly—experientially, "existentially"—a souvenirable postcard snap thereof. "Details" as microminutiate Americana neither register nor compute.

And you think of all the fraudulent mileage Ansel Adams got from such topography: choosing, mixing, framing, exposing silly rectangles of film with great American coffee-table intent. Romancing the stone, indeed! (Or maybe—great American benefit o' doubt—it was a grand act of Dada, a Man Ray imaging of this-rather-than-that-but-what's-the-diff?) Me, myself, I prefer the fly-by-my-car of structurally imposing anciency which NO MAN, certainly not an American, EVER BUILT. And I ain't saying "God" did either.

Look, this isn't even "untamed wilderness" (what would a tamer tame, mesas? raindrops? drops in temperature?)—it's the Moon, the Void. And in this void, Nothing—no assortment of nth-percentile rules or expectations—applies. Among the smattering of standard-issue whitebread humans who actually live here are those who not only build domes and hold artso film rites, some (we're told) even *worship the devil*. Most, I'm sure, also worship money, exploit Native Americans and vote for Reagan, but who said life was perfect—even in a perfect void?

Most of Arizona, next up, was an extension of this, though more groomed, perhaps, and color-coordinated; the Santa Barbara version (if you know what I mean) of No Place, really.

Kingman, finally, was the doorway, the anteroom, to Someplace. California's nearness was all too loud 'n' palpable, its grimy orange extending 'cross state lines to tempt and beckon every local Jane Blow (soon to star in a made-for-TV erection). If it snatches them in from New York and Paris, what chance you wanna give a poor dusty burg with Dreams so poor, so dusty it's actually named one of its larger streets ANDY DEVINE AVENUE? "Hey, Wild Bill, wait for me!"—how's *that* for desert role-model wish-hopin'!

It's a good thing the empirical scientist in me got to catch & sniff both New Jersey and California in a single week. Immediate sensory evidence can at times be useful; memory romanticizes *too damn much.* For ten years I'd held to the notion that Jersey and partner-in-crime Manhattan were atmospherically grimmer on an average day than L.A. on its life-snuffing worst. Well I dunno from average, or even from worst, but 30 yards (or some such figure) from Needles it was already smoggi*er* (by a factor like 50) than the N.J./N.Y. of not only five days previous, but of drastically mismemorized yore. And this was just *desert*, for fug sake; L.A. the "city" was still 250 miles down the road.

I'd never before approached California, Southern or otherwise, from this direction—a preferred route for Dust Bowlers and, one assumes, for Bobby Troup, author of "Route 66." Gateway to the garden (of Eden), to the pot (of etc. at rainbow's end). Well, seeing how tawdry and ugggggly the damn thing could be, and finally knowing in fact where it *came from* (from turf more pure, interesting and "spectacular" than itself; from a Nothing which knows its Being and its Place), I instantly KNEW—evidence enough—that the California Ruse must predate even the film industry. Realtors thought it up, or the academics, "historians." Lying to keep from crying! *Well, Mary Jean, I'm sure it'll pick up when we reach the sea . . .*

Follow. . . the sun.

And I did a 2nd take on Kansas: it had its *reasons.* Agriculture, physical isolation—reasons for being bland, modular, unaware. Southern California *has* no reasons; none, that is, dealt by geographic, geologic reality. In matters of mindset and heartset, Southern Cal is geography *denied.*

Or maybe it was just my dread of returning Home.

I'd been so long in transit, and it felt so *okay,* that I really didn't want to stop, and certainly not here. Around Pomona or Ontario, the smog so thick you could barely read the signs, traffic slowed, crawled: first traffic jam of the trip. Which made sense. All a venue of ALL CARS can offer, in the end, is the *illusion* of transit; cars *become* geography, er, real estate; the smallest units of propertied immobility. Or some such lunacy, some fitting Jim Morrison terminalism (to celebrate my less-than-joyous reentry).

This *was* the end, it hadn't been too rough a haul, and I realized two things. One, that L.A.-hater Jack Kerouac's biggest problem was he didn't drive, that by depending too exclusively on others for both general mobility and vectors into and out of place-coded predicaments and experiences, he was ultimately consigned to a sensibility—as both writer and man—too monochromatically that of the Passenger: passive and/or "out of control," restless of hand and foot, unaccountable, "not responsible." Heck, I'd only really had one car *problem* all trip (in a storm in New Mexico it didn't start, then did), and I hardly ever drove at night, so I'm not talking courage, adventure, tough-guy stuff or any of that. The daily stresses of wheeling into ferocious setting suns, of holding a curve while holding in a wicked piss, were irksome but by no means immense. The rewards were, big deal, rewarding.

But the whole thing is more than plus/minus, than a series of small but concrete "achievements." By handing the reins over to the Lew Welches and Neal Cassadys, what Jack missed out on was a heap of ORIENTATION. A means of viewing activity, basic functional NORMAL activity, from a vantage point which is also its CUTTING EDGE: the Zen of merely driving. An easy one (and, again, no big deal), but throughout life, except for rare practice runs, the King of the Beats was too cheesed out to bother.

Two: New York and L.A. are not contiguous. That's with a *g* ("adjoining, adjacent"); and, with an n, nor are they continuous ("linearly connected") by connections other than instantaneous: airplanes, TV. No surface passage is quick enough or smooth enough to pull it off, to *make* them continuous, so you've got to fly (or plug into network Death). "Bicoastal" scumbags (and pluggers into networks) are the bane of BOTH COASTS. That's it.

'Bye.